FIERCE

Book design by Nauset Press
Published by Nauset Press, LLC
Publishing contact: info@nausetpress.com

Library of Congress Control Number:
2019935749

ISBN-13: 978-0-9907154-5-0

Editor
Karyn Kloumann

Writers
Nancy Agabian
Betsy Andrews
Debra Brehmer
Kara Lee Corthron
Chicava HoneyChild
Robyn Kraft
Caitlin Grace McDonnell
Leah Mueller
Meera Nair
Edissa Nicolás-Huntsman
Jessie Serfilippi
Claudia Smith
Taté Walker

Illustrations
Anna Torbina

Cover Photograph
Organic Photography

Cover and Book Design
Nauset Press

**Consulting
Development Readers**
Linda Ganjian
Heather Klinkhamer
Leila Merl
Kate Novotny

**Reader's Guide
Question Development**
Stephanie Cohen
Heather Klinkhamer
Tiffany Morris
Margaret Seiler

Index
Heather Dubnick

FIERCE

Essays by and About Dauntless Women

Written by

Nancy Agabian

Betsy Andrews

Debra Brehmer

Kara Lee Corthron

Chicava HoneyChild

Robyn Kraft

Caitlin Grace McDonnell

Leah Mueller

Meera Nair

Edissa Nicolás-Huntsman

Jessie Serfilippi

Claudia Smith

Taté Walker

Illustrations by

Anna Torbina

Edited by

Karyn Kloumann

I am not free while any woman is unfree, even when her shackles are very different from my own.

— Audre Lorde

Contents

Preface

Distilling the essence of each essay
to a single word

༄

Defiant

Antiwar

Origins

Revelry

Provocateur

Blind

Audacious

Persistent

Present

Transcendent

Deliverance

Disappearance

Lyrical

Foreword and Introduction

*D*uring the spring of 2018, *The New York Times* and *National Geographic* apologized for a collective three centuries worth of implicit bias in their articles. Their apologies were intended to undo some of the damage of the past while acknowledging the importance of their role in helping to shape the future through a more equitable view of both women and minorities. The *New York Times* retroactively published obituaries of previously ignored notable women in a new section called "Overlooked."[1] Meanwhile, in their April 2018 issue, *National Geographic* apologized for past racist and colonialist prejudice and explained their objective to correct the record for their readers.[2] As shown by these two mainstream print media outlets, we seem to be in the midst of a cultural reevaluation. Coincidentally, this anthology, *Fierce: Essays by and About Dauntless Women*, is timely, although the idea for it has been brewing in my mind for over a decade. It took an additional three years to bring to fruition and crested with current social media campaigns such as #BlackLivesMatter, #NoDAPL, #MeToo, and #TimesUp—all significant movements launched by women of color.

Some of the questions raised in this book are no different from those posited by the suffragettes of the early twentieth century—not to mention first- and second-wave feminists—whereas others are more contemporary and esoteric. However, these are questions that still need to be answered, and not just in theory. As we move toward the one-hundredth anniversary of the passage of the Nineteenth Amendment (which granted women the right to vote in America), we must ask ourselves the following:

> *What does it mean to have representation?*
> *Is feminism relevant without intersectionality?*
> *Who determines citizenship and voting access and eligibility?*
> *How does one maintain agency over one's body?*
> *What does it mean to be accorded humanity?*
> *How does one acquire education and gain access to opportunities and*
> *   power in an unequal society?*
> *Can systemic oppressions be rendered obsolete?*
> *How can one be paid equally to men and garner economic parity for*
> *   similar work?*

These are a few of the broader questions considered in this book. Also, the *Reader's Guide* section at the back of the book is highly recommended as threshold into a deeper parsing of the issues and ideas evoked by each essay and brings each essay into focus with the fierce and dauntless spirits that motivated them.

The obscure and dusty biographies of women such as Margaret Cavendish, Julie D'Aubigny, Bricktop, Alice Ramsey, and Deborah Sampson are paired with contemporary personal narratives and analyses that breathe new life into these historical figures, showing how the past is inextricably germane to the present. The distinctive voice of each essay in *Fierce* has its truth, and to paraphrase artist and philosopher Adrian Piper, if any of these voices make you self-conscious about your beliefs and your strategies for preserving them, or uncomfortable or annoyed at reading them, or raise glimmerings of doubt about the veracity of your opinions, then this tome will have succeeded in blasting what Piper called "the illusion of omniscience."[3]

The system of gender inequality in Western society has long, deep, and stubborn roots. In *Women & Power: A Manifesto*, British classicist Mary Beard describes a moment in one of the earliest instances of literature, *The Odyssey*. During a party, Telemachus, the grown son of Odysseus and Penelope, sends his middle-aged mother back to her room like she is a naughty child and tells her to shut up when she protests the night's entertainments:

> ...*speech will be the business of men, all men, and of me most of all;*
> *for mine is the power in this household.*[4]

Two millennia after Telemachus' dominance display, a deeply entrenched pattern of patriarchal arrogance continues to reverberate across time and cultures as normative, affecting the livelihood, person-hood, security, and well-being of half of the population on the planet in ways both big and small. *Fierce* essayist Edissa Nicolás-Huntsman encloses a one-act play in her essay, which excerpts texts from public speeches by Ernestine Rose. At one point, during an enactment of the Second National Woman's Rights Convention in 1851, a "Chorus of Priests" drones to the Albany State Legislature about Rose:

> *She is indecent, an unevenly yoked woman, who should not be permitted to engage in public speaking. Why is she permitted to agitate the public? Let us use our power to silence her.*[5]

Unfortunately, this echo of Telemachus' arrogance continues to resound loudly even today. Some 167 years after the attempted silencing of Rose's speech, Senator Elizabeth Warren (D-MA) was shut down by Mitch McConnell (R-KY). On February 7, 2017, Warren read testimony aloud from Coretta Scott King's 1986 letter about the suitability of Jeff Sessions' confirmation.[6] Not unlike a snapping turtle, McConnell sniped defensively:

> *Senator Warren was giving a lengthy speech. She had appeared to violate the rule. She was warned. She was given an explanation. Nevertheless, she persisted.*[7]

The Senate sustained McConnell's objection, effectively silencing Warren. Later, Jeff Merkley (D-OR) was allowed to read King's letter without complaints.

In addition to public silencing, the parallel behavior of random men policing women's expressions, appearances, and moral virtue by demanding that they smile in public reinforces the idea that women have the lowly social status of children: "be seen, not heard." *Fierce* essayist Leah Mueller shares a fitting anecdote of a man scuttling away after her negative response to his question asking whether she was "a pure column of unspoiled light." Former US President Jimmy Carter said in a 2018 commencement address at Liberty University, "Recently, I've changed my mind about the biggest challenge that the world faces [...] it's a human rights problem and it is the discrimination against women and girls in the world."[8]

In seventeenth-century Germany, women artists were forbidden by guilds to paint professionally with oils; they were relegated to the use of watercolors instead.[9] This may seem like a quaintly arbitrary example of inequality, but it is not an exaggeration to consider that women today are still shut down subtly and blatantly in the office, the classroom, the bedroom, the political arena, and other spheres, both public and private. For example, although men named "John" make up only 3 percent of the American population, and women make up 50 percent of the American population, the *Glass Ceiling Index* exposed a statistical rift by calculating that the possibility of encountering a female CEO is about the same as finding a man named John in the same position.[10] *Fierce* essayist Debra Brehmer points out in her essay on Victorine Meurent and Laure that "capitalism was and still is a steamroller that does not respect difference or realignments of power."

Symbolically, the forty-fifth US president—a self-described predator[11] (and traitor, too?)—epitomizes the most galling, high-profile example of an unprepared, inexperienced candidate blundering stupidly into a job at the expense of the obviously more competent, intelligent, and qualified candidate, Hilary Clinton—likability issues aside. Even as she handily won the popular vote, Clinton's aspiration to helm the White House proved to be an edge too far for the electoral college to sustain, and according to exit polls, 53 percent of white women nationwide, boosted by wins in gerrymandered districts and the non-participation of people who didn't vote, bear responsibility for the current result[12] (pending evidence about Russian election meddling notwithstanding). This outcome implies an ethos that French-Algerian feminist Hélène Cixous describes in her essay "The Laugh of the Medusa": "Men have committed the greatest crime against women [...] they have [led] them to hate women, to be their own enemies, to mobilize their immense strength against themselves."[13]

Electing the hindmost dregs of the Republican lineup, however, has fomented a backlash of other-thinking female rage that has exploded in the pressure cooker of social media and resulted in measurable socioeconomic repercussions for specific men who previously inhabited some of society's highest-paying and most coveted positions of power. Perhaps it is the start of a long overdue cultural shift in which women, men, and those who identify as non-binary can all be human together, equally worthy of empathy and dignity.

During a 1986 commencement speech at Bryn Mawr College, the novelist Ursula K. Le Guin rallied,

> ...*when women speak truly they speak subversively—they can't help it: if you're underneath, if you're kept down, you break out, you subvert [...] I am sick of the silence of women [...] Speak with a woman's tongue. Come out and tell us what time of night it is! Don't let us sink back into silence. If we don't tell our truth, who will?*[14]

In the spirit embodied by Le Guin, and to further amplify diverse female voices, I asked twenty writers to share their personal and creative perspectives to bridge the muddy gaps of history—the dense hagiographies, the thickets of elisions and mis-characterizations—and burnish them with their specific contemporary focus and shine. Of the original twenty submissions, thirteen essays are published in this book—coincidentally, an ideal number for a coven, primed to change the tenor of the conversation about gender roles and societal norms.

This idea of a coven also led to the concept for the cover image, a variant on a witch's ladder, based on a nineteenth-century artifact: twine tied with feathers found in an attic in England alongside six brooms and a chair. It's purported use was to steal milk from a neighbor or to cause death, although modern users reportedly practice with the intention of positive outcomes.[15] Like a witch's ladder, *Fierce* straddles the space between positive and negative; it does so by advocating for awareness and the destruction of unreasonable and unjust power structures to make way for creating a more evolved and principled society.

⌁

A Brief Introduction to Each Essay

Each tag on the cover of *Fierce* is inscribed with a single word, chosen by each writer, distilling the direction of each essay. In the following introductory descriptions, the writers, their subjects, and each essayist's defining word are bolded. These truths, as varied as their subjects may be, are expressed in the thirteen essays that follow.

1) *Nangeli: Her Defiant Breasts*

Meera Nair dissects and excoriates the socio-political injustice and violence normalized by centuries of colonialist reinforcement of caste distinctions in nineteenth-century and modern-day India with her searing and personal essay about **Nangeli**, a low-caste woman who **defied** the law with a horrifying personal sacrifice.

2) *Baba Yaga Unleashed: The Night Witches*

Betsy Andrews writes about the "**night witches**," Soviet women pilots who coolly bombed the enemy during World War II. Andrews uses fairytale conceits to craft emotional images of their airborne violence, rooted in the twin catalysts of anger and patrimony in service of the broader sweep of war. Far from admiring the bold and ruthless destruction, Andrews' stance is resolutely **antiwar**.

3) *Origins*

Lakota writer and activist **Taté Walker** features **Ptesáŋwiŋ** (White Buffalo Calf Woman), a figure from Lakota oral history. Walker invokes Ptesáŋwiŋ to weave a tale of pre- and post-colonial feminism with personal and political threads, a tale backed by statistical evidence. Walker's storytelling forces an uncomfortable reckoning among readers of conscience with white and settler privilege, who—due to government-led genocide, media misrepresentation, and erasure of Indigenous people—often forget Indigenous women in their quests for justice. *Origins* compels readers to be better as allies, friends, and sisters.

4) *Reveling and Rebelling: A Look at the Life of Ada "Bricktop" Smith*

Playwright and author **Kara Lee Corthron** illuminates globe trotting nightclub owner **Bricktop**, who opened venues in Paris, Rome, and Mexico City. These nightclubs were enjoyed by twentieth-century luminaries including F. Scott Fitzgerald, Cole Porter, and Josephine Baker. Deeply layered issues of colorism, survival, and sexuality underpin the celebratory **revelry** of this essay.

5) *Firebrand: The Radical Life and Times of Annie Besant*

Writer **Leah Mueller** (who works as a professional astrologer and tarot-card reader) seeks to understand nineteenth-century theosophist, anti-colonialist, and activist **provocateur Annie Besant** vis-à-vis her own experiences, utilizing the mystical to parse the psychological implications of sexism.

6) *Victorine and Laure in Manet's* Olympia: *Seeing and Not Seeing a Famous Painting*

Debra Brehmer experiences a timely assessment of her metaphorical **blindness** in her pointed and trenchant essay about nineteenth-century artist and artist's muse **Victorine Meurent** and her little-known fellow model, **Laure**, in Manet's "Olympia."

7) *Audacious Warrior: Ernestine Rose*

Edissa Nicolás-Huntsman creatively envisions an unexpected intersection and overlap between herself, a twenty-first-century black, third-world feminist with Caribbean roots, and **Ernestine Rose**, an **audacious** nineteenth-century former-Jewish, European, freethinking abolitionist. Through her activism, Rose established the groundwork for better-known feminists such as Susan B. Anthony.

8) *Up from the Rubbish Heap: The Persistence of Julie D'Aubigny*
The seventeenth-century sword fighter and opera star **Julie D'Aubigny** lived several scandalous and outrageous lifetimes compressed into a singular life. Poet **Caitlin Grace McDonnell** compares her own **persistent** familial fighting spirit, including the life of her great-grandmother who fenced professionally in vaudeville theater as well as offstage.

9) *The Blazing Worlds of Margaret Cavendish*
Robyn Kraft examines the uneasy **presence** of women in the twenty-first-century male-dominated culture of fantasy and sci-fi by studying seventeenth-century duchess **Margaret Cavendish**, who is credited with being one of the earliest science fiction writers.

10) *Radiant Identity: Chicaba Herstories*
Chicava HoneyChild unearths the **transcendence** of **Chicaba,** also known as **Teresa, Sister Juliana of Santo Domingo**, an eighteenth-century kidnapped African princess who became a Spanish slave and later a Catholic nun after the demise of the woman who called herself Chicaba's owner. The source material is tainted by the agenda of second-party accounts. Although it is not known what Chicaba's true thoughts were, her spirit and resilience inspire.

11) *Under the Cover of Breeches and Bayonet*
Hundreds of years after **Deborah Sampson**, a gender-bending Revolutionary War soldier, trod the Earth, **Jessie Serfilippi** traverses Sampson's exact footsteps around present-day New York State. By cinematically documenting Sampson's life, Serfilippi finds self-agency in her own **deliverance** via a historical investigation that does not always align with desired outcomes about modern representations of sexuality.

12) *Rose-Poisoning: Beauty, Violence, and the Uncertain History of Zabel Yessayan*

Writer **Nancy Agabian** entwines her own generational family dynamics into her examination of the overarching idea of **disappearance** by investigating the life of **Zabel Yessayan**, an Armenian intellectual and writer active during the late nineteenth-century massacres that led to the early twentieth-century Armenian genocide.

13) *Trek Across a Trackless Land*

Claudia Smith depicts a **lyrical** romanticism in her essay. In the early twentieth century, before a continent of paved roads existed, **Alice Ramsey** was the first white woman to navigate the classic coast-to-coast American road trip. Smith, an academic and mother seeking economic stability in the American South, contrasts her own peripatetic road travels and cultural touchstones, including the film *Thelma and Louise*, by way of snapshot-like vignettes.

—*Karyn Kloumann*
July 24, 2018
Brooklyn, New York

Nangeli: Her Defiant Breasts

By Meera Nair

One morning in 1803 in Mulachiparamba, on a tiny sliver of land in the state of Kerala in Southern India, a young woman named Nangeli ducks out of her hut and goes to work as usual. She has skin the color of milky coffee and curly hair that hangs down her back. Her homespun sarong hugs her hips and legs, made strong by hard labor in the fields. As she sets off down the dirt path, fronds of the coconut trees high above her rattle and creak in the humid breezes that waft from the Arabian Sea.

In India then, as it is now, it is a curse to be a beautiful woman from the lower castes. I imagine Nangeli keeps her eyes fixed on the ground, as she has learned to look demure and submissive. She has trained herself to become invisible. She has to do this as a survival tactic, because to be noticed is dangerous. I imagine that she looks up now and then—a quick glance that she hopes does not catch on the barbed wire of a hostile glare—perhaps to catch a glimpse of her husband and love, Chirukkandan, as he drives a plow or scales a coconut tree. Her husband is from the Ezhava caste, as is she. In their tiny village of Chertala in Southern India, a lower-caste couple like them would only find work in the fields owned by the upper-caste families.

Nangeli and Chirukkandan. In the thin documentation on them I can find, my heroine sometimes shows up as "Nacheli." Who is she, then, this woman to whom I now give hair and breasts and attitude? This woman with a disputed first name and no last name?

Until recently, the area around her hut was called Mulachiparamba, which translates from Malayalam, the native language of Kerala, as "Field of the Breasted Woman." Nowadays, there are buildings where Nangeli's hut once stood, with stores painted blue and white that sell plastic cans and rope and cheap bras in bright colors. At night, the street dogs run free and howl in the streets. There is no memorial to Nangeli, no monument that anyone can show off or claim.

Fast forward for a moment to 2015: Nangeli's great-great-grand-niece, Leela Amma, tells the enterprising reporter from the *Times of India* who tracked her down that Nangeli's face lived up to her name, which means "beautiful one." The niece had heard stories, handed down from mother to daughter, generation to generation. The niece's family was poor, and they rationed out the story of their famous ancestor, stingily, like it was gold. It pleases me that this woman, Nangeli, who I think of as a heroine, was beautiful. I'm shallow like that.

Now, consider the antagonist, the erstwhile king of the Kingdom of Travancore who ruled vast lands, including Nangeli's little village. One in a long line of powerful rulers, the king's name stretches to a paragraph: Sripadmanabha Dasa Vanchipala Balaramavarma Kulashekhara Kireedapathi Manne Sulthan Maharajarajarama Rajabahadoor Shamsherjang Maharaja. Or Maharaja Avittom Thirunal Balarama Varma Kulasekhara[1]—for short!

The king's name indicates the ruling dynasty he is descended from, including honorary titles bestowed upon him and even the fortunate astrological sign under which he was born. In the principality, his family ruled for centuries, and his lower-caste subjects like Nangeli and Chirukkandan were subject to over a hundred laws designed, with calculated and brutal cruelty, to oppress and humiliate them. These laws were sanctioned by Hinduism, India's dominant religion, which reinforces the caste system,[1] a system that Professor Anupama Rao calls "inherited privilege," where people are born into their castes, much like race in America.

Nangeli and Chirukkandan live in a world where everyday interactions are codified into complex rules. For instance, "a Chovan [Ezhava] must remain thirty-six paces off, and a Pulayan slave ninety-six steps distant. A Chovan must remain twelve steps away from a Nair, and a Pulayan sixty-six steps off, and a Parayan some distance farther still. Pulayans and Parayans, who are the lowest of all, can approach but not touch, much less may they eat with each other."[2]

There are subtle variations among and within castes that are too complex and numerous to go into here. There are also geographical differences across the vast country of India, where certain castes dominate over others based on region. On the whole, however, the system is intricate and inflexible, inviolate. It is enforced through strict endogamy; to marry out of one's caste is to risk being ostracized or even being put to death. For Nangeli and Chirukkandan, it is an oppression from which there is no recourse or relief. They were born into their caste and cannot escape it, just as a black man cannot shrug off his skin. For people in the uppermost castes, however, the system is one of advantage; the structure creates a whole class of people over whom they can maintain power, exploit economically, and dominate with impunity.

⌁

11. "When (the gods) divided Purusha, into how many parts did they cut him up? What was his mouth? What arms (had he)? What (two objects) are said (to have been) his thighs and feet? 12. The Brahmana was his mouth, the Rajanya was made his arms; the being called the Vaishya, he was his thighs; the Shudra sprang from his feet."

This is the Purusha Sukta (the poem to the Cosmic Being), the Ninetieth Hymn of the Tenth Mandala in the Rig Veda. It is the first and most influential of the four Vedas, the sacred scriptures that arose from the Indian subcontinent around 1200 BC. At first glance, these two verses are explanations of how the four ancient classes, namely the priests (Brahmins), warriors (Rajanya or Kshatriya), traders (Vaishyas), and servants (Shudras) were constituted from the body of Purusha, the creator, "for the protection of this whole creation."[3]

At its most innocent, the hymn is a story of the origin of the universe, of a piece with other cosmogonies like the Genesis of the Old Testament. But unlike Genesis, the verses are not understood as poetic and hyperbolic explanations of cosmic phenomena. This verse and this verse alone is treated as an injunction, a divine law, and a mantra so sacred that it cannot be questioned.

It must be obeyed and enforced to codify ancient Indo-Aryan society.

Sanctioned, systemic oppression, Ambedkar's "graded inequality," which was conveniently backed by holy scripture, was the bedrock of Hinduism for 3,000 years.[4] It took an existing social order—namely, the natural sorting of ancient society into priests, warriors, traders, and workers—and "idealized the rule," Ambedkar says, blowing the golden dust of divinity over it and making it sacred.[5]

In the eighteenth and nineteenth centuries, the verses of Genesis 9:18–27 in the Old Testament, the curse of Ham, became a foundation myth for collective degradation, readily trotted out as God's reason for condemning generations of dark-skinned peoples from Africa to slavery in America. In the same way, the scriptural argument from the Rig Veda, the so-called sacredness of the original source, is what was used to justify the debasement and exploitation of millions of men and women like Nangeli. Because the Shudra servant sprang from the Creator's feet, he or she is to be treated as the lowest of the low, a being who exists to serve, and to whom it is not necessary to even extend basic dignity.

By the second century CE, caste-based discrimination was firmly embalmed into Indian thought via the ancient text, *Manusmriti*, or *The Laws of Manu*, the most influential of the Hindu *dharmashastras*, or law books that organize and lay down the code of conduct for human society. *The Laws of Manu* uphold the Vedic view that society is to be divided along the lines of those who know the Vedas (Brahmins), those who govern the land (Kshatriyas), those who trade (Vaishyas), and those who serve (Shudra). The worst punishments in the book, though, are reserved for the Shudras, whose "single activity" allotted by the Lord was "ungrudging service to those very social classes."[6] Dalit leader B.R. Ambedkar, a great thinker and theorist of caste inequality and architect of the Indian Constitution, argues that the consequence of the original hymn from the Rig Veda was far more influential than its meaning: "Besides dividing society into four orders, the theory goes further and makes the principle of graded inequality the basis for determining the terms of associated life as between the four *Varnas* [castes]."[7]

No discussion of caste in India can be complete, however, without noting the influence of the British, who colonized India from the eighteenth century to 1947. Although medieval Indians accepted *The Laws of Manu* as the standard, the text was loosely and flexibly applied in everyday life: "Different groups in different regions enforced their own lists of crimes and punishments," Ambedkar says. "The law therefore took on varied form[s] depending in the locale."[8] As the British consolidated their rule over the country, however, their administrators began to formalize what was an adaptive and inconsistent code into enforceable law. They "redoubled the importance of caste in daily Indian life, and gave the institution governmental legitimacy it had not enjoyed since during the time of Manu, if even then."[9] The end result was a further consolidation of caste difference and discrimination in society, backed by the full authority of the state.

When I visit India and see its great, modern cities flaunting monoliths of glass and steel, its opulent shopping malls and roads choked with Mercedes-Benz and Hyundai cars, or when I drop in to the nightclubs crowded with millennials who wear the same short skirts and unruly beards as their hipster counterparts do in New York and Paris, it is hard for me to make peace with the idea that a caste system derived from the Rig Veda—composed as long ago as it was—continues to influence my country of birth. I once asked a young Indian techie I knew in Bangalore if he knew the Chaturvarnya, or the four-caste hierarchy that has organized Hindu society for thousands of years.

He looked bewildered at my question. "I guess so. But who cares?" he said. "All that stuff is finished—look around you." He waved his hand at his coworkers, who stared at their screens in slick red-and-yellow cubicles. "You think I know who's what caste?" He sounded affronted.

I was tempted to ask him if his mom had a separate plate and glass for the maid in their house or if she stood a carefully calibrated distance away from the street sweeper. But I didn't. What would that have gotten me? He would have probably shrugged and said yes, laughing at his mother in the way my liberal friends in New York snicker about the racist uncles they have to tolerate at Thanksgiving. For most people in India, the social separation between people of different castes is an unremarkable aspect of everyday existence, something that they leave unquestioned. Worse, they find it not worth questioning.

As a child, my summer began the moment we stepped onto the Kanyakumari Express. The train took three days to wind slowly down India's middle before it brought us to the cool green oasis that was my grandparents' farm. One June, I entered the train car with my obviously middle-class family. Our fellow passengers looked up at us—me in my jeans, my fair, pretty mother in sunglasses and the latest non-crush sari—and jumped up, smiling and friendly, to move suitcases to make space for ours. I was pulling out my book and settling down when one of these strangers we had just met leaned over to my mother and asked, "Sister, what is your caste?"

That was the first time I became aware of caste differences and of people's need to classify us. On other journeys, when the same question was asked, I watched my mother smiling and smiling, saying, "We are Kshatriyas, Nairs from Kerala. My great-grandfather was a soldier in the king's army." I paraphrase, but that was the gist. She was eager to prove superiority, or at the very least, claim equality. (Many years later, I found out that although solid research exists that Nairs were renowned soldiers in the armies of various rulers of Kerala, the origin of the Nair caste itself is uncertain. Several conflicting theories exist, including one that says that Nairs are descendants of snake-worshiping tribes from Northern India.)

To my ten-year old ear, though, the subtext was clear. We were acceptable. Our family had the right blood and ancestry, and we were "the better sort of Indian" that Salman Rushdie lampoons in *Midnight's Children*. As I grew older, I would climb up into the bunk above the seats and stew there in an adolescent rage at my mother's lack of revolutionary fervor. I hated her eager submission and pandering participation in the charade of friendship that followed in the train compartment. I wanted no part of the unseemly sorting, the rush to self-congratulatory solidarity along caste lines. I would lie there with my jaw clenched, staring at the words in my book until they dissolved into squiggles, reveling in my smug, righteous virtue.

I will never become like them; I won't. I won't.

⁓

On most days, when Nangeli steps out of her hut and walks down the dirt road, she is naked from the waist up. As a lower-caste woman, she is forbidden to cover her breasts in public. Under the king's decree, only upper-caste women have the right to hide their breasts from the eyes of strangers. Nangeli's breasts need to be uncovered because they display a coda that is easily interpreted. Clothing, hair, jewelry—they are all part of an elaborate signage system, "the spectacle of the body" that is "replete with caste markers," as Professor Udaya Kumar points out.[10] Members of the upper castes read Nangeli's naked breasts as we would a flashing stop sign—as a strict warning to maintain their distance from her to avoid being polluted. The belief, outrageous and unscientific but deeply held, is that a lower-caste person transmits her impurity through the air and pollutes everyone else. In this worldview, the very body of a human born into the lower castes is corrupt and contaminated. Its mere shadow has the power to defile the higher-caste body. In the old days, high-caste dignitaries had a crier who ran ahead of them on the street, announcing their approach. Lower-caste passersby who were unfortunate enough to be in the path of the approaching personage would dive into the bushes or sink down into the ditch beside the road so that the exalted, worthy person wouldn't be tainted by the sight of them.

And yet, Nangeli's breasts, coerced into display, are also a spectacle attracting scrutiny and examination. Although she is not seen as a wholly human person, her body is not permitted to disappear.

She is thus simultaneously sign and spectacle.

The sign says to stay away, and the spectacle says, "Look at me." Her nakedness invites strangers to notice her sexuality. Her lower-caste status gives higher-caste people ritual sanction to stare, to visually possess her. The high castes restrict the availability of other bodies to Nangeli's by making sure she stays within her bounded space, but they increase their own access to her body by making more of her visible to their gaze.

In July of 2016, CNN reported that according to India's National Crime Records Bureau, more than four Dalit women or women from the lowest untouchable castes are raped every day in India. That amounts to twenty-eight women raped in a week. In many cases, upper-caste men commit these crimes. One woman was gang-raped in a village near where Bimetal Devi, age forty, lived. A reporter interviewed Devi. She said, "We cannot send our daughters unaccompanied to the fields to fetch water or even to school. Men from the upper caste stare at our daughters with lustful eyes."[11]

In 1803, lower-caste women who were caught covering their breasts had to pay a tax. The king, Maharaja Avittom Thirunal Balarama Varma Kulasekhara-1, invented a mulakaram, or "breast tax," for the rebellious ones. The tax was prorated to the size of the taxed woman's breasts—the larger the breasts, the higher the tax. In Travancore, women were punished for denying the upper caste their right to look at their breasts.

For Nangeli, nakedness is not the natural, pleasurable state that it can be for so many of us. John Berger argues in *Ways of Seeing* that "nakedness reveals itself. Nudity is placed on display."[12] In Nangeli's case, she is a perpetually sexualized object, her nudity a condition that has been thrust upon her to advance the fantasy of continuous control, to make of her what the upper caste wants her to be—a woman disrobed upon their command. She is an object, a degraded, stigmatized, sexualized thing. Nangeli is rendered powerless by decree and is expected to be available at all times to the implicit, possessing, panoptic, upper-caste, presumably male gaze.

The tax is a punishment. She may not withdraw her breasts and body from the spaces they are forced to inhabit. She may not attempt concealment. She may not dare to intimately and privately engage with her own body. The state feels no need to hide what it is doing: Nangeli is on display, at and for the pleasure of men.

In the 90s, I got a job and disappeared gratefully into the anonymity of one of India's giant cities. My friends and I inhabited spaces where no one asked questions about who we were. I was smart, creative, and enterprising, and I could write. My job—my identity, my power to fit smoothly into the fun but frantic world of advertising—came from these abilities alone, unhampered by caste. My world was Westernized, one in which I felt safe creating a life where I did whatever I wanted. I lived as if I wasn't a citizen of a country where twenty-eight lower-caste women are raped every week. In the cities where I lived, a new country was taking shape, one that offered neon-lit nights of vodka-imbibing, nightclubbing, boyfriends, and a house of my own, where, for the first time, I could live alone and independently.

I had a maid who came and cleaned my place every day. Radha was a stocky fifteen-year-old who, in spite of living with a father who was a drunk and threw water on her textbooks, was at the top of her tenth-grade class at her public school. She was a sad young thing. She went to school during the day, then to her second job cleaning a corporate office. By the time she dragged her stolid self to my house, it would be late in the evening. I was never home, so I gave her a key and told her that didn't care if she swabbed my floors at eight o'clock in the evening. Some nights, I would come home to gleaming floors, and there she would be, bent glumly over her books. I didn't ask why she studied so late in my house. She wasn't the chatty type, nor was I. I figured she put off returning to her family's chaos for as long as she could.

One night, I got home earlier than usual and found Radha squatting on the floor in a corner of the kitchen, scooping cold rice with her fingers straight from the pan into her mouth. She was eating leftovers from my fridge. She flinched at the sight of me, almost dropping the rice, before she scrambled up and stood staring at the floor.

In the dim-yellow light of the kitchen, I looked at her round, heaving shoulders in her threadbare tunic, my heart beating hard. I couldn't tell if I was embarrassed for myself or for having put her into this abject position. Perhaps both. I had just returned from a restaurant where my colleagues and I had eaten and drunk for hours. Radha hadn't eaten since that morning. Her mother, who worked as a cook, made my dinner and left it in the fridge. There were many days when I didn't eat at home.

"You can eat whatever is in the fridge," I mumbled and started to rush away. Then I remembered to add, "There's no need to sit on the floor."

A few months later, my mother came to stay. One evening, we were eating dinner when she looked up from her meal, abruptly furious.

"You let that servant girl eat on the same plates as we do?" she asked. "Why don't you have separate plate and glass for her?" My mother had trained in classical Bharatanatyam, a two-thousand-year-old dance form. She had represented her district in athletics in high school. She was the kind of woman who stuffed my old shirts and skirts into a suitcase and lugged them back to her farm so she could resize them to fit some poor farm-hand's wife or daughter.

Yet, she raged at me because I had let Radha eat from the plates we ate from every day.

How could you? What were you thinking? It's disgusting.

Radha's caste was low enough that the principal of ritual pollution and purity should have stayed firmly in place within our dynamic. Ritual pollution derives from bodily fluids such as blood, semen, saliva, feces, hair, nail clippings, and so on, and there were complex restrictions in place on the food and water touched or supplied by members of the lower castes. Granted, my mother was fine with Radha cleaning the house or folding her clothes—but the idea of eating from a plate that a Shudra might have, at one point, eaten from was too much to stomach.

I once thought that my mother's silly posturing on the train was as far as her caste consciousness went. Who was this person accusing me of being a communist and threatening to not talk to me or eat in my house from that moment on? It was all because I had treated a servant like a human being. Apparently, my mother's compassion and generosity were conditional. The rules of servitude, the rituals of separation and deference—we on our chairs, the servants on the floor, distance between bodies and food and mouth and fingers—had to be strictly observed. Only then would she continue to be her pleasant, kind self. The daily performance of inequality was necessary on Radha's part and ours, because that was what was required to maintain the whole rotten edifice of upper-caste–lower-caste interactions.

I often feel a tinge of guilt when I remember my mother's confusion and seemingly genuine feelings of betrayal that day. She couldn't understand why I wanted to do this to her, to force her to overcome her most deeply held beliefs. If I allowed myself to be honest, I would have acknowledged that she was afraid of what my repudiation meant. By breaching the separation between Radha's body and mine, I was conveying that the whole system that my mother had so carefully maintained was wrong—that it could be easily shaken.

I had discarded it easily, and to my mother, it likely felt as if I was disowning not only our traditions, but *her*. I was cutting myself off from that which most comforted her, the fixed intimacy of ritual. The rituals remained unexamined beyond that catchall "that's how it's always done," but knowledge rose between us, sharp and thorny. I knew more about her than she cared to understand.

My transgression—made worse because I was her daughter and owed her filial piety—was my explicit refusal to prop up the rules she lived by anymore. I use this incident as a milder manifestation of that other, more destructive fury that sets the upper castes on the lower ones. It arises without warning when the lower castes raise their heads, make more money, go to school, dare to cover themselves, drink water from the wrong well, stand too close, aspire to look like us, dress like us, or eat like us. That is when the poorest Brahmin or the most ignorant Nair will have them smashed back into the ground.

"How dare she? How dare she?" my mother had shouted at me.

⌒

The Bhotmange family lived in the village of Khairlanji in Maharashtra, a state in western India. They were lower caste but upwardly mobile. The husband, Bhaiyalal, and his wife, Surekha, owned some land; their children had bicycles, even a phone; and Priyanaka, their only daughter, was a good student in her tenth grade class. Surekha wasn't afraid to stand up for herself and was known to yell at the upper-caste villagers who trampled the family's crops.

Perhaps it was the relative prosperity of the Bhotmange family that irritated the dominant men and women of the village. Or perhaps it was the fact that Bhaiyalal wasn't afraid to exercise his constitutional rights. When some landowning villagers beat up a friend of theirs, Bhaiyalal complained to the police. The police complaint antagonized the upper castes even further against the Bhotmange family.

On September 29, 2006, Surekha Bhotmange, the mother, her two sons, Sudhir and Roshan Bhotmange, and her daughter, Priyanka Bhotmange, were dragged out of their house by upper-caste men after an altercation. The mother and her children were stripped, paraded naked, and beaten. Sudhir was told to have sex with his sister Priyanka in public, and when he refused, the villagers, both men and women, beat him and Roshan and mutilated their genitals.

Surekha and Priyanka were gang raped until they died. A policeman who was summoned but did nothing to interfere later reported that the upper-caste men raped the Bhotmange women's bodies even after they were dead. Men and women from the village kicked and tossed the corpses of Sudhir and Roshan before the crowd of onlookers. No one stopped them, and when authorities came to take statements from the villagers days later, every single participant in the horrific incident stayed silent in caste solidarity.

Bhaiyalal was the only one who survived. He had witnessed the entire incident, hiding from the mob behind a tree. He later managed to escape from the village and inform the police. Even after the police, politicians, local and state governments, and the media got involved, investigations into the horrors that had taken place were stymied at every turn. The state, the justice system, the police, and the entire upper-caste bureaucracy tried everything they could

to obstruct the course of the law. It took years of organizing, countless marches, and sustained protest by the lower castes for any measure of justice to be served and for the accused to be sentenced to life imprisonment.

The family's home was razed to the ground long ago. In the midst of the patch of dirt and grass left behind stands a cot, its metal parts slowly rusting. Bhaiyalal let it remain there as a remembrance, to remind the villagers of his family. In an interview, Bhaiyalal said, "I go to Khairlanji every year on September 29 to pay tribute to my family along with many community organizations and leaders. Nobody in the village talks to me." He travels with a police escort. "I feel there is still some danger to my life," he said.[13] That interview was recorded in 2016.

⌐⌐

Nangeli disobeyed the king's orders. She covered her breasts, hid them away. Refused to be on display. History doesn't tell us why she decided to suddenly reclaim her body, to repossess her breasts. She chose to cover up, knowing that she would be severely punished. Nangeli—illiterate and unschooled as she may have been—accepted the risks of concealment. She preferred to delight in the discreet and enclosed. Her gesture seems to shout, "The parade is over, and the spectacle is done."

I imagine her pleasure, her reveling in her insubordinate power to deny the state access and use her body in her own terms. I imagine her dragging the rough cloth across the skin of her chest, tucking one end into her waistband, pulling the other loose end over her shoulder. I imagine her sailing out on the reliable vessel of her body, the cloth on her breasts fluttering like a flag. Did she feel the thrill of transgression as she stepped out into the controlled spaces of her village? Did she feel the exhilaration of the forbidden act? Did her heart beat, "Yes, yes!" as she stopped "No more!"?

We know that she walked along the paths of the village with her breasts hidden, mimicking the modesty afforded the women in the grand mansions of the highborn. We know someone snitched and that the news traveled quickly to the authorities. As surely as the sun sank toward the Indian Ocean that evening, the parvarthiyaar, or tax collector, showed up on her doorstep to collect the King's dues. In a society that had turned her unclothed body into a display, a woman finding joy in the experience of privacy and relishing her autonomy was a threat.

ᒪ

When I was twenty years old, I landed my first job as a copywriter for a small advertising outfit in Hyderabad. On my first day at work, I met Shanti. She was a small-boned, birdlike woman who was full of intrusive questions. She liked to gush over me, telling me often that my cheeks were like mangoes, or my clothes were "tip-top." Her friendship was insistent and determined. I tolerated her. I thought she was lonely, and I wasn't. I could afford to be generous with my attention. I had quickly made friends with the other young twenty-somethings in the office who came from similar homes as I did and who had seen the same movies. We would squeeze into the back of Sharif's tiny old car to go hiking along the rocky hills that ringed the city or drive to obscure restaurants for dinner.

Shanti wasn't invited. She didn't speak English very well and felt uncomfortable around us. She was a strict vegetarian. Now, I wonder if I made up excuses to leave her out. She heard us laughing carelessly at lunch about the time when I lost my sandals in the river, or when the car stalled in the midst of a passing herd of cows. She didn't hide the fact that she eavesdropped and would ask me eager questions—*where, when, how?*—as we walked out into the warm evening together after work.

One Saturday, she invited me to lunch at her house. She begged me to come, saying that she had told her mother to make a special meal for me. I remember feeling slightly put out, imposed upon. However, I didn't want to come across as a snob, so I agreed. She lived in a small concrete house with the rooms laid out one after the next in a straight line. Calendars of brightly colored Hindu gods and goddesses hung on the wan walls of the living room. It was furnished with a couple of scratched metal chairs and not much else.

Shanti left me alone in the room for the longest time. A thick, striped curtain hung in the doorway and separated the room from the rest of the house, and behind it, I could hear voices and the discreet clatter of utensils. I could smell rice cooking. No one else from the family came rushing out to say hello, as would have been normal in my household. I thought it was odd. Where was her mother? Her sisters? Who leaves a guest alone in the living room, especially in a culture where a favorite saying is "Athithi Devo Bhava," or "the Guest is as God?"

Eventually, Shanti came out holding a plate of food. Rice, lentils, and a vegetable were all mushed together on an aluminum plate that was dented around

the edges. She set the plate on the floor and laid out a mat next to it.

"Please sit," she said, and I—dumbstruck—obeyed. Her smile was off-kilter and excited. "We are Brahmin, so I'm not allowed to eat with you," she said. "I'll eat inside, okay?" Before I could open my mouth, she turned and disappeared behind the curtain.

I hadn't thought of Shanti in years until I started writing this essay. Then, I remembered the throat-closing, helpless humiliation I felt that day. The way I slumped, blindsided and abject on the floor, staring at that damaged plate of food. It all came back: my resentment, my swift, hard revulsion toward Shanti, my brain stuttering, *How dare she, how dare she?*

⤎

I was born into a household that prized curiosity above all else. My father and I fought over the merits of Marxism at dinner. As a teenager, I fell in love with dead writers: Faulkner, Kafka, and Dickens, for a start. But for Shanti, this self I had constructed wasn't good enough. On Shati's floor that day, my identity was distilled to its base element.

To her, I was my caste. Inferior. Nothing more, nothing less.

It didn't matter to her that I was born into an upper caste, just one rung below hers. Even that one level of difference allowed her the impunity to expect me, as a matter of course, to sit on the ground alone and eat from a separate plate—like any servant would.

But worse than what she'd done to me was what I did to myself. Faced with her judgment, I became a Kshatriya, a Nair, fighting like my soldiering ancestors, my fist and jaw clenched for the caste identity I had tried so hard to discard. I remember wanting to fling the old, "Do you know who I am?" at her like a knife. We are Nairs. My great-grandfather marched in the king's army, and my family has owned land for two-hundred years."

The boasting words came rushing up. Never mind that I had acted, for years, as if this part of myself did not exist. As I ripped off my thin Band-Aid of rationalization, this submerged identity came swaggering out, bloated with pride and resentment, slinging blood and soil with the rest of them. Until then, I hadn't taken a hard look at the cozy pieties of my comfortable life. My safe little seditions and my kindnesses to those less fortunate had remained unexamined.

⤎

I remembered other moments. Eating with my grandparents at the large wood table on the farm, the windows and doors open to a summer day, I hadn't given a thought to the farm hands eating on the veranda. It was only later that the sight of the farmhands a mere few feet away from me, bent over their food, began to make me uncomfortable. Yet, for years I never challenged the status quo, tried to eat with them, or made any attempt to break the rules. I had given these demarcations no thought as a child, had accepted them as the natural order of things.

I've come to understand how that natural order was subverted for Shanti by the way relationships operated at our modern workplace in a big city like Hyderabad. There we were, of a lower caste than her, enjoying more privilege, better pay, coziness in our higher social status, and our cool weekend adventures.

The caste system and its oppressions have been reshaped in India. Progressive movements during British rule and after the country won independence in 1942 restructured the caste system and mitigated its oppressions. A constitution was written as a promise toward a modern, democratic nation-state, which contained protections for marginalized communities and guaranteed equal rights for all citizens. Other safeguards, similar to affirmative action in the United States, ensured reserved seats for the lowest castes and opened opportunities that they'd been forbidden from gaining before. In the cities, at least, there was a semblance of modernity, a blurring of once-rigid distinctions.

When I recall Shanti's attempt to humiliate me—a pointed reminder of her once-superior caste position—by relegating me to the floor, I see a futile backlash against the loss of power that she must have felt daily. In her eyes, I was a threat, someone who was challenging or upending caste norms, disrespecting scripture, and violating thousands of years of caste practice.

༄

Nangeli, too, had thrown down a challenge by covering herself. Someone complained—perhaps a neighbor, unhappy with the fact that she was flaunting the rules. The parvarthiyaar showed up at her doorstep one evening and demanded she pay the breast tax. The tax inspector was a direct representative of the king, a high-caste Brahmin with all the trappings of royal office. He could not have come alone. He and his entourage would not have stepped into Nangeli's hut, which would have been be unthinkable to them, and they would not have allowed her to come any closer to them than the dreaded

thirty-six paces. The usual crowd of villagers would have come to gawk; this was an exhibition, a public humiliation.

Did Nangeli stand bent over her hands covering her mouth so her polluting breath would not escape? It was, after all, the attitude of abject subservience that was required of her kind. The inspector would have announced her crime and his charge. Or did she stand there, her breasts insurgent, thrust out for the assessment that the tax inspector was obliged to conduct?

There would have been other rituals she followed. Respect that had to be paid. The status of the personage at her door required it. She would have brought out a sacred oil lamp and lit its five wicks before placing it at his feet. Also arranged next to his feet would be brown grains of unhusked rice in a wooden measure—the tax she had to pay.

Then, Nangeli would have gone to the back of her hut, to her banana patch, and cut a green leaf, shaped wide as a giant's tongue, off the plant.

Alone in her backyard that day, I imagine that Nangeli filled her hands with the soft fruits of her breasts for one last time and raised her sickle. Then, the drawn-in breath, the sudden severance, the inner steeling as she arranged her breasts on the leaf and laid them at the man's feet.

Her tax, paid in full.

⚶

Nangeli's death, her act of literally offering her body as a revolt, was the flashpoint that led to long, sustained, unrelenting protests. It took a few years, but finally the king withdrew the tax and allowed lower caste women to cover themselves. Nangeli was poor, lower caste, and a woman. The laws of the state controlled her humanity and her sexuality, prescribing the spaces her body could occupy. But the moment Nangeli raised her sickle, she went from a woman controlled to an uncontrollable woman. Her severed breasts lay in front of the watching world, an outrage that triumphed over the obscenities the state had forced upon her. To the state that had condemned her to be a useless display, Nangeli brought a rebellion that would never be forgotten. In that instance of her self-dismemberment, Nangeli owned her own story and became whole. ✤

Baba Yaga Unleashed: The Night Witches

By Betsy Andrews

*L*et us begin with the bombs. Some say they weighed twenty-five kilograms. Others say thirty-two, fifty, or one-hundred kilograms. On the airstrip, each armorer, the strongest of the women, hung three tons of them each night. Working gloveless in the pitch-black frost, they felt for the four racks beneath the lower wing, tucking the devices into the womb of the Polikarpov Po-2 biplane. From above their targets, the pilots cut their engines, dive noiselessly, and yank at a jerry-rigged umbilical cord to birth their loads, about 661 pounds of explosives per flight.[1]

Birth. It's a lousy metaphor. But it's apt. The German soldiers were desperate for sleep. The 46th Taman Guards Night Bomber Aviation Regiment needled them every three minutes[2] every night on the Eastern Front at Stalingrad, at Krasnodar, at Minsk[3] —24,000 combat missions[4] in all.

The Germans knew witches when they encountered them. Starting with the fairytale hag that Hansel and Gretel burned in the iron-doored oven within a gingerbread house, the Brothers Grimm mythologized an awful actuality. Nearly half of the estimated 90,000 people, mostly women, who were persecuted during the European witch hunts died in Germany.[5] From the fifteenth to the eighteenth century, Germany was the locus of the craze. With roots that stretched back beyond the Holy Roman Empire, one character that engendered long-lasting anxiety in Germans was the "night witch." Careening at pregnant women while they slept in their beds, ripping babies from their wombs and devouring them, the night witch was the midwife of terror.[6]

Nachthexen—or "night witches"—is what the German soldiers called the Russian women bombers in their Po-2s. Plywood-framed and canvas-sheathed, their trainer craft—crop dusters previously utilized to dump chemicals on collectivized fields—were almost toy-like. Their rattling motors earned them the nickname "sewing machine[s]," like the modern inversion of the fairytale's magical spinning wheel with its stupor-inducing prick. They bombed all night, every night, and sleeplessness was a theme. Pilots drifted off, "almost snoozing away"—just "a little nap on the way to the target."[7] No one—not the night witches, not the Germans—got "a wink of sleep."[8]

When the pilots deliberately stalled their engines, the Po-2s' susurrations took on a deeper menace: the wind that thrummed the planes' bracing wires *whooshed* through the gap between upper and lower wings like a hag's broom sweeping the blackness. It was the murmur of oblivion, the seemingly innocuous whisper of fear. The women in their planes plummeted so close to the ground that they could hear the sleepless Germans' cries of "Nachthexen!"[9]

Wehrmacht infantrymen smoked quickly and tamped out their cigarettes, lest the women spy the glowing red tips from the air. A rumor spread among the Germans that the night witches were subject to special injections that gave them cat-like vision, to see in the dark. This, too, was a typical Nazi fantasy, an updated Grimms' tale wherein a diabolical physician prescribes a magic potion. But it was not far from the truth. The Russian medics pushed uppers on the pilots, "pills nicknamed Coca-Cola to keep us awake."[10] Still, there was a much more potent drug keeping them going, "a super human psychic overstrain."[11] The adrenaline of war made bombing addictive.

Witches, "very ugly night witches."[12] Not women. They couldn't be. When the 46th Taman Guards were deployed, German radio announcers were sanguine.

"All Soviet airmen are exterminated," they reported. "Now, Stalin is introducing all-female regiments, which will be destroyed easily as well."[13]

But the night witches proved these German radio reports wrong. "They fight like wild-cats and are quite subhuman," wrote one German soldier to another.[14] Monsters, not women. Shape-shifters.

"We simply couldn't grasp that the Soviet airmen that caused us the greatest trouble were in fact women," wrote Nazi general Johannes Steinhoff.[15] "These women feared nothing. They came night after night in their very slow biplanes."

German radio changed its tune. A prisoner of war told the Soviet women that the radio stations had begun to warn the *Wehrmacht* troops: "Attention, attention, the ladies are in the air, stay at your shelter."[16]

A Nazi pilot like Steinhoff, who gunned down a night witch, imploding her plane like it was paper to flame, was rewarded with Hitler's highest honor, the Knight's Cross of the Iron Cross, a medal in the shape of a flare-legged X with a swastika at its center.

⁓

I fell into this topic—bombed into it, really—by accident. I assumed that the Russians had named the 46th Taman Guards Night Bomber Aviation Regiment themselves, World War II's only all-female flight battalion, the "night witches" in reference to their own Baba Yaga. A pestle for her control stick, Baba Yaga, the fabled hag of the northern birch forests, takes to the sky in a mortar made of wood, like the Po-2 with its open cockpit. She comes home to a hut propped on chicken legs, skinny as the malnourished limbs of the 46th, swimming in their military-issue men's pants. The eyes in the skulls of Baba Yaga's victims glow around the perimeter of her yard, impaled on a fence made of their bones. She keeps a spatula for seating guests so she can ferry them efficiently into her oven.

Violent but omniscient, Baba Yaga has the dark smarts that Vasilisa, the princess heroine of Russian folklore, employs to get bloody revenge against her abusers. When Vasilisa seeks her out, Baba Yaga puts her up to impossible tasks. If the girl does her job well, the witch helps her. If she makes a mistake, Baba Yaga roasts her in the oven.[17]

I thought it was romantic, the handle "night witches," an invocation to the ancient crone power, the mystical violence in every woman that has potential to remake the world.

⁓

"At first," observed Nadezhda Popova, 46th Guards squadron commander, "no one in the Armed Forces wanted to give women the freedom to die."[18] A couple of months into the slaughter, "freedom" was granted, and subsequently, many of them died, though many more perished as civilians. Over one million women served in the Red Army,[19] though nearly seven million Soviet women lost their lives in the war. Perhaps enlisting gave them a fighting chance at survival. The 31 of the 230 night witches who died[20] were but very few of the women who enlisted. They weren't the only female aviators. But as symbols, they were outsized. They were the subject of frequent wartime reporting in the Soviet and foreign presses. Twenty-four of them became Heroes of the Soviet Union. It was the nation's highest honor.

After the war, Stalin said, "The Soviet woman has the same rights as a man, but that does not free her from a great and honorable duty which nature has given her: she is a mother, she gives life. This is certainly not a private affair, but one of great social significance."[21]Women soldiers were summarily discharged. They were barred from military schooling, the route to careers in the Soviet Air Force. Russia needed babies and factory goods, and for these, it needed women, not witches. The title of "Hero of the Soviet Union" was swapped for that of Heroine Mother, a status rewarded with a Motherhood Medal.[22]

Motherhood under Great Father Stalin could be as traumatizing as flying a bomber plane. During the war, pilot Mariya Akilina said. "When I was in the hospital, a letter came to the regiment informing me that my two children, ages two and five, had been killed in a bombing."[23]

After the war, pilot Serafima Amosova-Taranenko said, "There was an earthquake in Ashkhabad in 1948 when Stalin was in power, and he ordered us not to tell anybody. [...] My daughter was born in August, and she died in this earthquake."[24]

Mothers or monsters; in the fairytales, they are flip sides of the same tossed coin. And this, I thought, is how men let women wage war: as monsters. Baba Yaga, unleashed, howled up out of the children's books and exacted revenge on Vasilisa's abusers.

But, no, I was wrong. The Russians did not name the night witches. Baba Yaga, folkloric stand-in for Mother Russia herself, was already dead, "liberated" from her land during collectivization. She had starved, along with seven million other peasants, in 1932. The Soviets were in the thrall of modernism, a narcotic so strong it turned Vasilisa, the princess daughter, into an addict. The narcotic had a pusher in Joseph Stalin. So taken was he with industrialization that he named himself after its raw material: steel.

"We are becoming a nation of metal," he boasted.[25] At Red Square spectacles on May Day, Aviation Day, Red Army Day, International Youth Day, and October Revolution Day, Stalin showed off what steel could make: tanks, artillery guns, aircraft.

Steel was what modern Russian airplanes were made of. Fearful of flying, Stalin nonetheless loved airplanes, especially those built for long-range flight. Hurtling between the extreme reaches of the vast Soviet Union, distance fliers masked the societal whiplash of forced mechanization in a sportive display of Stalin's reach. His favorite was Marina Raskova, navigator of the three-woman crew of the Rodina, a plane whose name meant "motherland." A converted twin-engine, long-range bomber, the Rodina crash-landed in hideous weather at the end of a 6,500-kilometer haul from Moscow to Komsomolsk in the Far East, setting a distance record for women but leaving Raskova, who had bailed in a parachute, to wander the taiga, lost for ten days.

It was 1938. One-fifth of the Soviet population had just been arrested.[26] Perhaps the flight of the Rodina was a muscle-flexing diversion from the Great Terror. When crew was rescued and returned to Moscow, the survivors of the wreckage of a vessel called "Motherland," Stalin was waiting for them with a parade. With a state dinner. With kisses. And with a speech about the ancient matriarchal roots of Russian culture: "Today," he said, "these women have avenged the heavy centuries of the oppression of women."[27]

Baba Yaga turned in her grave. Meanwhile, in the labor camps of Stalin's metal cities, the bodies of women prisoners who had been worked to death piled up like lumber.[28] On the wind-lashed Ural steppes, the Stalin Magnitogorsk Metallurgical Complex, Stalin's pride, cranked out Stalin's steel for Stalin's airplanes. Enslaved peasant women were among those forced to build its foundries and furnaces.

A Hero of the Soviet Union and a member of the Supreme Soviet, Marina Raskova was an accomplished Stalinist by October 8, 1941, when, four months into a Nazi invasion that Stalin had insisted would never happen—a

denial that had him purging advisors who gave him evidence to the con-
trary—she convinced him to sign Order 0099 to authorize the formation
of three women's air battalions.

"I've received 112 little princesses," wrote the commander of the 218th
Night Bomber Aviation Division, D.D. Popov, to 4th Air Army General
Konstantin Vershinin. "Just what am I supposed to do with them?"

"They're not little princesses, Dmitrii Dmitrievich, but full-fledged pilots," Vershinin replied. "And, like all the other pilots, they're going to fight
against the enemy."[29]

The New Soviet Woman: she might be sent to the front, or she might be
condemned to the Gulag, but she would suffer equally alongside her Soviet
brother, thanks to Dear Father Stalin. "For the Motherland! For Stalin!"
Equating the two, the official war cry of the Red Army invoked a kind
of ideological cross-dressing. Stalin, the autocrat, ripped the spatula from
Baba Yaga's grip and battered the sons and daughters of Russia with it.

"Happy skies, happy skies," Raskova said to the night witches before
they took off. Raskova did not survive the war. She crashed on the banks of
the Volga in 1943 while commanding the night bombers' daytime counterparts, the 125th Guards Bomber Aviation Regiment. She was given the first
state funeral of the war; they buried her in the Kremlin wall. Her adoring
troops, devastated, went on without her.

"We were innocent of life—our motherland was endangered, and we
would fight the Germans."[30]

Chatter-teethed in the Russian winter, sitting like eggs awaiting a crack-
ing in the wooden bowls of their cockpits—"a terrible, naked sort of feeling"[31]—as German searchlights ignited the gloom like a wick, burning their
vision and searing their perception so that vertigo set in, the violent, traumatized night witches flew catastrophic skies to fight a fight they believed in.

My lover says I should understand them. "I could see you making the
same choice," she says.

I say, "No. I would be like Anna Akhmatova, composing poems and
suffering outside the Leningrad prison while my son rots away inside its
walls."[32] I say, "No. I would be like Nadezhda Mandelstam, sitting in the
kitchen after a meager supper, awaiting the knock of the secret police, searing details into memory to write about them three decades later."[33]

Lenin called the secret police "the Cheka," a name that sounds, to

English-speaking ears, nearly diminutive, feminine. Stalin named them the GUGB NKVD, a gulp of Cyrillic alphabet soup standing for "Main Directorate of State Security of the People's Commissariat for Internal Affairs." It is a title that smacks of the banality of evil, though these proto-KGB were strong-arms, not paper pushers. Like the night witches, they worked only at night. It afforded them cover, though in a stroke of cruel irony, they wore identical topcoats so that their victims always saw them coming. They called their visits "night operations," a euphemism suggestive of a wet dream. The trench coats—long, black, and leather—supported the notion, a whiff of cartoon perversion standing in for another, much darker, dirtier one.

It's a dark, dark fantasy, this notion that I would wrap myself in my poetry and suffer severely for it rather than take up the uniform of Stalin's army with the belief that I'd be defending "our fair motherland, for our people whom the fascists had trampled."[34] I have no idea what choice I would make. But I do know something about being the violent, traumatized daughter of an autocrat. My father, frying pierogies for me while wearing his dead Ukrainian-American mother's apron at her cabin in the mountains, flew into a rage.

"Get me a spatula!" he'd scream."Quickly! QUICKLY!" and I'd jump.

He must have jumped, too. He must have jumped hard, racing across the hills of Korea's thirty-eigth parallel, a twenty-year-old kid from the Pocono mountains, the son of an immigrant coal miner with a hereditary foul temper. He must have jumped hard when he dragged a fellow soldier from behind enemy lines and back to the foxhole. He must have jumped—and then fallen really hard—when the shrapnel exploded in his body. The shrapnel, that leaden braille of history, bloomed blue and hard beneath his skin, sometimes falling out in the shower. His was the trauma of an industry manned by Eastern Europeans that fueled the American war machine. His was the trauma of the first frigid fissure in the Cold War that followed the incandescence of World War II. It is a cleft into which collective memory fell hard, a rupture nearly forgotten—until now, as the man who became the US president threatens the North Korean autocrat with "fire and fury," and the North Korean autocrat threatens a "second Korean War" in response.

I did not go to war. But I am my father's daughter, that hereditary foul temper blooming blue and hard under my skin when my father grabbed my arm hard in one hand and held me in place, a soft bullseye for his hard kick. Ever vigilant as a girl, I did not sleep a wink. My analyst—a man—says I should separate these things: history, politics, how I suffered as a child. I mustn't conflate the domestic tableau with the theater of war, or I will just keep on suffering. But what's a daughter to do?

In 1937, Nina Raspopova was denounced as an enemy of the republic. She was expelled from the Komsomol, the young Communists' league, and fired from her job at the glider school where she worked as an instructor. Fifteen days later, she was reinstated. By 1941, she was a senior lieutenant in the 46th Taman Guards Night Bomber Regiment. She had been granted the privilege to be shot from the sky, to crash-land, wounded and bleeding, to wander behind enemy lines, to watch bodies pile up in a field hospital, and once recovered, to be sent back to do it all over again.[35] This is how it goes. They were daughters. Just daughters. Dangling, without parachutes, in the treacherous skies of the blackest nights in history.

⌒

In 2011, Vladimir Putin's personal security force, the Federal Guards Service, put a government tender in for three million rubles' worth of NKVD-style black leather overcoats.[36] Apparently, repression is back in fashion. In November 2016, *The New York Times* reported that "Russia has gone slightly statue mad,"[37] a rash of kitsch in a country afflicted by nationalism. "Stalin all but disappeared after his death, but he is beginning to pop up in stone in towns around Russia."[38] The story ran three days before the United States elections. Fan of both torture and Putin, the man who became the US president misappropriated funds from the foundation bearing his name in order to purchase a six-foot, speed-painted portrait of himself. His daily briefing is a folder of clippings proclaiming his greatness.

Is it a wonder that the night witches are haunting me? The man who became president drops "the mother of all bombs" on Afghanistan. Motherhood. It's a lousy metaphor for the narcissism and the violence of the father.

"When are you going to write a book, Betsy?" my father kept asking in the years before he died. "When are you going to write a book about *me*?"

Cloistered to the point of imprisonment at Stalin's dacha in Kuibyshev, Stalin's daughter wrote to him. "Papa," she wrote, "why do the Germans keep coming and coming? When will they finally get a kick in the neck? After all we cannot give up all our industrial areas. [...] I kiss you many many times once again. Svetlana."[39]

Stalin, the Great Helmsman. Stalin, Supreme Commander. Stalin, our Shockworker, our Best of Best. Stalin, our Darling, our Guiding Star. Stalin, Gardener of Human Happiness. Stalin, Soviet Women's Best Friend. Stalin addressed a nation at war. "Cowards, deserters, and panic-mongers" would be crushed, he said.[40] What's a daughter to do? Svetlana, a teenager, "remained an idealistic Communist,"[41] even as her own family members disappeared. Stalin was purging close to home.

"Many years had to go by," Svetlana later wrote to a friend, "before everything that had taken place, not only in our family but all over the country, could range itself in my consciousness with my father's name, before I could realize that all of it had been done by him."[42] In 1967, Svetlana defected. By then, Stalin was fourteen years in his grave.

The man who is president of the United States insulted a US senator who had been a POW. "I like people who weren't captured," he said.[43] He sounded like Stalin. August 16, 1941: Stalin issued Order 270. All Russian soldiers who surrendered or were captured were deemed "traitors to the Motherland." Wives of captured officers were rounded up and sent to the Gulag, too. The man who is president of the United States campaigned against his opponent to chants of "lock her up," while his own daughter waved from the dais.

⸎

Can you understand why the night witches confuse me? I reach for empathy and come up ambivalent. It was the central committee of the Komsomol that selected the volunteers for women's aviation battalions. It was the Komsomol, too, that sent youth to help "dekulakize" the countryside:

If you were a good farmer, you got dekulakized—that is, you have everything taken away from you. They took everything away from us—everything down to the last crumb, including the house. Just the kids and myself were left. My husband was taken away in a black raven.[44]

With the help of the youth of the Komsomol, the NKVD turned the countryside over and filled the Gulag. Their cars were called "black ravens," like the sidekicks of a witch practicing very dark magic. Stalin in goth drag.

To be young and female in Stalinist Russia was to grow up with "the woman-soldier mentality," to see yourself as someone "whose foremost obligation was preparation for the great war anticipated by the entire society."[45] It was the big idea, this always-looming war that kept Soviet youth on their toes for Stalin.

At festivals as a toddler, you chanted, "Thank you, dear Comrade Stalin, for a happy childhood!"[46] At nine years old, you joined the Young Pioneers. At fourteen, you entered the Komsomol, the paramilitary clubs, the mega-paramilitary organizations, including Osoaviakhim—the Society for Cooperation in Defense and Aviation-Chemical Development—and there you learned chemical warfare, marksmanship, and parachuting. You learned to fly. To refuse to do so "was not an option."[47] When the Germans invaded in June of 1941, and war came for real, "young women knew exactly what to do: they were to discontinue their peacetime activities and head to the nearest military commissariat."[48]

Major Irina Rakobolskaia said, "We are a generation not from this universe."[49] A generation of a "sacrifice-oriented nature."[50] What was a daughter to do? Commit mechanized violence, dispassionately, as Senior Lieutenant Serafima Amosova-Taranenko said? "Our feelings were that we were doing a simple job," she reported, "just a job to save our country, to liberate it from the enemy"[51]

Or should we do so passionately and attempt to survive? Lieutenant Polina Gelman said yes: "We hated the German fascists so much that we didn't care which aircraft we were to fly; we would have even flown a broom to be able to fire at them!"[52]

‿

I wrote a poem called "Serbian Exile." It was 1995, during the civil wars in Yugoslavia, a nation cobbled together from the rubble of the First and then the rubble of Second World War. Rubble makes a lousy foundation. I spent time in Yugoslavia in the 1980s before it crumbled. I had friends there who found themselves fleeing to the West, going AWOL from conscription into a Serbian Army that was committing genocide. One of my friends, a gifted cameraman, ended up in Hollywood shooting porno flicks. He's in the poem. The poem ends:

while on a hill above Sarajevo,
the starving Serbian soldiers
have scratched up a field full of lily bulbs,

buds of the Bosnian national flower,
and have eaten them, wishing them onions.

My MFA advisor said that the poem was flawed. "It's about the wrong side," she said. Yes, but they were humans. Atrocities are human acts. This was what I meant by it.

Navigator Alexandra Akimova said, "When we saw the captured Germans, in spite of the fact that they were the enemy and had committed such atrocities in our country, we couldn't look at them without a throbbing of the heart. They were miserable figures in shabby clothes, absolutely starving, thin and weak, and we experienced a kind of pity even for the enemy."[53]

I am struck with the similarity between this description and the photographs of the victims of German concentration camps that are part of my legacy as a Jewish woman. It is nearly impossible not to be grateful to the Russians for stopping the Nazis. But suffering on both sides of the Eastern Front was pandemic. Stalin was less discriminating than Hitler was, but he killed just as virulently. "Ech," dear Father Stalin told his daughter, Svetlana, "together with the Germans we would have been invincible."[54]

I argued once with the boyfriend of a friend. "As a Jew," I said, "I believe it's my ethical responsibility to reckon with the piece of Hitler I have inside me."

"Hitler was pure evil," he replied. "I have none of him in me."

The guy was a good, churchgoing Christian. He was prone to categorical thought. I have nothing against good, churchgoing Christians, but I find categorical thinking imprecise when trying to really look at our world. Fight or flight: what if they're the same reaction? Topsy-turvy in the disorienting snare of the German spotlights, the night witches couldn't tell the heavens from hell.

So what can I offer the night witches? This: the refusal to see them either as Baba Yaga, the witch, or Vasilisa, the heroine. They were young women compelled to act in their time and place. What's a daughter to do? Paint flowers on your fuselage with a message for the Germans? "Revenge to the Enemy for the Death of our Friends."[55] Pull threads from your military-issue blue underwear to embroider the cloth that you stuff into your too-big military boots to help them fit?[56] Obey the male commander who has "decided to reward the girls" for combat readiness with "suits, coats, skirts, and a pair of high-heeled

Origins

By Taté Walker (Mniconjou Lakota)

There is a story about the way the pipe first came to us. A very long time ago, they say, two scouts were out looking for bison; and when they came to the top of a hill and looked north they saw something coming a long way off, and when it came closer they cried out, "It is a woman!", and it was. Then one of the scouts, being foolish, had bad thoughts & spoke them; but the other said: "That is a sacred woman; throw all bad thoughts away."

When she came still closer, they saw that she wore a fine white buckskin dress, that her hair was very long and that she was young & very beautiful. And she knew their thoughts and said in a voice that was like singing: "You do not know me, but if you want to do as you think, you may come." And the foolish one went, but just as he stood before her, there was a white cloud that came & covered them. And the beautiful young woman came out of the white cloud, and when it blew away the foolish man was a skeleton covered with worms.

—**Black Elk, from the handwritten draft of interviews conducted by John Neihardt**[1]

I was introduced to Ptesáŋwiŋ as I participated in my first inípi ceremony alongside other juvenile delinquents and Native inmates from the North Dakota State Penitentiary in Bismarck. It was the cold, early months of 2001, and I was seventeen and a ward of the state after

shoes."[57] Lose a heel in the mud of the airfield when the Germans bomb your plane and run to save it? Bathe in puddles and snowmelt?[58] Having survived Stalin's orchestrated famine that killed your mother, drop your bombs and dream "of a small village house, a piece of rye bread, and a glass of clear river water?"[59] When you lose control of your Po-2, whisper, not to Stalin, dear father, the Father of Nations, but to your mama to help you survive?[60] Cry, "Mama, oh bless me, let me make a soft landing?"[61] Sing and dance after completing a mission "because life is life," and you are young?[62] Never grow accustomed to the fear?[63]

"The very nature of a woman rejects the idea of fighting," said night witch Senior Lieutenant Alexandra Akimova forty-five years after the war. "A woman is born to give birth to children, to nurture. Flying combat missions is against our nature; only the tragedy of our country made us join the army, to help our country, to help our people. If the women of the world united, war would never happen!"[64]

I don't know about that. In a trailer at Creech Army Base in Las Vegas, Nevada, the women drone pilots of the United States Air Force guide hellfire missiles on people 7,000 miles away in Afghanistan and Iraq. A pilot with the diminutive nickname of Sparkle told a reporter for *The Daily Beast* that "you can't be that soft girly traditional feminine and do the job."[65]

It's a false dichotomy. The night witches scared the shit out of the Nazis.

"Nevertheless," said pilot Yevgeniya Zhigulenko, "after a night of combat, we never forgot to curl our hair."[66]

That's how daughters are. Variable. Dichotomous. Complex. Making do on the darkest nights in history. Daughters doing hellbent fathers' bidding and begging the ghosts of their mothers for mercy. Women, not witches, heaving bombs, hungry and exhausted, into the wombs of the Po-2s. Women hurtling off in subzero weather, icicles forming on their faces.

experiencing a series of unfortunate adolescent events. Like many teenagers, and especially those with unchecked mental health and abuse issues, I felt untethered—like I had no control over any part of my existence, including my mind, body, and spirit. Looking back, everything about this inípi setup was sketchy. (Whose idea was it to put teenage girls inside a pitch-black dome side-by-side with adult male prisoners?) My experience, however, was powerfully positive. Life-changing, even. Raised primarily in an urban Catholic setting, my Lakota foundations heretofore had only grazed the surface—think powwows and decorative pottery versus prayer and cultural pedagogy. As a white-passing individual, it was often only my name and brownish features that tied me to my Indigeneity. So, when the group-home leaders where I lived told me I was going to a sweat lodge, I really didn't know what to expect.

It was dark under the massive layers of blankets and tarps. About twenty of us sat uncomfortably close together, silent, and cross-legged upon carpet scraps that covered the frozen dirt beneath us. My breath *whooshed* out of my lungs as the first wave of sizzling steam hit my face like a slap. Someone started hitting a hand drum, and the first round of inípi began with a rousing prayer song to Wakáŋ Táŋka, the Great Spirit.

Though I sat motionless, my blood raced. With sixty fired stones emitting a liquid blaze with every drop of water thrown on them, sweat poured from my skin in a full-body cry. After what seemed like hours, the song ended, and the leader opened the door flap to allow in a blast of winter night air.

A few people left, too overwhelmed or physically unable to continue with inípi, of which there were three more rounds. I thought about leaving as well, but at the time, I self-medicated through cutting, and the intense heat from the stones felt a lot like the pain I often craved. It was definitely the wrong mindset to be in for ceremony, but there it was. I'm thankful I stayed, because as soon as the flap closed and we were again plunged into darkness, the spiritual leader spoke. He told us about Ptesáŋwiŋ, her power, and her gifts to the Lakota people of which we now took part. What immediately struck me about this woman was that she didn't take any shit from men. A beautiful woman, Ptesáŋwiŋ obliterated the first asshole who had impure thoughts about her body, leaving only his skeleton and a promise for other would-be rapists.

As someone whose body had been appropriated by others, and who often heard and saw the bodies of other Native girls being taken advantage of,[2] it was empowering for me to listen to a story about a strong Lakota woman who was looked upon—not simply remembered but acknowledged as a *living deity*—with reverence by Lakota spiritual (and male) leaders. My life thus far had showed me a world that ranked women as inferior to men, but this story, along with the experience of inípi, opened my eyes to new ways of thinking.

This would not be my only encounter with Ptesáŋwiŋ. In fact, since that first inípi, she has reminded me of her existence in many ways, usually when I'm feeling weak or burdened. As I've come to know myself and reclaim my Lakota history, culture, and contemporary experiences, I see her teachings and value in everything related to the work I do to promote Indigenous feminism. Though there are many stories of her appearances and gifts to the Lakota people some 500 years ago, the common thread among them highlights the fundamental connection between ceremony and femininity that still exists in Očéti Šakówiŋ communities today. The ideals she stood for flow throughout Lakota history and contemporary issues, and our discussions about the future are vital to not only understanding Lakota worldviews but also to the continuation of our culture.

Lakota Feminism: History

Then the woman [Ptesáŋwiŋ] spoke to the one who was not foolish: "You shall go home & tell your people that I am coming & that a big tepee shall be built for me in the center of the nation." And the man who was very much afraid went quickly and told the people, who did at once as they were told; & there around the big tepee they waited for the sacred woman.

—**Black Elk, from the handwritten draft of interviews conducted by John Neihardt**[3]

Recognizing the importance and impact of Ptesáŋwiŋ begins with an understanding about the Lakota people, including our broader societal structure, how we traditionally shared information, and the role femininity played in shaping our worldview. Within all of these philosophies lies the fundamental value of kinship and our relationships to each other and all living things, including and especially the land. The Lakota people are part of a larger governing body called the Očéti Šakówiŋ (Seven Council Fires), or what most outsiders erroneously refer to as "Sioux."[4] The Očéti Šakówiŋ confederacy consists of seven tribes of the same language family divided by three dialects: Lakota, Dakota, and Nakota. In the past, these tribes operated under similar—if not identical—value systems and nomadic lifestyles within specific regions of the upper

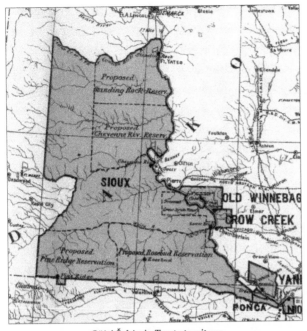

Očéti Šakówiŋ Treaty territory

Great Plains. Though many differences were apparent prior to colonization, today, the Lakota, Dakota and Nakota represent fairly synonymous experiences, so much so that when reading the word "Lakota," one would be safe to assume interchangeability with "Dakota" and "Nakota." Still, I use the word "Lakota" throughout this piece purposefully, because those are my ancestors, relatives, and stories I know. When reading the term "Očéti Šakówiŋ" here, I am writing of all three groups.

Like many Indigenous cultures, the Očéti Šakówiŋ did not pass on knowledge and history through written language, although important tribal events were kept pictographically upon annual winter counts.[5] Instead, information was shared through oral storytelling and song, and elders, especially grandmothers,[6] played the role of storyteller in Očéti Šakówiŋ life. Though the method was deemed unreliable and uncivilized by European standards,[7] this system of knowledge-sharing allowed for evolutionary thought and experiential learning, a distinct departure from the colonizing societies that were dependent upon rigid ideals trapped within a canon.

Recognizing the Lakota as a culture specializing in oral storytelling, it's critical to remember when talking about people and events such as those surrounding Ptesáŋwiŋ that many versions of her history exist, and that each is as accurate and honest as the storyteller. Thus, words ascribed to Lakota stories by the colonizers—words such as "myth" and "legend," which denote imagination over fact—are disrespectful, demeaning, and

wholly inaccurate. Context within the Lakota language, which includes communication cues like body language, is a huge factor, and the meaning of
words varies depending on the speaker, the listener, and the situation.

Interestingly, until recently, I only ever heard of Ptesáŋwiŋ from men, and
the story was never told to me as one that focused on the sacred feminine.
Instead, as Vine Deloria, Jr., writes, "The importance of the story was the
reception of the Sacred Pipe, not the woman herself as a personal object of salvation."[8] Though I'm a big fan of the late Deloria Jr., an influential Lakota author and activist, and though I agree that the story of Ptesáŋwiŋ is one that of
course focuses on sacred Lakota ceremony, Deloria's dismissal of Ptesáŋwiŋ as
a central Lakota figure and especially his use of the word "object" to describe
a woman is telling: colonial patriarchy rules the society in which we live, and
the mindset that women are inferior infects even our most celebrated heroes.

With this in mind, I've sought Ptesáŋwiŋ stories as told by women and Two
Spirits (an Indigenous understanding of "queer"), as I find their analyses to be
not only female-friendly but also integral to understanding the importance and
relationship between Ptesáŋwiŋ and the Sacred Pipe—or rather, the sacred
feminine and ceremony. Smith writes:

> The women in these stories are more than fertility goddesses and mothers,
> acting more as foundation figures for the tribe.
>
> Philomine Lakota, [who is] Hohwoju, Itazipacola and Oglala
> Sioux Lakota, teaches the Lakota language at Red Cloud High
> School on Pine Ridge.
>
> According to Philomine Lakota, the Lakota word for the tree of life is
> also used to refer to women. The word for the principal male translates
> to "the mouth of the tree of life."
>
> In other words, the male was intended to be the mouth of the
> woman, not to control her, and Philomine Lakota says that is one
> thing that has been lost in the culture.
>
> "A lot of people think that us women are not leaders, but we are the
> heart of the nation. We are the center of our home, and it is us who decide
> how it will be," Lakota said.
>
> "We have yet to relearn that."[9]

We color our experiences with bias, so when I say I read feminism as inherent within Lakota culture and tradition, versus it existing separately, I know many of my elders and contemporaries will not agree with me. But this is why the unwritten history of Lakota storytelling is central for understanding; our comprehension of the world is *meant* to change. As Deloria himself sets forth, Lakota society flourished for tens of thousands of years without the use of writing utensils, because we valued our shared experiences—our relationships to place and to each other—not to time and linear chronology.[10] "In Lakota terms, the customs that matter the most are the ones which relate the meaning of prescribed kinship behavior to other levels of order,"[11] such as tracking time via written history.

This devotion to kinship, as well as honoring femininity, is seen throughout Lakota origin stories. For instance, Íŋyaŋ, the stone, began as the only—and therefore the most powerful—spirit being. But he craved to exercise that power over others and so created Maká, the Earth. "But in creating her, he took so much from himself that his veins opened and all his blood flowed from him, and he shrank and became hard and powerless."[12] The story continues, and two other spirit beings are created—Škáŋ, the sky, and Wí, the sun. The four preside over everything.

Although some storytellers say the original spirit beings are genderless, most ascribe masculine or feminine qualities to everything with a name. That Maká is the only female among the four original spirit beings is pretty powerful commentary on what it means to be female in Lakota society. Unlike Škáŋ, who is supreme but immaterial, or Wí, who is chief of the spirit beings but immovable, or Íŋyaŋ, who experienced the ultimate karmic irony and went from almighty to powerless in his first act meant to dominate (a feminine entity), Maká is the most dynamic of the four spirit beings. She is the epitome of life, and although she is irritatingly described as quarrelsome, taunting, nagging, and complaining,[13] Maká fights to have only the best for herself and thus everything that lives upon and within her.

That's undeniably powerful feminine energy at work, and why virtually the entire world calls her "mother" (the Lakota often call her Uŋčí Maká, or "Grandmother Earth"), a relationship that requires no explanation. In recognizing something as necessary for life as the Earth is as feminine—and not just feminine, but the honored place of grandmother—the Lakota identified their interpersonal and communal bond with place, a tribal philosophy of interconnectedness and a social and spiritual structure that valued feminine energies among the top of their priorities.

This value system of an all-inclusive "we" is never more apparent than when Lakota people invoke the prayer, mitákuye oyás'iŋ, loosely translated as "all my relatives," according to Whirlwind Soldier et al.:

> *To teach and understand that creatures, man, animals, birds, insects, reptiles, plants, water, and air are integral to the survival of the people and earth as we know it is the heart of the culture. Mitakuye Oyasin reflects the physical, mental, spiritual, emotional and intuitive relationship that the Oceti Sakowin has with all aspects and elements of the environment.*[14]

Though dimmed by settler colonialism and assimilation, these values continue to be an integral part of contemporary Lakota life and ceremony. Sharing, giveaways, gift-giving, prayer, and land-based kinship (among other philosophies) continue to fly in the face of the ever-encroaching colonial mindset that places individualism, consumerism, and (white male) dominion over all else.

Indigenous Feminism: Interrupted

And after a while she [Ptesáŋwiŋ] came, very beautiful & singing, and as she went into the tepee this is what she sang:

With visible breath I am walking.
A voice I am sending as I walk.
In a sacred manner I am walking.
With visible tracks I am walking.
In a sacred manner I am walking.

And as she sang there came from her mouth a white cloud that was sweet to smell.

—Black Elk, from the handwritten draft of interviews conducted by John Neihardt[15]

Though most of my childhood and teenage years weren't immersed in Lakota culture, I did spend many of my early years living among my biological mother's brothers and sisters before she and my father divorced. And while sometimes these close proximities led to traumatic experiences, there were always sibling-like-cousins who I could play with, and a mother—even though she was not my own—was never far away. In this way, I always *knew* I was Lakota.

Siblings and cousins of the author (far back left)

But the idea that I was *different* never hit me until I got to elementary school. I never took a bath in order to scrub the brown from my skin, as some of my darker-complected relatives did. I didn't experience the educational violence and identity erasure known as Indian boarding schools that my mom and her siblings did while growing up on the Cheyenne River Indian Reservation. The casual observer only saw my father's strong genetics in me, which kept me insulated and privileged.

And then...

Dances with Wolves came out in 1990, when I was in first grade and living primarily with my father in the South Dakota border town of Rapid City.[16] All of a sudden, I wasn't "Taté, the weird kid with a weird name," but "Taté, the Sioux girl—let's touch her hair and see how many Sioux words she knows!" My classmates always understood I was Native, but now my identity could be exploited because Indian-ness was en vogue. I remember kids in my class coming up to me randomly with their index fingers as horns on the sides of their heads, telling me they were Native, too, because they knew how to say "tatanka" It made me simultaneously angry and proud, because pretending to be Native was finally cool, but I still didn't know how to say any more Lakota words than the white kid acting like a buffalo did. And when I'd cry in frustration and try to explain to teachers how this made me feel, I was kindly laughed at with a dismissive. "Oh, no, they're not making fun of you!" they told me. "They're just kids playing Indian—go have fun with them."

Of course, it still wasn't cool to actually *be* Native, because Natives were dirty and homeless and criminals (and usually all three) and very much "the problem" in Rapid City, according to its leaders.[17]

This was my first foray into the casual racism experience, which is to say the *American* experience—the American *way*. I've been inundated ever since: post-racial, Midwest nice, Southern hospitality, not seeing color, playing devil's advocate, bootstrap theory, preaching tolerance, and a host of other, similar ideas are euphemisms used to dilute, dismiss, and deny the existence of racism, especially among white liberals. Unlike hood-wearing KKK members, white liberals who engage in racist behaviors often go unchallenged despite actively upholding an oppressive status quo. The thought that the United States was somehow a post-racial society after Barack Obama was elected president is almost laughable when you consider how little progress was made on the Black Lives Matter front during his reign, and now, with the Donald Trump presidency running full-steam ahead.

White liberals like to showcase their diversity street cred without receipts. Like first graders running around with their versions of "Sioux" words in their mouths to show cross-cultural understanding and solidarity, white liberals act like the United States isn't still committing acts of genocide against Indigenous peoples in the name of economic prosperity and citizen safety. Romanticizing the Indigenous experience is a huge part of the problem, one we saw mighty big heaps of during the 2016 protests against the Dakota Access Pipeline, when thousands of non-Native people came to protect the Missouri River alongside the Standing Rock Sioux Tribe against oil interests. Daily reminders had to be sent out across the protector camps and allied social media that Standing Rock's Indigenous leaders were in charge, and that Indigenous women were the ones who established the initial resistance and protector camps and should also be listened to above others. So many white people were quick to forget their place.

White people want our beautiful culture if it's land-loving, tipi-living, and headdress-wearing, but few want the Indigenous leadership, historical trauma, and systemic settler oppression that comes attached to it.

Although it has been idealized beyond recognition to some extent ("teepee glamping," anyone?), the Lakota worldview of communal wellbeing clashed—and continues to clash—greatly with Western/Christian principles of individualism.[18] But this isn't the only major difference in values. Femininity was sacred to the Lakota. No person could own the Earth—a living, *feminine* being from which we emerged as humans eons ago, or the creatures upon her. In fact, Lakota origin stories describe how the Očéti Šakówiŋ descended from the Pté Oyáte, of "the Buffalo People." (Side note: pté is the word for female buffalo, whereas tatáŋka refers to the bull). Beyond this, the Lakota honored a girl's first menses with a coming-of-age ceremony (one of the seven sacred ceremonies delivered by Ptesáŋwiŋ and one for which revitalization efforts are underway today in South Dakota's tribal communities), and many elders make space for Two Spirit people in tribal histories and contemporary society.

Of course, pre-colonial life on the Great Plains wasn't perfect, despite Western attempts to romanticize and therefore commodify the traditional Lakota experience. Indeed, Abenaki writer Susan Hazen-Hammond retells several stories from the Great Plains and other tribal regions with complex themes of rape and abuse so disturbing as to question even the possibility of pre-colonial matriarchal societies: "There is no family so dysfunctional that it hasn't already starred in a Native American legend."[19] Some winter counts detail events of women seeking family protection from their abusive husbands to women being mutilated for infidelity.[20]

Yet these aren't stories about *systemic* violence perpetrated by law and policy, as is the case today against Indigenous women at the hands of the U.S. government and its version of justice. That's a vital difference between pre- and post-colonial violence. Yes, all violence against (all) women is terrible, but the problem for Indigenous women is exacerbated under occupational rule, where laws not only perpetuate but actively do harm. Within tribal stories of feminine mistreatment live undertones or overt statements of how the experiences of those women *also* adversely affected the people and communities around them and/or how those women *overcame* the challenges with which they were presented. Essentially: harming Native women harms everyone. That's a big message to take in, especially when compared to Western stories of femininity, such as those presented in the Bible (or in pop culture), which (continue to) objectify and seek to dominate both women and the land, and all are inferior, quite literally, to (white) Man.

Clearly, patriarchy *is* colonialism and vice versa.

It's no wonder, then, that genocidal efforts against Native people took us away from each other; to colonize our lands, the government had to systemically strip away the "we" from our communal identity. Scholar Roxanne Dunbar-Ortiz describes the following: The Indian Removal Act of 1830 forcibly relocated Natives away from their homelands;[21] the government-led buffalo slaughter of the mid-nineteenth century devastated Great Plains food and economic systems;[22] the Dawes Act (a.k.a. General Allotment Act) of 1887 privatized/destroyed reservation lands and encouraged tribal assimilation into the dominant white culture;[23] and federal- and church-run boarding schools forced children away from their families with the intention of eradicating Native identity.[24] Many more policies were forced upon us, and each tribal nation today has its own, unique story of surviving genocide. Holding onto some of our kinship philosophies has helped us to survive this long, and efforts to reclaim some of what was taken (land, ideologies, stories, etc.) have been underway the past 200-plus years. Make no mistake: Indigenous women are to thank for those reclamation efforts.

Indigenous Feminism: Current Understandings

Then she [Ptesáŋwiŋ] gave something to the chief, and it was a pipe with a bison calf carved on one side to mean the earth that bears & feeds us, and with twelve eagle feathers hanging from the stem to mean the sky and the twelve moons, and these were tied with a grass that never breaks. "Behold!" she said. "With this you shall multiply & be a good nation. Nothing but good shall come from it. Only the hands of the good shall take care of it & the bad shall not even see it."

—**Black Elk, from the handwritten draft of interviews conducted by John Neihardt**[25]

My storytelling voice—my writing, that is—developed in high school. I took newspaper production for several semesters and enjoyed writing the corny clips about which school in town was better (mine, obviously) and what motivated emo musicians to learn guitar (the better musician you were, the more acceptable it was to wear copious amounts of dark eye makeup). Somewhere during this time, the Fighting Sioux controversy came to a crescendo. Regional media took note of Native protests against the University of North Dakota's (UND) nickname and logo, which was backed by a Nazi-sympathizing, multi-millionaire alumnus set to finance a new UND hockey arena with the caveat that the "Fighting

Sioux" nickname and Indian-head logo had to be prominently displayed.[26]

I wasn't really up to speed on all things Indigenous activism, especially as it related to mainstream depictions and representation—I mean, I spent fourth and fifth grade at Cherokee Trail Elementary in Parker, Colorado, so to me, the Fighting Sioux issue seemed comparatively harmless. Plus, you didn't attack UND, which was where any North Dakota high schooler not going to Ivy League or the military wanted to end up. But my news-writing teacher encouraged me to research the issue and report on my fellow Native classmates' perspectives. Growing up, I was often one of the few, if not the only Native students in my class. But when my father moved us to Bismark, North Dakota in the summer of 1998, and I began attending the city's largest urban high school in 1999, I immediately gravitated toward the other Native students, who fully embraced me and my desire to fill the holes in my life with whatever Nativeness I could. Unfortunately, my Native peers were about as interested in protesting Indian mascots as I was—that is to say, there was no interest.

Internet use wasn't yet widespread, and when I asked my father to use the family computer, he dutifully inquired as to my purpose. I described the assignment. My lack of enthusiasm for the story and the bigger issue of Indigenous misrepresentation was evident, and I may have grumbled. In what would be one of the most most impactful conversations we ever carried out, my father—a white dude from New York who had spent a majority of his adult life working among Native people—offered a succinct and poignant summary of the Indian mascot issue that, for brevity's sake, went something like this: "No other race of people are subjected to the same kinds of modern racism that sports mascots exacerbate. Only Native people are.[27] For instance, you wouldn't find a team like the Fighting Blacks or the Fighting Mexicans. So why is there a double-standard for Native people?" My mind was blown, and instead of writing a news column, I wrote an editorial from my new perspective. The column was published, and the backlash came swiftly from both students and teachers in the form of name-calling and cloaked racism. (Think, "It's an honor, Taté. Wouldn't you want your head on the gymnasium wall?") But something even bigger happened: I had support. I had Native students and other teachers thanking me in the hallways for speaking out, and several of my non-Native friends actively supported me as allies, even going so far as to write letters to the editor against the team name and mascot.

The year was 2000, I was sixteen, and I was officially politicized.

Advocating for accurate representation of Indigenous peoples has been at the core of my activism since I started writing about Indian mascots as a teenager. Misrepresentation is like gateway racism. It invariably feeds into all of the other ills that Indigenous people face, because how we're depicted in mainstream media, from blockbuster movies to news articles, impacts how much outsiders choose to care about our other issues, or what some condescendingly refer to as "more important things" for me to worry about—things such as substance abuse, low economic and academic achievement, high death and suicide rates, deplorable housing standards, loss of language, domestic violence, and a host of other issues. Readers might be shocked to learn that I do, in fact, care about *all* of these issues and more. That's what being human is—the ability to take in multiple streams of complex information. No one issue is monolithic for any human being. As Audre Lorde wrote, "There is no such thing as a single-issue struggle, because we do not live single-issue lives."[28] This is one of the many reasons that stereotypes of Indigenous identities, much like other identities, simply cannot be separated out in a simplistic way.

Ptesáŋwiŋ not only represents complex femininity, but she is also how we learned to follow where Indigenous women lead. Though her supernatural abilities make for a more compelling story, and though some those larger-than-life qualities may have been mythologized to the point of unattainable fantasy, I argue hers is an ever-present story detailing the inherent life-bringing and life-protecting powers within every Indigenous "womxn,"[29] including those without female reproductive organs and those who embrace what are considered masculine qualities. In handing over a sacred pipe that tangibly exists to this day, Ptesáŋwiŋ's greatest gift was showing us that Indigenous women are the heroes we've been waiting for and have had protecting us all along. Because despite the US government's many (and continued) attempts to cleanse itself of Indians, Indigenous women have been at the forefront of efforts to keep their people and cultures alive and vibrant by taking their place at the head of social justice movements. Sampling a selection of contemporary Indigenous organizing efforts—including media representation, ending violence against women, and environmental justice—reveals Indigenous women at the heart of them all.

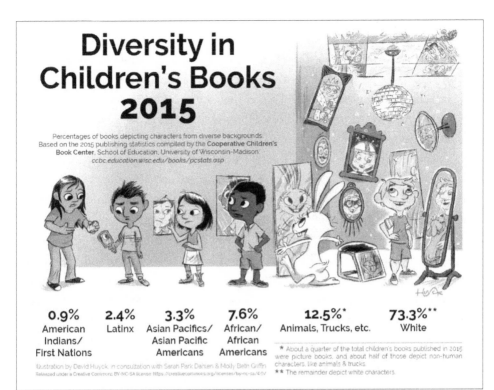

Media Misrepresentation and Erasure

A powerful illustration depicting racial diversity in children's literature began circulating in mid-2016.[30] Drawing on 2015 publishing statistics compiled by the Cooperative Children's Book Center at the University of Wisconsin-Madison's School of Education, the image showed five children (Native American, Latinx, Asian Pacific, African American, and white) and a bunny standing in front of various mirrors; the more mirrors the child (or bunny) had in front of them, the more that demographic was depicted in children's literature. The Native American child is holding a compact mirror in the palm of their hand; Natives showed up in fewer than 1 percent of all children's books. This contrasts greatly with the white child, whose race made it into 73.3 percent of all books. The bunny represents all the animals, trucks, and other non-human characters that made it into books. This category has the second-highest number, 12.5 percent, which is nearly identical to the number for the other four races combined, 14.2 percent. Did you catch that? Children of color have a better chance of reading about a non-human character than they do reading about a person who looks like them. There's something very wrong with that.

For me, the numbers in this illustration aren't the most troubling issue (though they are, indeed, troubling). Look again at the white kid surrounded by mirrors of all shapes and sizes reflecting an assortment of characters back at them. In the mirrors, the child sees themself as an astronaut, a firefighter, a superhero, royalty, young, and old. How great it must be for a child to be able to identify with such a wide array of representations. As an Indigenous person, I wouldn't know. There's power in that kind of media recognition. When you're seen as multifaceted, never mind being seen *at all*, it's likely others will see the issues that matter to you, and it's also likely you'll see yourself and the potential person you might become—a hero, a professional, or simply happy.

Compare that to the Native child, whose mirror can barely reflect one whole eyeball. This is what happens to Natives beyond age and across all media platforms: we are barely there—or missing. And if not missing, then misrepresented, which is the same as being actively erased. Books aren't the only platform lacking Native representation. Every media platform, from movies to television shows to news organizations, has a Native identity problem. We're depicted as historical props and background pieces, comedic sidekicks, or fantastically supernatural—and we're rarely more than one-dimensional. There are thousands of unique Indigenous tribes across the Americas today, and yet, most non-Native people think "long, dark hair, headdress, and scantily-clad brown skin" when asked to describe someone Indigenous to these lands. If we're shown in a contemporary light, you get poverty porn directed by an outside lens. And Native women? We're hypersexualized to the max.

Media Hypersexualization and Real-World Violence

"Well, most women are hypersexualized," some might think. Yes, white women face negative images of their gender in the media, but not to the extent of women of color and especially Native women, and definitely not with the same consequences. The hypersexualization of Native women in pop culture is based on settler perceptions of our race and the white man's relationship to us, essentially, a sexualized frontier of manifest destiny. As explained by Arvin, Tuck, and Morrill:

> ... *Manifest Destiny is often taught as a positive or benign development strategy that afforded the expansion of a new, important, and superior nation. However, when Manifest Destiny is reexamined at the intersection of colonization and patriarchy, it is evident that the strategy is not*

at all benign, but a convenient rationale that has permitted genocide. Manifest Destiny relied upon gendered and arrogant notions of the dominion of man over the earth, the divination of the founding and expansion of the United States, and narratives of American exceptionalism, which still are employed to defend the country's role in global politics and occupations. Manifest Destiny, somewhat after the facts, became the explanation for the atrocities of settler colonialism, more for those who benefit/ed by settler colonialism so that they might more easily stomach their own complicity in ongoing colonization.[31]

Entertainment media shows that Native women, like land, exist for the white man's prerogative, from Pocahontas, to Tiger Lily, to the unnamed dead wife of the protagonist in the Academy Award-winning film *The Revenant* (2015), which received rave reviews as a pro-Native film despite the violence inflicted upon its Indigenous women characters. White women indeed face hypersexualization, but, like the white child in the illustration above, that have their choice from a range of depictions within the media they consume—a choice Native women do not have.

Furthermore, the hypersexualization faced by Native women materializes as contemporary genocide: Native women experience violence (harassment, stalking, abuse, rape, murder) at rates more than double to ten-times the national average, depending on where they live in the United States and the type of violence committed.[32] According to the National Institute of Justice,[33] more than 84 percent of Native women have experienced violence in their lifetime: 56.1 percent sexual violence; 55.5 percent physical violence; 48.8 percent stalking; and 66.4 percent psychological aggression by an intimate partner. The same study found Native female victims were 1.5 times as likely as white female victims to be physically injured, 1.8 times as likely to need services, and 1.9 times as likely to miss days of work or school, likely because Native women were 2.5 times as likely as white women to lack access to needed services. What's more, despite recent updates to tribal criminal authority to prosecute non-Native perpetrators of violence, many Native women never see their abusers or rapists brought to justice, according to the Indian Law Resource Center:

An unworkable, race-based criminal jurisdictional scheme created by the United States has limited the ability of Indian nations to protect Native women from violence and to provide them with meaningful remedies. For more than 35 years, United States law has stripped Indian nations of all criminal authority over non-Indians. As a result, Indian nations are unable to prosecute non-Indians, who reportedly commit 88% of the violent crimes against Native women on tribal lands. ... Federal and state officials having authority to protect Native women and girls are failing to do so at alarming rates. By their own account, between 2005 and 2009, U.S. attorneys declined to prosecute 67% of the Indian country matters referred to them involving sexual abuse and related matters. Even grimmer, due to the lack of law enforcement, many of these crimes in Native communities are not even investigated.[34]

Media hypersexualization experienced by white women in no way compares to that faced by Native women, because (a) white women have access to positive, accurate, and contemporary images with which to combat their hypersexualization; and (b) will not be subjected to the systemic perpetrations of that hypersexualization and attached real-world violence Native women have been plagued by since the time of Columbus.

Native Women Fight Back: Science, Social Media, and Standing Rock

Violence statistics are difficult to overcome, especially when researchers and authorities spin them as blameless natural occurrences, like an "epidemic," purposeful language that legal scholar and Muscogee (Creek) citizen Sarah Deer discusses extensively:

Using the word epidemic *fails to acknowledge the agency of perpetrators and those who allow the problem to continue. The word also utterly fails to account for the crisis's roots in history and law. Using the word* epidemic *to talk about violence in Indian country is to depoliticize rape. It is a fundamental misstatement of the problem.*[35]

Like Deer, Native researchers across disciplines are pushing back against accepted norms. A 2015 study conducted by a team of psychologists, including Tulalip tribal member Dr. Stephanie Fryberg, showed, "that the invisibility of Native Americans in the media undermines self-understanding by homogenizing Native American identity, creating narrow and limiting identity prototypes for Native Americans, and evoking deindividuation and self-stereotyping among contemporary Native Americans."[36]

Fryberg represents one of many Indigenous women who have taken the lead in fighting against misrepresentation on several fronts the past several decades, and her work is foremost when activists discuss the science and mental health issues associated with the racists portrayals of Natives in pop culture, especially as those representations impact Native youth. What's more, there are literally dozens of studies like the many Fryberg herself has conducted showing the dangers of media misrepresentation and erasure. That is to say, the fight against Indian mascots and inaccurate (or nonexistent) media portrayals is *not* what many gaslighters like to call "political correctness run amok" or Indigenous people being too sensitive. Fryberg and others give us staggering amounts of peer-reviewed science as undeniable evidence that these issues matter and feed

Author (right) with her cousin at the Standing Rock NoDAPL camps

into other areas of life and death significance for Native people.

This is why accurate Indigenous representations created by actual Indigenous people are so vital across the media spectrum. Interestingly, we're seeing this occur for contemporary Indigenous women more and more, at least on one mainstream stage: social media. Platforms such as Twitter, Facebook, Tumblr, and Instagram serve as modern-day fires around which to tell stories. These web-based campsites have become havens for Native women and those inspired by them to advocate for social justice issues including violence against Indigenous women, environmental rights and protection, language and culture revitalization, youth empowerment, food sovereignty, Two Spirit reclamation, and every other area they care about. Those of us who regularly engage within these Indigenous social media spaces witness and experience not only powerful commentary and free education but also gain effective advocacy methods for our own use.

These spaces also function as a means for outsiders to learn about our issues, which of course, aren't being covered (or are covered insufficiently or inaccurately) by mainstream news media outlets, where Indigenous journalists are scarce. Direct from Indigenous women on the ground come photographic and video evidence of the many injustices we face. In the spring of 2016, for instance, few people knew about the Dakota Access Pipeline and its route through the Missouri River on legal treaty lands a stone's throw from the borders of the Standing Rock Sioux Tribe in North Dakota. That any of us know about this pipeline today is because of the ongoing fierce efforts of Indigenous women like Bobbi Jean Three Legs, a youth worker in Standing Rock who led young Native people on cross-country awareness runs; and Standing Rock historian LaDonna Brave Bull Allard, who offered a place for hundreds and thousands to stage a mass water protection when she founded the Sacred Stone Camp on her own land. These two Indigenous women were among hundreds who inundated social media using tools like hashtags and Facebook Live video to pump out their messages for help and prayers and calls to action to allies across the world.

Environmental Justice and Pre-Feminism

The movement to combat environmental violence committed by extractive industries (e.g., those that remove oil, metals, coal, stone, etc., from the Earth) showcases the kind of value that Očéti Šakówiŋ and other Indigenous people place upon the land and water. To us, it is worth risking everything for, which, if you think about it, is what we've been doing since colonists came to the Americas with an obsession to dominate through resource extraction (e.g., bodies, slaves, gold, and land). But protecting Uŋčí Maká isn't simply about resources. As evidenced by the reproductive health issues, high rates of cancer and other illnesses, and chronic social stressors inarguably caused by and linked to extractive industries (directly or indirectly, such as via toxins and other contaminants released into the air, land, and water), *violence against the Earth is violence against Indigenous women.*

Tekatsitsiakwa Katsi Cook, an Akwesasne Mohawk midwife and women's health advocate, puts it this way: "We must never forget that it is at this most critical window of development in the mother's womb, the child's first environment and first relationship, where the embodied wealth of indigenous nations is determined."[37] That Indigenous women's bodies—and therefore future generations of Indigenous people and cultures—are intimately tied to the fate of the Earth is a common refrain among the many who advocate for both the environment and those who call for an end to the disproportionate rates of violence Native women face. In addition to feet-on-the-ground lobbying and legislative efforts, those on the front lines of the anti-violence movement have also used social media as an effective messaging tool, primarily through the missing and murdered Indigenous women hashtag #MMIW.

Whether in the physical world or the digital world, resistance movements led by Indigenous women who root themselves to and grow awareness for issues facing their families, communities, or ongoing ancestral conflicts and/ or endeavors are indeed doing feminist works. As shown through Indigenous histories like Ptesáŋwiŋ and others, these works are decolonizing in nature and demand that we—all human beings—honor that which is sacred: women's bodies, land, water, and Indigenous cultures. These works predate first-, second-, and third-wave feminist concepts, which my ancestors simply referred to as "life." Owning property, filling leadership and other decision-making roles, and other responsibilities many would consider a "man's work" were normal occurrences for Indigenous women pre-Columbus.

I think this is why many Indigenous women leaders today don't see themselves as feminists. Fundamentally, feminism was built for white, middle-class women who had never experienced gender equity. Native women, on the other hand, are reclaiming spaces our feminine ancestors enjoyed for generations. I've listened to citizens of tribes from across the United States and Canada who tell stories about how their Indigenous languages never had gendered nouns; in fact, gendering language would have been absurd considering that many of these tribes recognized more than two genders. Other stories tell how it was only after male settlers refused to treat with the female leaders of matriarchal societies that those tribes began adopting more leadership roles for men.

For the tribes of the Great Plains, our storytellers describe how roles for men and women changed once our primary food source was all but destroyed. Because we were traditionally a nomadic people that followed the Plains buffalo herds throughout the upper Midwest, the purposeful, US-led destruction of that food source and the confinement of our people to concentration camp-like reservations meant our men had nothing to hunt or provide for their families or communities. The government created dependency for commodity goods. This lack of role and responsibility removed masculine purpose, and many of our men turned to addictive coping methods such as alcohol. And it was the women who stepped in to fill the void and become providers, because our women are survivalists. Our men fell into the patriarchal trap that tells them women are inferior. Boarding schools further perpetuated this lie to the extent that even the women began believing they were second- and third-class entities, despite continuing to keep our cultures and languages alive.

It wasn't until I met Anishinaabe activist Winona LaDuke for the first time in the spring of 2015 that my ideals of feminism were fundamentally shaken by someone I considered to be an icon within the movement. LaDuke's work is comprehensive and inclusive, but she's most known for her decades-long leadership in the areas of climate change, renewable energy, sustainable development, food sovereignty, and environmental justice. She was also a founding member of the Indigenous Women's Network, which was established in 1985. LaDuke writes:

> *In some communities, a concern surfaced that we were organizing a "women's liberation" movement that would separate us out from the men; some people said that instead of making divisions we should be trying to keep our communities together. In the planning circle, we talked through this issue all along, because all the women involved were interested in healing and uniting our communities, not dividing them.*

We brought out continuously that the Network and the gathering were work "within the vision of our elders." None of us felt that we were doing something totally new that was simply adopted from the women's movement. We believed that what we were doing was a natural part of the growth of our communities. Indian women have always been encouraged to work together in sisterhood societies and other women's circles. For us, the Network reflects tradition, particularly because it is an informal group of women. To those who brought up the issue of divisiveness repeatedly, some of us would say, "trust us a little—we are from the community, after all, and women don't just get together to gossip."[38]

Had I read some of LaDuke's writings about that experience, I might have been more prepared for her comments about feminism. I had gone to see her speak at a nearby university. In discussing food sovereignty, she encouraged people to produce and cook their own food, that as a society we've come to rely on mass food production, and that our relationship with food today is based primarily on how much we consume and how hot (or cold) it's supposed to be before we can shove it down our throats. The mass production of food—those mega farms and ranches that destroy land, water, and air quality as they attempt to feed millions—has removed US citizens, especially Indigenous people, from our traditional food knowledge. The feminist movement of the mid-twentieth century, LaDuke said, had a huge hand in widening that divide. She said feminism encouraged women to stop slaving away in the kitchen and live life unencumbered by food preparation, relying instead on restaurants and meal delivery. Feminists also frowned upon agricultural food production. White, middle- and upper-class women helped create a society that demonized dirt as dirty, LaDuke said. LaDuke's presentation that night lasted nearly two hours, and her views on feminism were more surface-level-afterthoughts than purposeful commentary. Yet, her feminist critique stuck with me, because OMG she was right! Hadn't I experienced some of the same condescension from white feminists after they learned I'm a queer mother who values my family, community networks, and tribal sovereignty above all else? Don't many of them aspire to the same CEO positions, the same government and political roles, and the same normative nation-building that white men enjoy? Much like our country's founding fathers, white feminists want independence. Independence from rigid and unfair cisgender roles and expectations, yes, but white feminists also seek freedom from beliefs and behaviors reflective of Indigenous traditions and responsibilities deemed dependent and subservient, such as community- and land-based caregiving that is inclusive of multiple gender and sexual identities.

Here we see what LaDuke was communicating, both at her university speech and with her writings about the foundations of the Indigenous Women's Network: at its core, white feminism exists within the framework of settler colonialism (land dominance), industrialization, capitalism, consumption, and, therefore, heteropatriarchy—all things that contradict the worldviews and communal value systems of many Native nations.

Indigenous women leaders like LaDuke, Cook, Brave Bull Allard, Three Legs, Fryberg, and Deer have always existed. We are mothers and relatives, landowners, trauma survivors, lawyers, midwives, scientists, storytellers, artists, and water protectors. We are all of these things and more. Or none and something different. Boxes and labels created by Western dominance structures don't fit. Finding and uplifting Indigenous women's work, voices, and movements is crucial to overcoming the negative effects of colonialism and made easier today with the proliferative qualities of social media. Consuming their work and learning from it is a step forward into a more just society and also helps pave the way for the next generation of resilient thought leaders, whom the gifts of Ptesáŋwiŋ prophesied.

Indigenous Feminism: Into the Future

Then she [Ptesáŋwiŋ] sang again & went out of the tepee, and as the people watched her going, suddenly it was a white bison galloping away & snorting, and soon it was gone.

This they tell, and whether it happened so or not I do not know; but if you think about it, you can see that it is true.

—**Black Elk, from the handwritten draft of interviews conducted by John Neihardt**[39]

And so I crawled out of the hot, humid darkness of inípi. The toxin-filled sweat and tears that fell from my body rose steaming into the winter night air like the prayer of an ancestral newborn, and I was filled with an energy as old as femininity itself. This first inípi marked for me the beginning of a lifelong journey led by the Lakota belief and ceremony that had heretofore been missing from my life. That it was a woman—Ptesáŋwiŋ—who provided the foundation upon which much, if not all Lakota ceremony is based is no coincidence; after all, the structure of inípi is representative of the womb. In much the same way, feminism is an integral aspect of Lakota existence; though we struggle mightily on many fronts, our spirituality and ceremony—what makes us foundationally Lakota—depend wholly on feminine energies to continue.

White Buffalo Calf Woman came to the people because we were starving, had no direction and needed spiritual guidance. Ptesáŋwiŋ gifted us with a food source—the buffalo—that functioned as an all-purpose survival tool, since every part of our animal relative was honored with use; she also served as a social stabilizer, providing the Lakota with interpersonal relationship codes of conduct, including the balanced roles and responsibilities of masculine and feminine humans; finally, she served as a liaison to the Lakota spirit world, sharing with us the knowledge of spiritual communication and purification through ceremony.

Did Ptesáŋwiŋ ever truly exist? I suppose answering that question rests largely on how you define truth and seek its sources. Like most Lakota origin stories, no definitive version of Ptesáŋwiŋ exists, which allows for socio-evolutionary retellings, an elemental difference from unchanging Western histories. For me, I see evidence of Ptesáŋwiŋ in every Lakota belief and behavior. Her feminine essence resonates across today's Lakota resistance, existence, and resilience. She gave us the tools to be better, and being better started with honoring and respecting Indigenous womxn in all their forms.

Retelling and reinterpreting stories like that of Ptesáŋwiŋ is crucial to understanding our culture, but also ourselves as powerful womxn. We lost some of our feminine understandings and appreciation as white settlers and their patriarchal notions bulldozed Indigenous people and values. But by using new technologies to tell our own stories, Indigenous womxn are once again rising. With our fists in the air we grasp tightly to that which colonialism always seeks to rip away: Our feminine power. We are not just the backbone of our tribal communities, we *are* our tribal communities. Like Ptesáŋwiŋ, we change form to fit the needs of our communities: sustenance, leadership, and prayer.

This essay is dedicated to the Sacred.

Reveling and Rebelling: A Look at the Life of Ada "Bricktop" Smith

By Kara Lee Corthron

*I*n the summer of 2011, I was opening a show I'd produced. It had been a long, painful, fraught process that gave me two lasting "gifts:" severe GERD and the knowledge that I would never produce again under any circumstances. The day after opening night, I remember feeling freer than I had in about a year. To celebrate, my husband Tom took me out to see a movie. That movie was *Midnight in Paris*. I fell madly in love with the film, and though I can no longer stomach any Woody Allen films—the Dylan revelations were simply too much—I'm grateful that this movie came into my life when it did.

The film has been out for quite a while now, so hopefully what I'm about to write won't serve as a spoiler. On my second viewing of the film, a particular moment stuck out for me: a bored Zelda Fitzgerald suggests to Scott that they leave the party they're currently attending to do "Bricktops." He energetically agrees. I remember thinking, "What the hell is a bricktop? A drink? Some old-timey drug?" Somehow, I kept this strange word in my mind and decided to Google it later. I did and was surprised by what I found. Bricktop was neither a drink nor a drug but a woman who became an institution at a young age and stayed that way until her death.

She was christened Ada Beatrice Queen Victoria Louise Virginia Smith in Alderson, West Virginia on August 14, 1894. Her father, Thomas Smith, died when she was only four years old, and that's when her mother picked up the family and moved to Chicago. They lived on State Street, where Smith's mother, Hattie, ran a boarding house, and where little Ada began to exhibit an orneriness that would never go away. She loved seeing shows at the nearby theaters, but one of her favorite youthful pastimes was sneaking into saloons and crouching down on the floor to see what was happening in the forbidden back rooms hidden by Western-style swinging doors. Because she was fair, bony, and had an unmistakable head of fiery red hair, she didn't blend into crowds so well. All the saloonkeepers knew her by name and would shout at little Ada to get herself home before they sent for her mother.

Ada Smith was black, though she'd never use that word to describe herself. "Colored" and "Negro" would be her words of choice. Her fair-skinned mother was mixed race, black, and Irish, born into slavery three years before the Emancipation Proclamation was signed. Ada's father was of a brown hue, as was her older brother, Robert, and her older sister, Ethel, was a light, golden-brown. Ada's oldest sister, Etta, was fair with blond hair. Everyone called her "Blond Etta," so eventually she just became "Blonzetta." I bring up the interesting variety of complexions and hair colors in Smith's family because this era, post-reconstruction into the early years of Jim Crow, was when many of our American ideas about colorism began to take serious root.

Young Ada, who was by all accounts a happy kid, also saw the painful realities of the adult world around her. She loved performing—mostly dancing, but she sang some, too, and always jumped at the chance to showcase her talents. Occasionally, on Sundays, Hattie volunteered at local jailhouses. One Sunday, she took Ada along because she thought it might bring joy to some of the inmates to see a sweet, cheerful child perform. In her autobiography, *Bricktop* (the chief source of research for this essay), Smith fondly remembers one man for whom she performed called Jack the Bear. He was a young, handsome black man with a winning smile who adored Ada and showered her with praise. When she got home after performing for him, Ada asked her mother if she could go back with her the following Sunday so she could visit Jack the Bear again. Hattie grew quiet, and after a moment, she explained that it wouldn't be possible; Jack the Bear was scheduled to be hanged the following day.

I also loved performing and showing off when I was little, despite my lifelong shyness. But I can't imagine what it must have felt like to know I'd given someone such joy the day before that person was to be put to death. In her autobiography, Smith doesn't reflect long on this moment from her childhood, but I wonder if it solidified a need within her to make people as happy as she possibly could—sometimes at her own expense.

I'd intended to begin this chapter by addressing this question, "How does a fair-skinned, American black girl born into the working class become the hostess to the world's aristocracy?" It's a good question, and that is exactly who she became. In her Paris nightclubs, first Le Grande Duc and later Bricktop's, Ada hosted European royalty, a who's who of ex-pat American writers, artists, and anyone who had a fondness for champagne and classy entertainment—provided they could get in and didn't have a foul mouth.

As compelling as the question is, I can't answer it. One of her friends once suggested that Smith had been a queen in a former life, but Cole Porter corrected this friend by saying, "No. An empress." From the moment, she was renamed "Bricktop" by a flirtatious saloonkeeper in New York City. Bricktop was determined. *Driven.* What fascinates me is that for a long time, I don't think she knew what she was driven by or driven to do. She spent her later teen years and her twenties performing in vaudeville shows and saloons, but when the opportunity for her to run her own business came along, she simply said, "Yes." It turned out that she was better at it than any of her peers.

Ada "Bricktop" Smith is an interesting icon for a variety of reasons, not the least of which was her racial ambiguity. She never shied away from calling herself a Negro when the situation called for it, but there were times when I think it would've been fair to call her a "Negro of convenience."

In the 1910s, Smith got her start as an entertainer by performing as a dancer and singer in vaudeville, in the TOBA circuit, which was specifically for African-American performers.[1] These were minstrel shows. A popular tune she'd perform went like this:

> *Coon, coon, coon, I wish my color would fade,*
> *Coon, coon, coon, to be a different shade,*

Coon, coon, coon, morning, night and noon,
I'd rather be a white man, 'stead of a coon, coon, coon.

In her autobiography, she recalls these days without any kind of judgment against the tastes of the time or the folks who gave her that song to sing. In fact, if she has any judgment at all on the matter, it's reserved for modern-day sensibilities, "Try to sing that now, and you'll get crucified. [...] But it didn't bother me to sing that kind of song. That's what you did in a minstrel show. It's what audiences wanted, and if you wanted to be on the stage, you gave the audiences what they came for."[2]

Smith was very much a woman of her time. To resist singing such a song or performing any song-and-dance act that demeaned the race was not in her nature or her interest. She adapted to get ahead in whatever endeavor she threw herself into. Being a black girl was useful to her in her youth since she had no problem with minstrelsy, and it eventually got her into the saloon back rooms she'd been daydreaming about since childhood.

It was also convenient for her that when she first arrived in Paris in 1924, her blackness was seen as an asset. Jazz was all the rage in Paris, and Parisians couldn't get enough of black Americans. This confluence of events was coincidental, but Smith quickly ascertained the truth of the situation and had no problem benefiting from it. When she first arrived, she performed at the intimate Le Grand Duc, but she eventually took ownership of the club, and though she still performed (often *while* counting money and/or yelling at her wait staff), she hired more performers to headline—these were always jazz musicians, mostly black, in the American style. She felt there were plenty of places to find European atmosphere. She wanted her clubs to feature African American talent and culture. It was a brilliant business model, and it was an astounding success in the twenties and early thirties.

However, the close legacy of slavery—as evidenced by Bricktop's fair complexion and quite frankly, that of my own family—occasionally caused problems for her in Europe. In 1927, she traveled to Berlin during the summer and began scouting out a location to open a German chapter of Bricktop's. There, she encountered racism in oddball ways. After bringing some of her musicians for a trial run at a German nightspot, for example, a German woman became infatuated with one of them and confided to Smith about it. Here's how that exchange went: "She came running to me and said, 'They don't smell bad.' I said, 'What are you talking about?' She said, 'We had been brought up to think that all black people smelled bad. He smells good.'"[3]

But the confusion about Smith's race actually went much further and ruined her chances of expanding her brand to Germany. Angry about her insistence on using only her own musicians whom she'd hired in Paris, she was sued by an ad-hoc group of Berlin nightclub owners. She had friends in Berlin who helped her find a lawyer, and when the case went to trial, she was stunned by the real reason she'd been brought to court. "One of the things the judge said to me was, 'Why, you are not even Bricktop. Not only did you misrepresent the musicians, you are impersonating Bricktop.' I said, 'But I *am* Bricktop!' He said, 'Bricktop is a *black* woman.' 'But I *am* Negro,' I said. '*I* am Bricktop.' Well, the whole courtroom went into laughter, and it was in all the papers. Too bad it didn't help my case."[4]

Though this incident was a pretty big setback for Smith both financially and professionally, compared to what her fellow African Americans were experiencing back home during the late 1920s, she was quite privileged—something she didn't realize until her reluctant return to the States in October of 1939, just ahead of Hitler's occupation of Paris. She was protected. During her heyday, Bricktop counted among her friends Cole and Linda Porter, F. Scott Fitzgerald, Jack Johnson, John Steinbeck, Josephine Baker (more on that later), Pablo Picasso, Man Ray, Sophie Tucker, Lady Mendl, Tallulah Bankhead, and the Prince of Wales, to name a few. Nobody with serious ill intent could get near Bricktop in those days. And though it may never have been conscious on anyone's part, it's hard to believe that Bricktop's fair skin wasn't an asset in this regard. She was an anomaly, a curiosity. A black woman who could pass for white but chose not to. In a ThoughtCo.com piece, "Colorism" is defined as "discrimination based on skin color. Colorism disadvantages dark-skinned people, while privileging those with lighter skin."[5] And it affects everyone. Long before the phenomenon had a name, it certainly affected (and *in*fected) the minds of Americans who afforded light-skinned African Americans more privileges in society, as evidenced by the paper bag test, to use one example.[6] Smith lived and thrived in a very specific bubble.

My experience is so different from Ada "Bricktop" Smith, it's laughable to compare the two. Still, although I can't imagine serving as a hostess and confidant to the world's elite and enjoying it (and she did), I've lately been thinking about the bubbles in which I live. For the past sixteen years, New York City has been my home. My community is made up almost entirely of people I've met through my career in some way. I am a playwright, and in 2017, I became a published novelist. The groups I move in tend to be comprised of educated critical thinkers, and all of them are on the progressive spectrum, from baseline liberal to left-wing radical. Logically, I know that there are many, *many* people in this country who don't share my views and who probably wouldn't be able to have a single conversation with me without becoming enraged—assuming it were a conversation in which I was actually revealing my true opinion about the state of the world. But I've been shielded, just by how I've chosen to live my life, from certain ugly realities about present-day America. On November 9th, 2016, I couldn't believe the America of my nightmares had come to fruition, and I felt... like a fool. Like I'd intentionally blinded myself to the size of the division in this country and the dangerous resentment simmering beneath the surface.

Reading Bricktop's autobiography, I had a few moments of impatience with her because of my hindsight knowledge. The longer she was determined to stay in Europe in the 1930s, the more frustrated I became. "Get out, you fool, before you end up in a death camp!" crossed my mind more than once, but now I think again about the morning of November 9th, 2016. I had to teach a ten o'clock playwriting class that day, and I walked into the building not quite knowing what I should do, or if anything we did mattered anymore. A few of my students were crying. One wondered if she'd ever get to see her play through to production for fear of being deported because of her Muslim name. All of us were intelligent, and none of us had predicted the outcome of that election.

It would have been frighteningly easy to remain in Paris had I been in Smith's place. We can't always know what's coming, especially when it's un-fathomable. I'm grateful she got out when she did. Leaving isn't really the answer or even a real solution for progressive Americans today, but now that my bubble has burst—as Ada's was—I intend to do all I can to prevent the new administration from finding a safe bubble of its own. Still thinking about Smith in terms of race and her relationship to her blackness, I'm interested in bringing up a particularly cringe-worthy role that she played in the lives of some of her friends and clients. I'm certain Madame Bricktop, as she was sometimes called, would want to slap me across my impertinent face for what I'm about to suggest, but I believe she was often *Mammified* by whites.

Seen as the caretaker of all things, people in Bricktop's orbit sometimes leaned on her in a strange way, and for the most part, she allowed it. One example that stands out for me is her relationship with F. Scott Fitzgerald. On one occasion, he'd been picked up by two police officers for drunk and disorderly conduct. He told them, "You can't lock me up. I'm a friend of Madame Bricktop."[7] This actually worked for him, and they dropped him off in front of Le Grand Duc. Smith wouldn't let him come inside in his condition because he was far drunker than usual. He refused to leave without another drink, so she sent him home in a taxi with a bottle of champagne. Moments later, the taxi driver brought him back, furious because Fitzgerald had apparently kicked out every window in the cab. Smith convinced him to give the driver enough francs to practically buy the cab, and then Fitzgerald turned to her and said, "See, Brick, I'm not responsible. I was just trying to teach you a lesson. You've got to take me home."

She goes on to say that the whole charade of him not going home unless "Bricktop took him home" happened on numerous occasions. Sometimes, she'd get to his place, where Zelda would already be sleeping, and he'd persuade her to go back to the club with him to have more champagne, and then they'd do the whole thing over again. Obviously, Smith had a choice here and could've told him to knock it off, but because she depended on big spenders and heavy drinkers like Fitzgerald for her livelihood, she was in a precarious position. But Bricktop relays these moments as funny anecdotes from her early days in Paris with no ill will toward the great writer at all. I, on the other hand, see a grown white man manipulating a black woman into babying him, and for what reason? I have no idea. Maybe he just had a warped crush on her. In any event, he was a brilliant writer, but he was also a man of his time, and I'm sure he thought nothing of inconveniencing a young black woman who was just trying to run her own business. All because he wanted her mother-like attention for himself.

Fitzgerald was a special case, but Smith's overall leadership style closely resembled that of a stern mother figure, not unlike the way her own mother ran her boarding houses in Chicago. Regardless of any age difference (sometimes there wasn't one at all), Smith seemed to readily take on a maternal role and serve as confidant and advisor. She even advised mega-star Paul Robeson, who she barely knew, not to leave his longtime wife to marry the white British woman with whom he was having an affair, largely because it would've meant career suicide for him. He took her advice. At the same time, Bricktop prided herself on keeping her private business *private*. With few close exceptions, she never revealed much about her personal life while taking on the problems of countless others. This tendency brings me back to the caricature of the Mammy. Mammy always puts everyone's lives before her own. Mammy always has some kind of wisdom to share. Mammy always cleans up all the messes. Don't misunderstand me: Bricktop was *nobody*'s slave. She did things how *she* wanted. Even in her later clubs, like the Minuit in Mexico City where she came up against definite mistrust of her managerial skills mainly because of her gender, she took no shit, as she recalls in her memoir.

> *When you have a percentage arrangement, the silent partners start resenting the big slice of the profits they have to pay out to the active partner. That happened at the Minuit. My percentage was a hefty one, and I was eliminated. I left, and took the business with me, and my big-deal silent partners were left with nothing but headaches.*[8]

Bricktop didn't shuck-n-jive. Still, I wonder if even on a subconscious level she knew that the Mammy role—at least as far as she was willing to take it— would be good for business. Her clients were loyal and loved her as though she were a family member. However, she felt that depth of fidelity for few people.

It might sound like I'm making Smith out to be something between a victim of her era and a calculating captain of industry, and I honestly don't think she was either. She was complicated, so she had contradictions. Two brief quotes from her autobiography are worth noting here. On running Bricktop's in Paris, she writes, "Every night there was something new, and I loved every minute of it."[9] On why she often turned down party invitations, she says, "If you'd spent your entire life catering to people when you wanted to punch some of them right in the nose, why should you go to parties?"[10] I believe both of these statements to be completely true, if at odds with one another. As I was reading her book, the second quote took me by surprise because it comes rather late in the narrative, and up to that point, she'd rarely said anything negative about anyone or her work in general.

After I thought about it, though, it made perfect sense. Sometime during the late twenties, though she's vague on exactly when, Smith suffered the first of a series of nervous breakdowns. Her condition was serious, but to her great fortune, she wasn't given any of the rather frightening prescriptions for "nerves" doled out at the time, such as electric shock treatment. Instead, her doctor told her to express her inner rage in any way she could. Smith didn't really think she had any inner rage and strongly objected when the physician suggested she start cursing people out (she could not *stand* cursing). But she needed to function and get back to work, so she began a bizarre ritual of walking around the streets and alleys of Montmartre in the early morning hours, screaming as loudly as she could. She swore by this practice, "After walking down the street screaming for a while, I'd feel fine, and in a few months I didn't have to scream anymore."[11] Her neighbors found this behavior charming. It became a little joke. If someone happened to be in a boulangerie early in the morning for a fresh baguette and asked about the awful racket outside, the response would be, "Oh, that's just Madame Bricktop getting rid of her nerves."

Despite my theories and projections from my twenty-first century worldview onto Bricktop's life, I think she did the best that she could—better than that, actually. Her relationship to herself as a black woman was something she could not ignore, but simultaneously something she couldn't waste too much time focusing on if she was to get ahead. And she did.

Smith's ability to cut herself off from her own personal needs in order to put the needs of others first, including the needs of her business, didn't much shift when it came to her romantic life. There were only two men who seem to have left a significant impact on her: Walter Delany, a pimp she fell in love with in her youth while performing on the west coast, and Peter Ducongé, the musician she married during her golden years in France. The Delany affair was doomed from the beginning. For Smith, he attempted to go straight and find legitimate work with questionable success, but his real problem was his addiction to opium. She's fuzzy on the details, but I don't think they were together more than a matter of months. Ducongé was her husband for several years before their marriage ended in disaster. He cheated on Smith with a young woman from a dance revue that Bricktop had taken under her wing. She cared so much about this girl that she allowed her to live in her home, which was how the affair began. But even before their marriage dissolved, Bricktop and Peter often lived separate lives. In the summers, he'd go on tour, and Smith would travel to new European cities, sometimes with friends, but sometimes on her own, which she preferred. She mentions "fooling around" with many different men over the years in Paris, but rarely with any kind of passion. There were rumors, however. Smith offhandedly addresses them:

> *I had some romantic involvements, and I could have had romantic*
> *involvements with women, but I never liked women. Consequently, I*
> *was never big on the orgies that some people had. You were either in*
> *on them or you weren't. I didn't play. Even meeting a bunch of other*
> *women for lunch wasn't my disposition.*[12]

It's interesting that she compares romantic involvements with women to having orgies. At any rate, in Jean-Claude Baker's biography called *Josephine: The Hungry Heart,* he states, "I'd heard rumors of a long-ago affair between Josephine and Bricktop, and the rumors, it turned out, were true. Bricktop told me so herself, after Josephine's death."[13] Of course, based on her above assertion, she denies the truth of this in her book. For all we know, Jean-Claude, who essentially adopted Josephine as his mother though he was fully grown at the time, was adding a little spice to his book that might not have been entirely true. Nonetheless, Bricktop had quite a lot to say about Ms. Baker:

> *Her reputation for performing nude too often overshadowed the fact*
> *that she was born to wear couturier styles, or the fact that she had a*
> *live, wonderful, natural talent.*
> *Also overshadowed was the fact that she was still a kid, and she*
> *was one of the most vulnerable stars I've ever met. At the time, Negro*
> *female entertainers were still a rarity in Paris. Naturally, Josephine*
> *and I got together.*[14]

The two women definitely had a strong friendship for a time, though Smith seems to have seen herself as more of a big sister or mentor to the younger and more naïve Baker. But when Josephine began a relationship with Pepito de Abatino, Smith became enraged. She describes it this way: "The night Josephine showed up at Le Grand Duc with Pepito, I couldn't believe my eyes. I didn't hesitate to tell Josephine how I felt. 'What are you doing with this bum? He can't even pay for a glass of beer.'[15]" Josephine and

Pepito's relationship only deepened, much to Bricktop's disappointment. "Pepito came to control more and more of Josephine's life. He put a kind of guard around her. You couldn't get near her. Pepito especially didn't want Josephine to have anything to do with Bricktop, because I'd told her what he was from the beginning."[16]

No one will ever know for certain if Bricktop's negative feelings about Pepito dipped into jealous-lover territory. It strikes me, though, that even the betrayal she suffered at the hands of Peter Ducongé and Hazel—whose last name she pointedly refuses to reveal in the book, and who was another young up-and-coming talent much like Baker—didn't seem to ignite the passionate rage she had reserved for Pepito de Abatino. Was Bricktop repressing more than the need to curse out some folks? When she walked up and down the alleys of Montmartre screaming her nerves away, was she also screaming for a specific happiness that she didn't believe she could rightfully have? She was ultimately quite fulfilled in her platonic relationships, much more so than in her romantic ones. She writes, "I wish I could say that my relationship with Peter remained as constant and satisfying as my relationship with Cole Porter—but of course, they were two different kinds of relationships, and I think it's always easier to maintain friendship than love."[17] Perhaps that was enough for her. I just can't help wondering if the time she lived in limited the possibilities she set for herself. *Bricktop* was published in 1983, and Smith passed away several months later. If she'd lived at a slightly later time and had been able to witness the power and longevity of the gay-pride movement, she might have been able to talk about her love life with more candor. And without shame. Possibly.

Bricktop seems to have had a unique code of morality. I'm not sure how to define it. She didn't judge heavy drinkers (who were good for business), drug users, or pimps. She knew many who felt that the wild nightlife of late twenties Berlin was depraved, but she didn't see it that way at all. She just saw people trying to forget the horrors of a devastating war. Though she denies any personal connection to homosexuality, she had no judgment for the LGBTQ people that she knew in her life. At the same time, as I've mentioned, she had a strict "no cursing" policy in her clubs, she didn't allow unescorted women to enter her clubs (and the escort had to be a man), and she was absolutely against interracial marriage.

Later in life, after the age of fifty, she became a devout Catholic. Upon her return to Europe, she set up Bricktop's in Rome, was captivated by the Pope and Vatican City, and began donating much of her income to Catholic-based charities such as a camp for Italian children orphaned after World War II. Why the sudden spiritual shift? Her mother wasn't particularly religious, though she did believe in good works. I think Bricktop might have struggled with a very old paradigm, the Madonna/whore complex. She had a need to be a "good girl," but all her instincts, going back to her childhood when she'd sneak into Chicago saloons, went against that ideal. Or maybe this is too simple a theory for a woman with as many contradictions as Bricktop had. She admired the women who sat in front pews with their rosary beads and who attended mass every morning and confession almost as often. *And* she couldn't deny how much she liked staying up all night, drinking too much Rémy Martin, and giving the rich and fabulous the time of their lives.

I have a similar inner struggle, though in my case, it's political rather than spiritual. I admire hardcore activists who consistently inconvenience themselves by traveling to protest after protest, or who write brilliant op-ed pieces, and/or make persuasive speeches all in the name of what's right and just in the world. I could never devote my life to that kind of work because it's not the sum of who I am. I do sometimes march, and in the past two months, for better or worse, I've signed and shared roughly three trillion online petitions. But I also need time to daydream, to write, to binge-watch *Gilmore Girls* on Netflix, and to sing in karaoke booths. I find it hard to justify "fun" as an enterprise, given the state the world is in. I imagine Bricktop had trouble with that, too.

Beyond fun, why all the strange rules? No unescorted women? No interracial marriage? And I should clarify: interracial dating and fooling around were totally fine, as far as Bricktop was concerned. She just drew the line at marriage. There's a theory that we all keep wearing the hairdo and/or style of clothing from the part of our lives when we felt safest—and possibly happiest. This isn't the case with me, hair-wise, but I certainly dress a lot like I did in college. In fact, I still wear some of the actual clothes I wore in college. It's also why you see many elderly women with outrageously out-of-date hairdos. It isn't necessarily that they don't know how styles have evolved, but they're unconsciously clinging to an earlier time. The twenties were Bricktop's golden time, and back then, it was common practice to bar women from entering nightspots without gentlemen escorting them. Supposedly, this was to discourage solicitation (i.e., a pimp couldn't bring say, seven "dates" into a club.) I have a feeling this policy did little to deter prostitution, but perhaps I'm cynical. Anyway, Smith continued this practice into the sixties, when most places had long-ago abandoned it. Also, Bricktop was born and raised in an America, where interracial marriage was not only unthinkable, it was dangerous. So she adapted and held onto that belief. I can't exactly explain her irrational hatred of foul language, but she was a lady with a capital "L" and proud of it. Smith was rigid and liberal at the same time. To her credit, she wasn't a hypocrite; the rules she expected everyone else to follow were rules she strictly abided by herself.

For the past few years, I've had this burning desire to write about Madame Bricktop in some way. I'm holding up a mirror now, wondering what, if any, of Bricktop I see in myself. What is this strong connection I seem to have with this woman who died when I was in kindergarten, beyond the fact that we're both black, we were both born in rural areas, and we share the astrological sign of Leo? One of the principal characteristics I think of when I think of Bricktop is her determination. Whatever she set out to do, she threw herself into it one hundred percent. She never half-assed anything when it came to her career. I have a touch of this determination myself, along with an insatiable need to achieve in my field, which is both good and bad. At first, Smith committed wholeheartedly to being a stage performer, and though her focus veered into nightclub hosting, she continued performing her entire life and sang songs for groups when specially requested, even into her eighties.

John Steinbeck once said, "When Bricktop sings 'Embraceable You,' she takes twenty years off a man's life."[18] Though she wasn't the best singer around, she could sell a song like no one else could, and no one ever forgot having heard her sing. For a long time, I thought I was going to be an actor, and I threw myself into that role with all of Bricktop's intensity. Being an actor in New York City in the early-aughts often meant showing up to cattle-call audition lines at 5:30 in the morning just to be seen. But I did it while that was my focus, and I committed just as hard when my career turned to writing.

Smith also loved supporting other artists. In fact, discovering new talent was a crucial part of her job. It's not something that I think about too much, but I feel the same way. I think this is why I'm usually exhausted by the end of a semester: I truly commit to my teaching and to encouraging students who are exceptionally gifted—so much so that I sometimes end up taking a temporary (and unplanned) break from my own work while my classes are in full swing. I'm still trying to figure out the life/work balance thing, but I think it's important to help young artists. All of us have needed help at one time or another, and we will need help again. It's not just good karma; it's making our community a kinder and more generous place to work.

But what about those times at the end of the semester when I'm completely drained, overwhelmed by deadlines and all the things that haven't been taken care of in my life? That is when it's really easy for me to collapse, just as Bricktop did when she had her nervous breakdown. Bricktop suffered from depression, as do I, and it is a *beast*. It took me a long time to finally get treatment, and I'm convinced that had I not, I wouldn't be functioning right now. I might not be here at all. Admirably, Smith sought help at a time when nobody recognized depression as a real illness. I'm proud to say that Bricktop and I are both depression survivors. She made it, and so will I. She also had some traits that weren't as laudable, a few of which I share. Decadence would be one. Did I mention her love of Rémy Martin? I'll let her speak to that herself:

> *Speaking of Rémy Martin, it was partly the fault of that champagne that I started putting on so much weight around 1929 and 1930. I hadn't been skinny since I was a teenager, and since my teens my weight had run around 135. I was what I'd call well made. After a few years in Paris, though, my life-style began to take its toll. We drank an awful lot of champagne. We also had dinner very late at night, then went and lay down, and then got up and went to work. No exercise. Then we worked until six or seven o'clock in the morning, and then we went to the bistros until nine or ten o'clock, had another big meal, then went home and went to bed. In no time at all I shot up from about 135 to about 175. I still had those 'singing legs and feet,' but the rest of me got to be almost too much for them to carry around.*[19]

I'm not there yet, but I can see it happening to me on my bad days. As I write this section, my husband and I have just indulged in the ultimate decadent meal. Something we allow ourselves about twice a year and, sadly, we've been looking forward to it all week: a bucket of KFC. I mean, *yikes*. The difference is that I have more knowledge about what I'm putting into my body than Smith did, so I can't claim ignorance. And it is a slippery slope...

I can also be secretive, though not to the extreme that Smith was, however; she rarely confided in anyone. I do a lot of quiet observing, especially in crowds. It feels easy and natural for me to sit and listen to people reveal everything about themselves, while I say nothing. I've had plenty of conversations, during which I barely said more than "Hmm," that have gone on for over an hour and some-times *well* over an hour. This isn't necessarily a bad thing; in fact, I pride myself on my listening skills (and listening to others is a skill that a lot of people don't have), but I could stand to share more. And I could definitely learn to ask people for help more often—a lesson Smith had to learn more than once.

Am I in self-denial the way Bricktop might've been? At times. No, I'm not about to come out. I'm happily married to my husband, and though I've had fleeting attractions to women in the past, at this point I think it's safe to say I'm not hiding in any closets. But I'm not always honest with myself at all. Here's an odd confession: every New Year's Day, I vow that the year in question will be the year that I finally learn to drive a car and get my license. I've probably made this resolution to myself for about a decade, and it hasn't happened yet. I haven't even come close. This isn't because I enjoy lying to myself, but I ignore a lot of the real obstacles that get in the way of the things that should be accessible to me but aren't. I imagine we all do this to some degree, but there are times that this self-denial feels pretty intense, and it's connected to my secrecy. I'm so secretive about certain things that the people closest to me probably wouldn't categorize me as secretive at all. I'm just good at keeping them away from what I won't re-veal. (Truth: I just deleted a sentence here where I obliquely revealed something about myself in such a way that no one really could've pieced together what I was talking about, but I decided to not even take the chance.)

> *I'm at peace with myself. Not many people can look back on their lives, as I can, and say that if they had to do it over, they'd do it just about the same...*
>
> *One of the reasons I am at peace with myself is that I've tried very hard to live my life without hurting anyone, and I have no intention of changing at my age.*
>
> *It's a good philosophy. Ciao, babies.*[20]

Those are the parting words in *Bricktop*, the autobiography that I've quoted all through this essay, which Smith wrote with the assistance of historian James Haskell. I sincerely hope to be at peace with who I am when I begin to feel that I've reached the end of my life. I want to try to live, in my life right now, a bit more like Bricktop did. She exemplified revelry to me. Pure *joie de vivre*. She approached her life with an attitude of "why not?" Despite being born black, female, and working-class in 1894, if she set her mind to do something, she did it. She wasn't dominated by feelings of inferiority. She sought out joy in her life and work, and she found it.

Ada Beatrice Queen Victoria Louise Virginia "Bricktop" Smith lived her life the way she chose and on her own terms. Whether it was becoming an entrepreneur or traveling the world. From the twenties up until her death, she was always her own person. There was no precedent for what she accomplished. No guides or mentors for her to follow. She just did it. When I began my research after seeing *Midnight in Paris*, the first question that came to me was this, "Why have there been no attempts to tell her story in mainstream culture?" Apparently, a movie was in the works during the seventies, which prompted Smith to move to Hollywood for a brief period, but it never panned out.

I've thought about this a lot. Being a playwright, I've wondered: *Could her life be a play? A musical?*[21] It's possible, but it would be a challenge. She embraced the joyous, delicious, and often decadent aspects of life, but she was always pragmatic and always worked hard, determined to be the best. Therefore, she didn't fall into the traps that far too many of her contemporaries did. She loved her champagne, as I've said, but she wasn't an alcoholic. Though she suffered from depression, she never struggled with any kind of drug addiction, and she never had any run-ins with the law. Our cultural lust for drama (and let's be real: trauma) often neglects the stories of people who lived fascinating lives and who ultimately lived WELL. Bricktop lived for a long time, dying at the age of eighty-nine, and she lived very well. No demented tragedies or juicy flings or blood feuds with celebrities. Just a long, full, and phenomenal life. She deserves to be remembered and revered. We can share her countless stories (read up on her, as I've barely scratched the surface here) and bask in the memory of her revelrous light (yes, I just invented the word "revelrous.") Maybe we can all learn to approach our own days with just a touch of her *joie de vivre*.

Ciao, friends!

Firebrand: The Radical Life and Times of Annie Besant

By Leah Mueller

I became interested in Annie Besant when I picked up a copy of *Think on These Things* by philosopher Jiddu Krishnamurti at a used bookstore. I was a young adult, hoping to address both my internal confusion and my bewilderment about the events unfolding on the planet. My ensuing research about Krishnamurti gradually led me to descriptions of Besant, an Englishwoman who was his mentor and later became his legal guardian.

As I read, a portrait emerged of a dynamic, passionate, contradictory woman. She was a crusader for the radical social causes of her day, including birth control and workers' rights, and she was a spiritualist seeker of truth during her later years. She sparked my interest because she threw her entire being into every project she undertook and never failed to attract attention. Annie's potent combination of spirituality and political activism fascinated me, due to my own passionate interest in both subjects. Often, politics and spirituality appear to emanate from opposite worlds, but Annie fused them together, seemingly with little effort.

In the beginning, Annie seemed destined for a life of mundane comfort. She was born on October 1, 1847 in the fashionable Clapham section of London. Her parents, Emily Morris and Dr. William Wood, lived a comfortable middle-class existence. However, her father's death rendered the family penniless five years later. This reversal of fortune proved challenging for young Annie in that it resulted in her traumatic expulsion from the family home.

When Annie was five, her mother persuaded family friend Ellen Marryat to take over Annie's care. Undoubtedly, her mother was already overworked; she had her hands full running a boarding house for boys at the nearby Harrow School.[1] Ellen assumed the caretaker role willingly and went to special lengths to make certain that her surrogate daughter received a good education.

Because Marryat was an Evangelical Calvinist, she insisted that Annie read the Bible, *Pilgrim's Progress*, and *Paradise Lost*. Annie didn't require much urging, honing her early oratorical chops by reciting entire passages from these books.[2] Marryat also took Annie on a life-altering trip to Holland, France, and Germany. Annie readily learned to speak the languages of these countries, which fostered a lifelong interest in travel, communication, and intellectual inquiry.

Annie's Calvinist upbringing also sparked her spiritual quest, which existed under distinctly conventional constraints at the beginning but transformed gradually into the opposite. She married a Church of England clergyman, Frank Besant, in 1887, and they had two children. However, it is hard to imagine a more unlikely couple, and Annie and Frank separated after only six years, mainly due to Annie's growing anti-religious sentiments. In her autobiography, Besant writes, "We were an ill-matched pair, my husband and I, from the very outset; he, with very high ideas of a husband's authority and a wife's submission holding strongly to the 'master-in-my-own-house theory', thinking much of the details of home arrangements, precise, methodical, easily angered and with difficulty appeased; I, accustomed to freedom, indifferent to home details, impulsive, hot-tempered, and proud as Lucifer."[3]

A year later, she met Charles Bradlaugh, a self-described atheist and freethinker. Bradlaugh was the leader of the National Secular Society.[4] Bradlaugh's belief system had an enormous impact upon Annie. It echoed her own growing doubts about the existence of a supreme being. She promptly joined the society and wrote numerous articles for their newsletter before becoming the organization's vice president only one year later. Drawing upon her early oratorical roots, Besant became a lecturer for the group's various social causes, which were extremely progressive for that period. She advocated fiercely for the political rights of women and eventually formed a partnership with Bradlaugh, which they named the Freethought Publishing Company. Four years later, Annie divorced Besant, although, in accordance with the custom of the times, she chose to retain his last name.

The Freethought Publishing Company published articles that many people considered scandalous. They wrote passionate screeds about trade unions, women's suffrage, and education. Besant and Bradlaugh eventually landed in hot water when they were brought to trial for obscenity in 1876 for republishing a pamphlet from forty years prior that advocated birth control within the confines of marriage, originally written by U.S. Charles Knowlton, a U.S. physician. He received a light sentence for selling an indecent work. The incendiary pamphlet titled *The Fruits of Philosophy, or The Private Companion of Young Married People* had been circulating around London for quite some time, without much fanfare. When Besant and Bradlaugh republished it, however, the little book provoked a feeding frenzy, proving the old adage, "There is no such thing as bad publicity."

Following publication, the two of them set up shop at the Guildhall, where they sold five hundred copies in the first twenty minutes. Shortly thereafter, they were arrested, which wasn't exactly a surprise given that they had notified the police ahead of time about their intentions. During the three-month interim period between their arrest and trial, they managed to sell a total of 125,000 copies.[5] Besant mounted a passionate defense in favor of the pamphlet, claiming that access to birth control was essential, especially for impoverished women. She did this nearly forty years before Margaret Sanger did the same with her pamphlet titled *Family Limitation*, which was prosecuted by the Comstock Act in the United States.[6] Highlights of the trial included a testimony by physician C.R. Drysdale, who claimed that the lactation method of birth control was both insufficient for the nourishment of a growing infant and ineffective for the prevention of pregnancy.

People who seek an organic system of birth control occasionally use the lactation method to this day. It is predicated upon the theory that unrestricted nursing suppresses ovulation and therefore prevents fertilization. Having employed the method myself after the birth of my second child, I can attest to its complete lack of efficacy. I resumed ovulation after only two months of nursing, even though I did not supplement with bottle-feeding. Fortunately, I was able to convince my partner to get a vasectomy, which is a nearly foolproof method of birth control, but I assume this was not at all popular in England at the end of the nineteenth century.

Drysdale cited examples of female patients who had borne twenty-five children despite constantly breastfeeding their infants.[7] Bradlaugh and Besant argued along similar lines, stating, "We think it more moral to prevent conception of children than, after they are born, to murder them by want of food, air and clothing."[8]

The solicitor general was unmoved, stating that *Fruits of Philosophy* was a "dirty, filthy book" meant to spur women into having sex without worrying about the consequences of their behavior.[9] He loudly proclaimed:

> *...no human being would allow that book on his table, no decently educated English husband would allow even his wife to have it...The object of it is to enable a person to have sexual intercourse, and not to have that which in the order of providence is the natural result of that sexual intercourse. That is the only purpose of the book and all the instruction in the other parts of the book leads up to that proposition.*[10]

The jury's eventual decision was rife with ambiguity because they felt the book was "calculated to deprave public morals." However, they decided to "entirely exonerate the defendants from any corrupt motives in publishing it." A six-month sentence was handed down then repealed. Besant and Bradlaugh were eventually freed without punishment, under the condition that they cease their mission of publishing and promoting the book. Needless to say, they paid no heed to the verdict and continued to print and distribute *Fruits of Philosophy*, as though nothing had happened. In addition, Besant decided to write and distribute her own birth control book titled *The Laws of Population*. Authorities were scandalized—it was terrible enough for a woman to publicize a birth-control-themed book that had been written by a man, but it was unforgivable that she should write one herself. *The Times* newspaper called it an "indecent, lewd, filthy, bawdy and obscene book." Her still-bitter ex-husband, Frank Besant, took advantage of the situation and hauled Annie back to court, where he managed to persuade the jury to allow him custody of their daughter, Mabel.[11]

It's reasonable to assume that this loss was difficult for Annie, though she remained committed to her larger goals. Her husband's priggish and vengeful mistreatment only seemed to propel her more forcefully into social causes, especially ones that revolved around women's rights. She continued to speak out for birth control, although she was not a proponent of free love.[12] It is possible that Besant's Christian upbringing had left her with a certain modesty, which persisted despite her fierce advocacy for a woman's right to maintain ownership of her own body.

꒦

Almost 150 years after Besant's trial, the issue of women's reproductive rights remains murky and frustrating. Abortion has been legal in the United States since I was fourteen. Lawmakers passed the bill at a time when the activism of the 1960s was finally bearing fruit, and liberal laws were being enacted with surprising swiftness. When abortion was legalized, I remember thinking, "Wow, this is certainly forward-thinking of them. But future politicians will never be able to leave this law alone. They'll challenge it over and over again." Even at fourteen, I was acutely aware that I resided in a male-dominated nation that embraced fundamentalist Christianity with passionate fervor. Pregnant women were expected to keep their babies or give them up for adoption. Abortion was a form of murder. However, the same people who condemned abortion also railed against birth control. This struck me as hypocritical in the extreme, and I was careful to use birth control once I became sexually active a couple of years later.

I have thought about my prescient observation many times since then. In 2016 alone, twenty-six different states enacted anti-choice laws. Leading the pack is Louisiana, which managed to pass seven different laws restricting a woman's right to obtain an abortion. These laws include a ban on abortions due to fetal abnormality and an extension of the mandatory delay law from 24 to 72 hours. The unstated objective of the mandatory delay law is this: the longer a woman has to wait to get an abortion, the more inclined she'll be to forgo it.[13]

Louisiana is not exclusive in its endeavors to disallow women's reproductive freedoms. Indiana, with Mike Pence at the helm, also passed the fetal abnormality bill as well as measures to control the donation of fetal tissue.

Arizona, South Dakota, Pennsylvania, Ohio, and Michigan enacted a host of new laws, many of which slashed or eliminated federal funding of clinics that offer abortions.[14] These restrictions are terrifyingly draconian given that abortion has been legal for over forty years. Every year, the pro-choice movement loses a little more ground, and the issue of women's reproductive rights remains a political football.

⤶

Besant's romantic attachments continued to be complex and often turbulent. Some of them were platonic in nature, perhaps due to sexual shyness resulting from her strict religious upbringing. Annie was smitten with playwright George Bernard Shaw, although he was known to be gay. She had a long-term romance with Bradlaugh and a particularly turbulent affair with Edward Aveling, a Darwinian scholar and founding member of the Socialist League and the Independent Labour Party.[15] But Besant became increasingly passionate in her advocacy of various progressive social causes, and this created a schism between her and Bradlaugh, who was a liberal. She embraced socialism with a growing fervor.

In 1888, she heard a speech by Clementina Black about working conditions at the nearby Bryant and May match factory. Besant became increasingly incensed about descriptions of fourteen-hour shifts, extremely low pay, and a system of stiff fines for minor infractions such as dropping matches or going to the bathroom. Most horribly, many of the workers developed a type of bone cancer known as Phossy Jaw, a highly invasive condition that causes the entire side of the jaw to turn first green and then black. This condition was mostly attributable to the high levels of phosphorus present at the plant. Sweden had long banned the use of phosphorus in the manufacturing of matches, but British lawmakers argued that such a ban would constitute an impediment to fair trade.[16]

Besant penned an article titled "White Slavery in London" for her newspaper *The Link*, which created a sensation. Her descriptions of working conditions were graphic and terrifying:

> *Born in slums, driven to work while still children, undersized because under-fed, oppressed because helpless, flung aside as soon as worked out, who cares if they die or go on to the streets provided only that*

Bryant & May shareholders get their 23 per cent and Mr. Theodore Bryant can erect statutes and buy parks? Girls are used to carry boxes on their heads until the hair is rubbed off and the young heads are bald at fifteen years of age.[17]

Bryant and May attempted to intimidate its employees into signing a paper stating they were just fine with their working conditions, but a large group of them refused to do so. The company fired the group organizers, and 1,400 factory employees promptly went on strike.

The editors of several other newspapers joined forces with Besant. Reporters decried Bryant and May's squalid conditions and spoke out boldly in favor of a new workers' union. The workers formed their own Matchgirls' Union and installed Besant as their leader. After only three weeks, the company agreed to an end to the fines system, and the workers returned to their jobs. The story gained national attention, as it was the first time a strike by unorganized workers had received so much publicity. Workers in neighboring factories took notice, and new unions sprang up in other industries as well.[18]

Besant continued her tireless campaign against the use of yellow phosphorus, joining forces with other activists such as William and Catherine Booth. They contrasted the pay and working conditions at Bryant and May with the much better ones at the newly formed Salvation Army match factory. Social pressure mounted, and by 1901, Bryant and May's managing director agreed to discontinue the use of phosphorus. This triumph, decisive as it was, took over thirteen years to achieve, and countless workers sickened and/or died before it was implemented. Still, Besant's passionate advocacy for the match workers had a lasting impact on the labor movement—it continues to this day.

I wonder what Besant's reaction might be if she could see our current political climate. Undoubtedly, she would be horrified by how slowly the United States has advanced since her activist heyday in the early 1900s. "Socialism" is still a dirty word in many circles, and labor unions are being decimated in favor of "right-to-work" laws. Many of our nation's systems are socialist in nature such as the post office and social security. Labor strikes are largely responsible for the existence of workers' rights like mandatory overtime and the eight-hour workday, but many of our citizens remain stubbornly unaware of this.

I consider myself to be a Democratic socialist, but I have a hard time uttering those words in many circles. Our nation's two-party system seems to have a stranglehold on the mindset of its citizens. I began my voting life as a proud Democrat. However, over the years, the party has drifted so far toward the center that it no longer seems interested in the fate of the middle and working classes. The federal minimum wage hasn't risen in ten years. This doesn't affect me much, but it does impact my adult children, along with a whole generation of millennials. In addition, conservative voters often confuse socialism with communism—probably a holdover from watching civil defense films when they were students in public school (which is also, ironically, a socialist institution).

The official website of the Democrat Socialists of America is adamant about the distinction:

> *Socialists have been among the harshest critics of authoritarian Communist states. Just because their bureaucratic elites called them "socialist" did not make it so; they also called their regimes "democratic." Democratic socialists always opposed the ruling party-states of those societies, just as we oppose the ruling classes of capitalist societies. We applaud the democratic revolutions that have transformed the former Communist bloc.*[19]

It is disheartening that Democratic socialists still have to fight for the same rights that Annie Besant championed—fair wages, safe working conditions, and right-to-strike laws. If anything, we seem to be moving backward as existing rights are stripped away, one by one. I am encouraged by the number of Americans who have recently taken to the streets in protest of the new presidential regime. So far, the majority of the demonstrations have been peaceful in nature, but several have already turned bloody.

Of course, bloody conflict is nothing new. Few people today picture Annie Besant when they hear the words "Bloody Sunday,"[20] but Besant played an invaluable role in that conflict. Massive unemployment had created intense civil unrest in London, and people took to the streets in droves to protest. On November 13, 1887, police attacked demonstrators, beating them with truncheons. A bloody battle resulted, with police horses charging at the crowd, many arrests, and countless injuries. Two men succumbed to their injuries and died a few days later. The incident was immediately dubbed "Bloody Sunday." The event didn't occur in a vacuum; protests had been occurring with increasing frequency across London for some time, particularly in Trafalgar Square. Besant had already set up the Socialist Defense Organization to help folks who had been arrested. The group offered both moral and legal assistance for jailed demonstrators. She enlisted the help of wealthy supporters, who showed up at jails at all hours of the day with bail money for those who needed it. The revolution was well funded and was therefore a force to be reckoned with. Annie's old love, George Bernard Shaw, described Bloody Sunday in this manner: "[It was] the most abjectly disgraceful defeat ever suffered by a band of heroes outnumbering their foes a thousand to one."[21] His view was a characteristically cynical one. Still, the large number of arrests and injuries and the two casualties made it difficult for most people to think of Bloody Sunday as any sort of victory.

Bloody Sunday helped put Besant on the map as an organizer. The government had recently passed the extremely unpopular Coercion Act, which suspended most civil rights indefinitely. Besant spoke at the protest but was not arrested, probably due to her gender. Afterward, she led a procession through the London streets as riots erupted around her. Many of the demonstrators were thrown into Millbank Prison. Besant showed up at the prison with bail money and escorted the jailed protesters to freedom in person, a gesture that instantly transformed her into a heroine. The incident caused much friction in her relationship with Bradlaugh. He had always been the more politically moderate of the two, and he was upset because she hadn't asked permission before deciding to lead the march.[22] However, the two of them found common ground during the later Matchgirl Strike, so their schism was a temporary one.

Meanwhile, Annie's popularity—or her notoriety, depending upon one's political persuasion—continued to grow rapidly. Her involvement in the Bloody Sunday riots put her on the map, and she wielded enormous power, which enabled her to be fully effective during the strike against Bryant and May. Annie's reputation as a socialist firebrand was secure, and ironically, her own bank account flourished as a result.

Later, however, Besant experienced a growing disenchantment with her philosophical belief systems. Atheism no longer appealed to her, and she sought to fuse her socialist ideals with a spiritual philosophy. She was introduced to Hinduism after joining the Theosophical Society in 1889, and she found herself increasingly drawn to India. Wikipedia describes theosophy as "a collection of mystical and occultist philosophies concerning, or seeking direct knowledge of, the presumed mysteries of life and nature, particularly of the nature of divinity and the origin and purpose of the universe."[23] It is considered to be an offshoot of Western esotericism, which fuses knowledge from the ancient past with present spiritual concerns, with the goal of discovering a bridge between the two.

In 1893, Besant secured an invitation from Colonel Olcott, president of the organization. Olcott was living with society co-founder Madame Blavatsky on the River Adyar in a former maharajah's palace, and the society had grown so large that he wanted Annie to help him manage its various branches. Her arrival in India was greeted with enthusiastic fanfare, with hordes of cheering people clamoring to hear what the famed rabble-rouser had to say. As always, Besant was far from reticent about sharing her opinions with the masses. Although the Indian government had decreed that theosophists could not be involved with politics, the charismatic Annie easily convinced them to abolish that rule. Almost immediately, she was hailed as a new leader in the movement, despite the fact that Olcott had observed the decree without argument and was upset by her defection from the law.[24]

Olcott, a Buddhist, remained in Adyar, whereas Besant lived in the Hindu city of Benares for six months out of every year. She took to wearing a white sari and sandals. White was the traditional Hindu color of mourning, and Annie claimed to be in perpetual mourning for India because the country was still subject to British rule.[25] Perpetual mourning didn't deter Besant in her mission of improving the lives of the people who surrounded her, however. Despite her frenetic pace, Annie found the time to write many books, including a translation in Sanskrit of the *Bhagavad Gita*. In 1898, she founded the Central Hindu School and College in Benares, and a few years later, she started the Central Hindu School for Girls. In 1907, when Olcott died, Annie took over as president of the Theosophical Society, a post she held for the rest of her life. She chose Charles Webster Leadbeater, a former Anglican priest, as president of the organization. Leadbeater had resigned from his previous post with the society due to unproven charges of perversion toward young boys.[26]

Besant and Leadbeater collaborated on a remarkable book titled *Occult Chemistry*, which sought to explore the connections between clairvoyance and the structure of atoms. Many of the conclusions stemmed from a weekend that a group of theosophists spent in Surrey in 1895. The stated purpose of the gathering was to "escape malevolent thought-forms" and utilize clairvoyance to observe atoms directly. They felt this was possible because an individual's "conception of himself can be so minimized that objects which normally are small appear to him as large," and, though "each object is in rapid motion," it was necessary to use "a special form of will-power, so as to make its movement slow enough to observe the details."[27]

Besant and Leadbeater believed that atoms could be observed with "etheric eyes," which allowed them to notice distinct shapes within the atomic structure, including "spikes," "dumbbells," and regular polyhedral arrangements such as the Platonic solids. In addition, they postulated that atoms contained a substructure made up of *anu*, the Sanskrit word for atoms.[28]

The book's premise might seem absurd to scientists today, but it was taken seriously by many prominent individuals at the time it was written. Besant and Leadbeater had extensive connections within the scientific community including with scientists Oliver Lodge and William Crookes, who shared the duo's interest in mysticism. Crookes, a member of the Theosophical Society, was open to the possibility of an invisible world populated by spirit beings.[29] Other scientists expressed greater skepticism, but the book created a stir within the community that persists to this day.

꙼

The Theosophical Society had an enormous impact upon the current New Age movement, and vestiges of its philosophy can be found at metaphysical fairs across the world. I am a professional astrologer and tarot reader, and I often purchase booths at psychic expos as a way of advertising my services. I am an intuitive counselor and take a pragmatic approach to my business. For the most part, I work with clients on here-and-now concerns like employment and relationships.

I consider myself to be more of a pagan than a Christian or New-Ager. My own brand of spirituality is Earth-based, and I observe seasonal cycles, celebrating solstices and equinoxes. I look for God when I'm in a forest or beside the ocean. However, my clients come from a variety of backgrounds. Many of them identify as Christians and feel a mix of guilt and curiosity about intuitive readings. They have internalized the message that it is sinful to seek spiritual insight from anyone except Jesus, but their need for self-awareness trumps their shame. I speak to these clients gently, emphasizing my belief that intuition is a natural facility all of us possess to varying extents. I reassure them that their religious convictions can exist concurrently with their desire to find their best options. Most of the time, they find this comforting.

I encounter a large number of people who are intrigued by the idea of an alternate, unseen reality. Aura photographers are almost always the most popular vendors at such shows, and customers wait patiently in line for hours to purchase a color photo that depicts the molecules of their energy field. No one ever has a black aura—they almost always present in soft, pastel shades, with an occasional red or forest-green thrown in for good measure. White is still considered the ultimate color of divinity.

Like Besant and Leadbeater, many of the most adamant new-age practitioners began their lives as fundamentalist Christians before eventually making a break with the church. However, they still carry some of the vestiges of their early religious conditioning. The theosophists' concept of "malevolent thought-forms" is analogous with today's New-Age idea of "bad energy," (i.e., any emotion that can be perceived as pessimistic or gloomy). Negativity appears to be synonymous with the Christian concept of the Devil, and it must be avoided at all costs. Sexuality is often viewed negatively and is therefore repressed.

Once, at a metaphysical expo, a man approached me and demanded to know whether I was an "unspoiled column of pure light." I replied that I was not, and he reacted with disgust. Shaking his head, he scuttled away in search of someone who would give him an affirmative answer. Perhaps I should have said yes, but I would have been lying. I puzzled over his choice of words. Unspoiled? How was that even possible? The mere act of existence was bound to create some spoilage. Why would anyone want to consult a person whose life was free from any perception of darkness? How compassionate could such a counselor be? I doubt whether such an individual could even exist in our chaotic, messy world. The incident was an amusing reminder of the paternalism that permeates the New Age movement—many of its male adherents are either looking for a messiah or, worse, imagine themselves to be one. Whether male or female, it seems that many of the people at metaphysical shows are searching for truth everywhere except within themselves.

In April of 1909, while wandering on the seashore in Adyar, Leadbeater discovered Jiddu Krishnamurti, a fourteen-year-old Hindu boy who wore a soulful, pensive expression. Young Krishnamurti enthralled Leadbeater. He claimed that he had never seen a boy with an aura "so free from selfishness" and predicted that he would become a great speaker.[30] This was news to his secretary, Mr. Wood, who had been helping Krishnamurti with his homework and saw nothing remarkable about the young boy. Nevertheless, Leadbeater was beguiled and introduced Krishnamurti to Besant a few months later. Besant took Jiddu and his younger brother, Nityananda, under her wing, declaring that the former as "the new World Teacher." She helped form an organization called the Order of the Star in the East and installed Krishnamurti as its head.[31] Besant felt strongly that the theosophists had predicted Krishnamurti's arrival, and she wanted to make certain that the planet was prepared for what the World Teacher had to say.

Despite the rigors of continuous travel with the two boys, Besant continued to throw herself passionately into her political activities. By 1910, she controlled two newspapers, the *Commonweal* and *New India*. She joined the Indian National Congress in 1913 but stood in opposition to many of the other political luminaries of the day during the 1914–1918 war. When Gandhi and other citizens called for a cessation of ongoing opposition to the Raj, Besant resisted, stating that "England's need is India's opportunity."[32]

Besant was unimpressed by Gandhi's practice of passive resistance. Though she admired Gandhi, she felt that his philosophy fostered disrespect for the law, which was ironic, considering her own reputation as a political firebrand. Her opposition to the highly influential pacifist distressed the Indian National Congress, and she lost her position as their leader.[33] Thus began a period of slow decline in political power for Besant, which allowed her to devote more time to spiritual pursuits. Though she was entering a period of her life that would be fraught with difficulties, she continued to work on behalf of her adopted homeland. In a 1918 article in *New India*, she wrote, "I love the Indian people as I love none other, and [...] my heart and my mind [...] have long been laid on the altar of the Motherland."[34]

Leadbeater assumed the lion's share of Krishnamurti's education, but he lacked patience with the boy. The pressure of becoming a world teacher was often too much for Krishnamurti to comprehend. Leadbeater was frequently annoyed by the youth's slack-jawed expression while concentrating and sometimes hit him on the chin to get his attention.[35] Krishnamurti's relationship with Annie was somewhat warmer, and he referred to her as *Amma*, the Indian word for "mother." His own mother died when he was a child. Besant and Leadbeater eventually took it upon themselves to adopt the two brothers. At first, the boys' father, Naravaniah, consented to the adoption. Later, he tried to regain custody but failed.[36]

Accounts vary wildly about the reasons for Naravaniah's alarm. Adherents of Blavatsky pinpointed Leadbeater and described him in particularly scathing terms. They suggested that Besant used exceptionally poor judgment in allowing him to rejoin the theosophists after his initial expulsion due to unproven charges of perversion. They insisted Leadbeater had admitted under oath to sexual violation of young boys and claimed that Krishnamurti had little use for the man. One writer even suggests that Krishnamurti might have been a target of Leadbeater's advances.[37] Other sources postulate that Naravaniah was angered by Besant's lack of proper care for the two boys and felt the boys' adoption had violated rules of caste.[38]

In cases of sexual assault, I tend to side with the alleged victim rather than the accused perpetrator. Long ago, I worked for a telephone crisis line, often fielding calls from rape victims. I learned that all too often, they feel terrified and ashamed and choose to remain silent about their experiences. It is far more common for a person to refuse to come forward with details of abuse than it is for one individual to falsely accuse another of sexual assault. Though the exact details about Leadbeater's relationship with the boys in his care will never be known, the fact that he had already been asked to step down from the Theosophical Society due to charges of "perversion" is deeply troubling. It seems as though it would have been better for her to install another woman as president, but Besant resided in a paternalistic society and often chose to surround herself with men. I'm sure she had her own reasons for reinstating Leadbeater, but she remained uncharacteristically mum about them. If Leadbeater did assault young Krishnamurti, I can only hope that Besant was unaware of it.

There is no evidence that Krishnamurti ever spoke about the alleged sexual assaults. Details remain murky, possibly due to his reticence about exposing either Leadbeater or Besant. It's entirely possible that if Krishnamurti was assaulted by Leadbeater, he felt great shame, and possibly even blamed himself for it. In this sense, little has changed in 150 years. However, as of this writing in 2017, many victims have come forward to report rapes and other forms of harassment they received at the hands of powerful, often famous men. The floodgates have opened, and people are far less likely to remain silent about sexual abuse than they were even a few years ago. I consider this to be an amazing, positive development, but long overdue.

The custody battle was long and bitter. Besant lost the case in lower court, and the brothers were made wards of the state. She appealed and was defeated again. After she took the case to the Privy Counsel, the boys were allowed to testify, since they were ages 15 and 18 by then. Jiddu and Nityananda spoke positively of their experiences with Besant, and the courts responded by ruling on her behalf.[39] It is easy to postulate that Besant's wealth and white, European heritage gave her an advantage over the boys' father—hers was a privileged status that transcended paternity. One can only imagine how painful it was for him to have to relinquish custody of his sons.

Krishnamurti had little to say publicly about his experiences with Leadbeater, but he spoke positively of Besant. He appreciated the fact that she trusted him to make his own decisions, and once said, "Dr. Besant was our mother, she looked after us, she cared for us. But one thing she did not do. She never said to me, 'Do this' or 'Don't do that.' She left me alone. Well, in these words I have paid her the greatest tribute."[40]

There is a puzzling duality to Krishnamurti's words in the above statement—an equation of love and affection coupled with a certain detachment, a "leaving alone" of the young boy. It is impossible to know whether Annie, preoccupied as she was with world affairs, was able to devote much time to nurturing. Perhaps her own lack of maternal comfort as a child had left its mark on her, resulting in a kind of coldness that permeated her most intimate alliances. Very little is written about Besant's relationship with her own children, and it is possible that she was more preoccupied with spiritual and social justice matters than she was with mothering.

For many years, Jiddu and Nityananda traveled across the globe with Besant, lecturing on behalf of the Theosophical Society. In 1925, Nityananda died of tuberculosis, which devastated his brother; the two of them had been exceptionally close. This loss created a gradual transformation within Krishnamurti, accompanied by a growing disenchantment with the Theosophical Society.

Three years later, he stunned its members by withdrawing from the group, claiming, "I maintain that the truth is a pathless land and you cannot approach it by any path whatsoever, by any religion, by any sect."[41]

Krishnamurti continued to lecture worldwide, though not on behalf of any organization. He remained adamant about an individual's need to seek truth on her or his own terms. He denied being a guru or a World Teacher, and emphasized that if people sought divinity, they needed to look within themselves. This was ironic because Besant herself had written that:

> ...blind belief is the road to equally blind scepticism; you place a student on a pedestal and loudly proclaim him to be a prophet, despite his protests; and then, when you find he has made some mistake, as he warned you was likely, you turn round, pull him down, and trample on him. You belabour him when should belabour your own blindness, your own stupidity, your own anxiety to believe.[42]

It is highly probable that Krishnamurti and Besant harbored some lingering, secret resentment toward each other. Still, the two maintained a friendly relationship, at least on the surface. Krishnamurti visited Besant periodically at Adyar, and he was present at her deathbed shortly before her demise, eight years after he left the group.

Powerful until the very end, Besant continued to advocate and lecture on behalf of India. She fell ill in 1931 but remained active as president of the Theosophical Society until her death on September 20, 1933. In accordance with her wishes, Annie's body was cremated. Some of her ashes were deposited in the Garden of Remembrance at Adyar. Another portion was transported to Bombay and eventually to Benares. Bhagavan Das deposited them in the middle of the Ganges river from a decorated boat. Yet another portion of the ashes remain at the Centre at Huizen.[43] Scores of people attended a ceremony in her honor at the headquarters of the Theosophical Society. Reverend Leadbeater spoke at great length, calling Besant "one of the World's greatest women."[44] After Besant's death, her secretary, N. Sri Ram, wrote the following tribute:

> Dr. Besant was nothing if she was not wholehearted and whole-souled in all that she undertook, in every aim and every inner impulse. Almost

always, as I know from personal knowledge of how she affected various people, they were struck with the extraordinary magnetism that seemed to surround her, the brightest energy, which seemed to leave her at the end of the day almost as fresh as at the beginning.[45]

Besant juggled many roles in her lifetime; she was a freedom fighter, a passionate advocate for birth control and workers' rights, and an unconventional spiritualist. Her fiery spirit scorched the usual expectations of a woman's role in nineteenth- and early-twentieth-century society. Yet, she was not without flaws—she sought worldly power at the cost of personal relationships and was often driven by ego. But few people would deny that Besant was a bright light shining fiercely—a powerful woman who labored tirelessly to illuminate the darkest corners of injustice.

I continue to search everywhere for answers to my internal and external dilemmas, and forty years after my purchase of *Think on These Things*, the search for enlightenment remains nebulous and difficult. My research about Besant reinforces my belief that male dominion is a blockade that strong women must resist. Feminist progress remains maddeningly slow. Annie Besant didn't just apply pressure; she literally blasted the walls down. For that alone, she has my undying admiration.

Victorine and Laure in Manet's *Olympia*: Seeing and Not Seeing a Famous Painting

By Debra Brehmer

*S*he is both innocent and seductive. I only know her through photographs in books and paintings spied at various museums over the course of a lifetime. But when I see her, peering from the bed, park, or street, I recognize something that is deeply part of my own constitution and psyche. I see a woman in a role that has been held by a man or by centuries of men. Imagine the sediment, the layers, and the buildup of all those desiring looks, as well as the disappointed and scrutinizing ones. Like dust or varnish, the looking accrues as an invisible haze over the paintings.

Edouard Manet's favorite model, Victorine Meurent, appears in nine of his works from 1862 to 1874. She is Olympia in the eponymous painting of a naked prostitute being greeted by a black handmaiden bearing flowers (1863). She is also the central naked woman in *The Luncheon on the Grass* (1863). She is the woman at the train station with her daughter (*The Railway*, 872–73), the woman with a guitar on her back coming out of doorway onto the street, eating cherries (*Street Singer*, 1862). She is a matador with a purple headscarf, a pink cape, and a yellow scarf in her pocket, her body twisting in formal rhythm within this triad of blooming colors (*Mademoiselle V in the Costume of an Espada*, 1862). Collectively, these and other portraits of

Meurent become almost a tribute to the roles of women during this period of great societal change and early industrialization in France. Whether Manet himself was conscious of ennobling and empowering women is a curious and perhaps unanswerable question but one worth pondering.

Much has been written about Victorine since the art historian Eunice Lipton saved her from obscurity by researching her life and publishing *Alias, Olympia: A Woman's Search for Manet's Notorious Model and Her Own Desire* in 1992.[1] Lipton spent years searching for remnants or records of Victorine, who, in earlier, inaccurate accounts, had been killed off at a young age as an impoverished, debauched alcoholic who plunged into decrepitude after Manet stopped using her as a model. Lipton discovered that Victorine (1844–1927), in reality lived into her eighties in the town of Colombes on the outskirts of Paris with a woman named Marie Dufour, and that she had earned acclaim as a painter herself. Victorine, daughter of a hat-maker, laundress, and bronze finisher, started modeling at age sixteen in the studio of Thomas Couture. She taught violin and guitar to private students while also modeling for Edgar Degas, Puvis des Chavannes, and Alfred Stevens. She seems to have stopped modeling for Manet by the early 1870s and resumed her own art studies in the evenings at the Academie Julian. In 1876, records indicate that a no-longer-extant self-portrait painted by Victorine was included in the official Salon, the annual or biannual state exhibition that could make or break an artist's career. It was the same year that Manet's entries were rejected. Her work would be accepted and exhibited in the Salon six times. In 1903, Meurent was accomplished enough to be admitted to the Société des Artistes Français.

Prior to Lipton's research, Victorine's history had been written incorrectly, which tells us something about how many histories are written. We think there is research and authority behind published accounts that intone knowledge and fact. But the assumptions of Victorine's demise might very well have traveled another channel of recited anecdote, a path that echoes the transmission of gossip into fact, a tone recanted by sloppy storytellers, angry colleagues, or spurned husbands and wives of the millennia who, over beers with friends, dismissed their tired female coworkers and wives, writing their narratives, shortcomings, and inevitably sad demises with bitumen and regret. Yes, all of this trickles into history.

‿

As I careen across farm fields in a rented minivan, driving two of our children across the country to college with my ex-husband, he tells me of his best friend's long, loveless marriage; their separate bedrooms; her shrew-like nature; and her controlling, manipulative personality. The best friend has long had a mistress but refuses to divorce because of money issues. I cannot judge their situation or marriage, but I wonder about the twenty-five years of child rearing that led to his great pride in their three children. What role did the so-called shrew play as she dedicated much of her moral bearing to the massive and important job of tending, nurturing, and raising the kids while her husband toiled at a corporate job with requisite after-work drinks and collegial softball games?

The worn categorical typecasting of women feels warm and familiar, like a wool coat one throws on to take out the garbage. The telling of stories becomes the recanting and writing of facts. If told often enough to the right people over beers in 2017 or absinthe in nineteenth century Paris, or in a rented minivan on a highway in Indiana, the stories become an official history. They bleed around the edges and become distorted, just as Victorine Meurent's story seeped stereotypically toward ruin and debauchery. Art history sometimes feels noble with fresh-pressed pages giving us orientation and direction, as if the authors know why a painter or painting is magnificent, why someone is greater than someone else, and why the lesser deserve the fringe to which they have been consigned. Then again, art history just as often feels like a hat full of random shreds of paper assembled by drunks and presented authoritatively, as hopeless a terrain as any cogent notion of "truth."

Many years ago, in art history class, Olympia gave me the hope and promise of autonomy and strength. She stared back at her audience, fully in control. The previous centuries' reclining nudes looked demurely downward or coyly unaware of an audience, ready for the consumption of male viewers. Olympia felt like a feminist breakthrough in the modernist period, a clamorous interruption of the status quo as Western culture was about to pirouette toward redefined freedoms and empowerment. Finally, a naked woman was in control of her own body.[2]

I sat in the lovely cocoon of the dark lecture hall, excited to learn about these pictures and their rootedness to society, how they absorbed the conditions of their time and could often be translated, decoded. My professor was young and handsome. He wore white shirts, jeans, and motorcycle boots, and his diction was a delicious mix of street talk, humor, and erudition. What a spell Olympia cast. When her image hit the screen, she became a touchstone after hundreds of years of reclining nude goddesses embraced by polite society because the mythological subtext suggested elevated thought and taste. Human beauty had become equated with spirituality and purity in quattrocento Renaissance Italy as a metaphor for God's coding of perfect geometries into human anatomy—(e.g., Leonardo's drawing of *Vitruvian Man* from 1490). For the next four hundred years, paintings of prone, naked, come-hither, silky-skinned beauties were not only de rigueur soft porn, but like room fresheners, they perfumed the world with heightened intellectual and moral values.

When I was in my twenties, before I married, I went to Paris to gaze at *Olympia*, a trip that functioned as a mini-feminist pilgrimage to the Jeu de Paume where she was then housed. Nothing could live up to the giant image projected in the lecture hall or hold up to the weight of assumptions and needs for strong women role models with which I had arrived. But she felt, appropriately enough in a building full of pictures and histories, like a bookmark that guides one's return to a meaningful passage. I had claimed her as a personal symbol, and although she was just a painting and couldn't be balm for my rage no a candle toward my societal impotence and invisibility, I did feel that I was Victorine as Olympia. I was the short girl who was sort of pretty but not beautiful, who says, "Fuck you, go away," just like Olympia seems to be saying to her unseen suitor. I was the girl who, despite her self-immolating interior insecurity, had agency, attitude, and a fairly secure sense of her own aptitude.

There is something I have never told my therapist. For whatever reason, I chose not to relate the story in the private confines of a small, protected space with a person I trusted, but I will tell it here to an unknown audience. Like Olympia, I was asked to model and pose. I was only a child, perhaps seven or maybe ten years old. My brother, who was five years my senior, had me take off my clothes and pose on the back of the couch while he sat in the arm chair across the room. I had no idea what this game was about, but he seemed assured that it was worth playing.

He never touched me, he just looked. In my small girl's body, I felt exposed and chilled as we performed a game that I knew could only be played when our parents were away, in spite of not knowing what it was about. He was a mean brother who tormented me. In response, I wanted to please him because it might adjudicate the abuse. But there was no pleasing. His cruelty gave him a power that he must have needed to survive psychically. I was the victim and the foil, innocence that melted like wax in the hands of his entitlement. He simply could not allow me to flourish while he suffered. My vulnerability magnified his power.

In this regard, I most certainly was Olympia—not an artist's model but a pawn, giving up her body as a matter of fact. The act of being naked, witnessed, and rendered—of being fully consumed—was and possibly still is a normalized female condition. Manet to Victorine to Olympia represents an equation of seer, individual, and the molding of individual into a fictionalized identity, thus becoming a vessel for consumption and fantasy. I look at Olympia, and even though she has been re-envisioned by Manet as a reclining nude with some agency and strength as she stares the viewer down, it is still Manet's conception of a painting and a moment created by a white male author whose intention is not really known. Manet might have wanted to address the entire history of the nude and reframe it within contemporary terms, vis-à-vis the philosophies of his radical friends Emile Zola and Charles Baudelaire, the writers and theorists of the time who called for more truth, more reality, and a grittier look at "what is."[3] But it is unlikely that Manet was thinking about female power as he painted her gaze, looking so directly at us: not "come-hither" but "don't come near unless I allow it."

Does it matter who we claim as emblems of power and triumph, despite the uncertainties of intention? Although academic studies might assure us that there are more probable interpretations of intention and content to fill in the many cracks of meaning in historic works, the viewer tends to fall in love with an artwork out of their own interests and needs. We identify with monumental works by the likes of Velazquez, Van Gogh, Goya, Michelangelo, Leonardo, and Monet because they nebulously confirm something we need to remember to stay fully alive, not because analysis of the work brings us greater knowledge of centuries past.

Unfortunately, there were precious few female artists in the pantheon, making my attachment to Olympia one of necessity. At least we now have Louise Bourgeois, Alice Neel, Betye Saar, and many others noted in art history survey books. Options of influence and inspiration seem plentiful within the contemporary global condition of connectivity. But can history really be rewritten? The Western canon, with all of its historic art monuments—the works people fly to Rome, Paris, Madrid, and Amsterdam to experience in person, from Michelangelo's *David*, to Leonardo's *Mona Lisa*, to Vermeer's *Girl with Pearl Earring*, to Van Gogh's *Starry Night*, to Picasso's *Guernica*—was crafted by white males.

Of course, we know this simple fact, but even now, it causes disbelief. This isn't possible, is it, that only white men created all the important works? As we cut and paste powerful women artists into the margins of this ironclad substratum, I wonder if their work will ever absorb the onerous weight of male forebears. Authority has its own scent. We follow the pheromones to the pivoting heel of Michelangelo's *David* at the Accademia Gallery in Florence, where buzzing droves of worshipers spasmodically discharge digital recording devices. I love this history and these works. I even love the buzz of hungry tourists. I have sat on the floor of the Academia at the foot of *David* and drawn in my sketchbook for hours, translating the mighty contours that anchor the young and old to the ache of beauty.

I glance at my bookshelf and see the course I followed, loving the masters but trying to find orientation from the female art historians of the 1980s onward—Whitney Chadwick, Griselda Pollock, Lucy Lippard, Linda Nochlin—who provided footholds to guide my way up the insurmountable mountain of male greatness. That is why Eunice Lipton's small book on Victorine Meurent became a precious object; it showed me a way to love this corrupt history while changing its terms. We can accept the greatness of monumental works, but we can also reinterpret them according to our own cultural perspectives, which are now shaped and buoyed by trails of women theorists as well as women artists who are only now coming into full agency. I like to shuffle the deck: a Frieda Kahlo portrait might hang next to *Mona Lisa*, one asserting pain and interior discord, the other a formula for the ultimate sublime. Kara Walker's *Sugar Sphinx* could assertively tower alongside Michelangelo's *David* (David is only half the size of Walker's 35-foot-tall *Sphinx*). A blinged-out reclining black nude by Mikalene Thomas could exist in consort with *Olympia*. They cannot fully exist without one another. Their sisterhood begins to crochet a new infrastructure in art history because it doesn't destroy the past but illuminates it.

One could align the works they love like a family photo album, tracing the contours of personal history and personality along the electrical wires

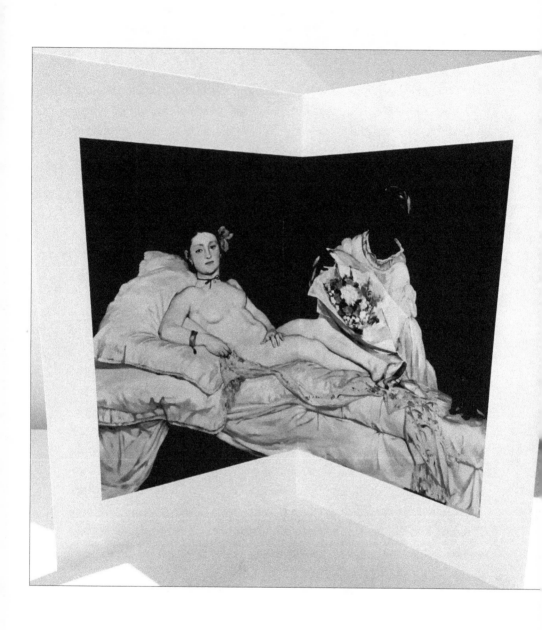

that solder Van Gogh's stars to Agnes Martin's devotional lines and grids and then to the voluptuous peeled orange at the feet of Victorine Meurent in Manet's *Girl with a Parrot* (1866). Those who love art end up going through life picking bouquets of unconscionably perfect moments of communion with things we've stood in front of, things we've stared at that mirror and illuminate our own needs, wants, desires, and confusion.

Although Olympia enhanced my strength and inspired me when I was in my twenties, I hadn't thought about her for a long time. Eunice Lipton's book was buried high on a bedroom bookshelf alongside other dusty feminist tomes. I just drove my last of three children to college. I'm alone. I am so *not* Olympia as my middle-aged body becomes a foreign terrain, my hair grays, and my eyes wrinkle. I am no one's sexual fantasy. But that is not fully why I've lost interest in Olympia. When I studied art history in the 1990s, we didn't think much about the Eurocentric whiteness or gender bias. Now, it makes my skin crawl. The emotional content of occlusion, omission, being disregarded, unseen, manipulated, used, demeaned, and dehumanized is the history of the industrialized world. Capitalism was and still is a steamroller that does not respect difference or realignments of power.

With each passing decade, Olympia loosens her spell over me, not because a male author invented her, but because I now realize she looks like a wan white girl. I am no longer interested in thinking about pronouncements or displays of categorical whiteness. Her body is like a street lamp, so bright it blinds. Her challenging gaze has not proven to eradicate the history of the prone female nude as serving only one purpose, to offer at the altar yet another full-bodied sacrifice to those who seek to behold and devour. I can still summon some sentimental love for Olympia and Victorine, but my affection is tinged with disappointment as her ambiguous half smile cracks through the narrative of tough urban prostitute, a wink and a joke for the confused nineteenth-century top-hatted viewers.

The painting was notoriously controversial when it was shown in the 1865 Salon because it toppled the conventions of the nude, erasing its idealism and leaving only a dirty, all-too-real prostitute bracing herself for yet another client. Although I admire Manet's interruption of a tired conceit and his seemingly empowered rendering of a modern woman, I now stumble upon the realization that Olympia has stolen the show. In the countless essays, interpretations, and graduate theses written about this painting, in the hundreds of thousands of times she flashed in a lecture hall, we didn't see the other half of the painting—the black maid.

I confess that I only see her now as I write this essay. In the process of asking myself why Olympia seems so much less interesting to me at this stage of my life, I realize that we were force-fed Western art history as a narrow slice of objects and attitudes that supported the forward momentum of capitalism via colonialism. It was—and in some ways still is—a fantastical, distorted, manipulative tale intended to justify the oppression that builds palaces. We can't blame poor Olympia for her whiteness and entitlement because Olympia is asserting herself from the fictive margins of a compromised life as a prostitute. It's not her fault that we didn't see or care about the black maid.

It is the much larger, embedded, systemic structure of Western society that we must blame. This confidently scaled painting (51.4" x 74.8"), despite the many labored and well-researched texts that give it form like pleats in the structure of a hoop skirt, has a meaning completely indivisible from its overt content or narrative. The painting is, for me, a mirror to the cultural efficiency of blindness. It is about what I didn't see versus what I have chosen to see and marks a rather frightening void in my own consciousness. I didn't see the black maid, and I didn't care about the black maid. And this is how we live in the world: thinking that we know or that we see, secure in our sensitive liberal perspectives, and utterly blind.

With humility, I print out an image of Manet's *Olympia* and fold it in half. The black maid occupies fifty percent of the painting. She looms as large as Olympia, almost as a mirrored image. It is a double bill. Rarely has she been written about beyond quick mentions. Her value to the painting was historicized to emerge out of the vogue for Orientalism and Harem subjects via the Romanticism and neoclassicism of Ingres, Delacroix, and Jerome. The black maid is likewise considered a vestige of colonial expansion, shifting urban space, and industrialization's new condition of leisure time, whereby a household maid would indicate middle-class stature. The maid might also be some kind of nod to France's abolishment of slavery a mere fifteen years before the painting was completed. She is now employed and free, and she suggests personality and individuality.

The painting is almost divided in two by a vertical line that appears to be the edge of a wall. Olympia's face is framed on a brown background with a draped curtain to the left, which formally presents her as a staged prize.

The black maid occupies the other full half of the painting. Her name was Laure, according to Manet's journals.[4] She is framed against deep green curtains in the background. Olympia is naked except for a ribbon around her neck, a bracelet, and slippers. It has often been noted how increasingly erotic these vestiges of contemporary clothing make her compared to the legions of historic nudes presented as distant mythological beauties. The maid is fully clothed in a pink dress trimmed with a white neckline. She wears a headscarf, which suggests Caribbean or African origin. In her arms is a giant bouquet of flowers wrapped in white paper. It seems as if one of Olympia's suitors has sent her a token of admiration. Taken as a whole, the painting seesaws between oppositions: black/white, clothed/unclothed, horizontal/vertical. When we add the black maid, the painting becomes a perfectly balanced visual fulcrum for shifting states of being; one age gives way to a new, industrial one, and history is amended and advanced in a fabricated bedroom.

Despite Olympia's direct, outward gaze, the painting is actually a conversation between maid and mistress. In recent years, female academics such as Darcy Grimaldo Grigsby and Emma Jacobs asked many of the same questions that Eunice Lipton asked in her groundbreaking study of Victorine Meurent in the 1990s.[5] All we really know of the black model's biography, however, is what Manet jotted in a notebook in 1862: "Laure, very beautiful Negress, rue Vintimille, 11, 3rd floor."[6] Lipton doggedly decided to find out who Olympia was, as a real person. The resulting book tells the story of her research as well as a personal narrative whereby Lipton decides to reject academia and move to Paris with her artist husband to spend years looking for any trace of Victorine's life. Nothing has been uncovered about Laure other than Manet's note. Perhaps we will never know her story or the consequences of her life because her trail is too obscure. But nonetheless, as Laure comes fully into focus in the painting, she provides a parallel discussion. That discussion is not only about what she meant in 1863 as part of Manet's composition but also about racial prejudice and the grip of hegemonic authority in shaping perspective: the black holes in art-historical research, the utter possibility and reality of fully ignoring something standing right in front of us, and the impossibly narrow purview of our constructed worlds.

Manet, at this time in his career, was interested in examining how art could be resuscitated to serve a changed contemporary world. Like Eunice Lipton, he had to look back to consider the present. The classic traditions of reclining nudes, religious paintings, and historic and political narratives had frayed by the mid 1800s. After the French revolutions and reconstructed democratic governments, painting no longer solely needed to serve the infrastructures of church and state. Manet appropriates and quotes the conventions of historic works to amplify new concerns and conditions. He doesn't disregard the past but amends it, updates the operating system. He takes Titian's *Venus of Urbino*, blows off the dust, and lovingly turns a timeless reclining nude muse into a present-day individual, not a perfect goddess but someone just up the stairs or in an adjacent room, someone you might see at any café in Paris. He drops the distancing veils of symbolism, mythology, and moral imperative, and instead "represents" an experienced reality.

But what about Laure? Doesn't it make sense that she has a role to play here as well? Now that I finally see her, I also see that her composition in the painting feels very familiar. Deep in our bones, we know the reclining nude in all of its vicissitudes. And deep in our bones, we also know another historic female trope, the only other role as deeply ingrained as the reclining nude: the Madonna and child. As I look at the black maid, I see the pyramidal composition developed in the Renaissance. Leonardo, Raphael, Titian, Bellini, and Michelangelo all churned out Madonna-and-child paintings that utilized the same perfect triangular form that Manet used to render the black maid. Often swaddled in white, like the maid's flowers, each permutation of Madonna holds the baby Jesus toward the viewer. Is it coincidence that Manet may have tackled two historic conventions in this painting? The larger question might be whether it is possible that art historians have overlooked this as a consideration because it is almost unconscionable that the black maid could carry equal interpretive significance to *Olympia*.

Art-historical discussions of the black maid have mostly treated her as an addendum, essentially unimportant to the iconography and value of the painting. During the Renaissance, the triangle or pyramidal compositional form emerged to suggest stability, to ground religious narratives to the present day, and to bring them from the mystical disembodied states of the Medieval world into the flesh and blood reality. On the Earthly realm, the sacred and profane met with new relevance. Could a black maid be a mother and a Madonna? Could her flowers be a sacrificial offering of promise and hope for a new era?

She is, after all, mothering Olympia by serving and tending to her needs.

This is how I want to see it: Venus, the goddess of love, meets the Virgin Mary in a third-floor walk-up, 7th arrondissement, Paris. They know the weight of their roles, even if no one else does. Olympia looks at us, and her challenge becomes not one of simply looking but of seeing. To look back is to have agency and power, and to see is to be free from the constraints of the shaping forces of culture. The black maid looks dubious in her role, eying Olympia with a slightly questioning gaze. Is this a mise-en-scène of sacred and profane presented like a vaudeville skit? These characters seem to want something from us. They are historic relics sealed in a painting. They are what was left behind as thought and gesture in a porous form of communication called a painting. They are stuck on that stage, not for us to consume but seemingly still imploring us to think, act, or simply notice.

Victorine and Laure are my sisters. I know both of their roles intimately as well as the space between them. They are vixen and mother, strong and weak, seen and unseen, loved and vilified, idealized and demeaned, needed and shunned, pampered and serving.

Perhaps Victorine always dreamed of her afterlife outside of Paris, when her looks had faded and she could no longer model or work the clubs with song and guitar. It pleases me that her housemate was a woman— perhaps her lover or partner. Olympia was a renegade. So was Victorine. But what of Laure, who has no last name? We will most likely never find out much about her life. Yet, nothing can eradicate the fact that she plays a full and important role in this famous painting. Even centuries of blindness and disregard cannot fully erase her. 🙠

Audacious Warrior: Ernestine L. Rose

By Edissa Nicolás-Huntsman

A Warrior's Life

The most famous picture of Ernestine Louise Susmond Potowski Rose was taken when Ernestine was in her mid-forties, the same age as I am now.[1] The photo reveals her polished elegance and uncharacteristic physical appearance: unbound, curly black locks hang over her shoulders. This is in contrast to her contemporaries, whose hair was uniformly worn parted down the center, pulled into uptight buns, and topped with bonnets in frigid imitations of puritanical desexualized piety. Rose is dressed in her typical stylish and flamboyant French fashion: a dark dress with an ultra-feminine white blouse accented with a needlepoint lace collar, elongated ruffled sleeves, and an elegant brooch at her throat. She looks nothing like her American friends. In the photograph, Ernestine poses with a delicate hand on her cheek and a wry smile on her lips. She seems to be listening. Her large, dark eyes sparkle, exuding confidence. She is looking at me.

Over 150 years separate us, but our fates parallel each other like echoes in time, mine because of a society with well-established basic human rights, which Ernestine envisioned and manifested. That wasn't the case in nineteenth-century Poland, where Rose was born. Although we are not yet where Rose wanted us to be as a society, we stand upon the foundation she built with her literal blood, sweat, and tears. The Ernestine L. Rose depicted in the photograph is a refined version of the courageous young girl who fractured every outmoded social norm she encountered. When Ernestine faced repression in the form of an arranged marriage at sixteen, she left home. When I could no longer tolerate physical, mental, and emotional abuse, I forged a new identity.

The child is set out by the door, waiting for a wolf to knock, to blow the house down. There are wolves. This is not a fairytale.

Ernestine L. Rose, a supreme-justice paladin, resisted all forms of moral corruption including the internalization of oppression. Remarkably, in a world constructed to support the pack mentality of tribalism, she held no prejudices. Ernestine rejected the privileges of assimilation, including monetary gain and popularity. A volunteer soldier, she selected a humble life with few luxuries as a means of advocating freely and broadly for all of humanity. And when she finally saw her labors come to fruition in the first-ever Woman's Rights Convention in Worcester, Massachusetts on October 23, 1850—for which Ernestine served as chair on the committee on civil and political functions[2]—she asserted, "I claim our rights on the broad ground of human rights."[3] Rose was a pilgrim who saw God in everyone. This is an odd thing to say about her, given that she admitted publicly from childhood that she was an atheist, asserting repeatedly, "If I have no faith in religion, I have faith, unbounded, unshaken faith in the principle of right, of justice, and humanity."[4]

I am drawn to Ernestine L. Rose in the way that one existentialist drifter finds another. We are both immigrants, recognizably other. We are kindred spirits traversing continents in search of an elusive homeland, transgressing internal and external boundaries. We share a bond as perpetual outsiders, fighting our way into institutions only to stand at the perimeters, marginalized by societal norms, our identities, and our beliefs: I as a black, Latina, third-world feminist with unknowable Caribbean roots; Rose was an Eastern European Ex-Jewish humanist feminist with an erased past. Neither one of us could accept our cultural inheritance, nor would we forsake our own conscience for temporary comforts, even at great personal cost. Even my hair is unconventional, as was hers.

The past I carry in my subcutaneous layers, out of sight, waiting to erupt. When I finally understand the extent of my brokenness, I begin to repair the elements of myself that are tattered. My flesh, marked and ravaged by experience, has little recourse. My mind is as thin as threadbare sheets, allowing unwanted images, memory, and voices to taunt me from within.

Rose, a constant emigrant with an informal education, became one of the most vocal women's-rights advocates of the nineteenth-century. After migrating coasts, east to west, I pursued a formal education in my late twenties into my thirties, landing in an Ivy League college by sheer force of will. I clawed my way through graduate studies because I dreamed of serving under-represented students like myself, but I remained an adjunct professor for ten years, ostracized by the racism of academia. Rose was a true socialist and concerned herself with international human rights, believing that "all human beings, regardless of color or sex, should have the same rights and the same freedoms."[5] Unfortunately, then as it is now, her views were out of step with mainstream perspectives. Yet, she acted as a barometer for her contemporaries: "I will not stand idly by to witness their anti-Semitism, their anti-immigrationist sentiments, their unconscious racism."[6] Her resistance cost her numerous friends and family members. I, too, have been unwilling to tolerate injustice and violence, and so, have walked alone.

My mother's constant disparagements, her slaps, insults, criticisms, complaints, and admonishments, lead me to believe I am inadequate. I am a counterfeit, my identity subverted to the needs and wants of others. I am a blank canvas, ready to be defined, colored, and rendered by the subject.

Against the bile heaped against her by adversaries, she railed, "In principle I know no compromise, I expect no reward, I fear no opposition, and can therefore afford to pass by in silence the outpourings of a bitter spirit [...] whose pen was dipped in the venom of bigotry and intolerance."[7] In each moment, Ernestine L. Rose shaped her own destiny.

The Eyes of Child

Ernestine's father was a rabbi, most likely in the emerging fundamentalist Hasidic tradition.[8] These rabbis, mythical cabalists, so-called "Wonder Rabbis,"[9] were believed to possess God-given powers to perform miracles and were surrounded by followers who sought their wisdom. In many ways, it was a most ideal moment for a rabbi to start a family. In 1809, the year before Ernestine's birth, Czar Alexander and Napoleon Bonaparte, the self-appointed "Emperor of the World,"[10] began a protracted and costly battle of wills involving enormous resources and armies.[11] Many of the 100,000 Jews in the region joined Napoleon, hoping to earn their liberation.[12, 13] Napoleon used the Jews and the long-contested Polish-Russian-Austrian geographic region of Galicia, now the Ukraine, to reward the monarchs who complied with his demands and accepted him into their aristocracy.

The Potowski home was a hub of social activity, political debate, and intellectual intensity. Owing to Ernestine's wealthy mother's death before she reached adolescence and the absence of a brother and heir to whom the rabbinate would pass, Ernestine received preferential treatment and special privileges.[14] These benefits included high-level literacy, debating skills, and social etiquette[15]—accomplishments that distinguished her from Christian Slavs, who were largely illiterate, as well as her Jewish male counterparts, who would have received only a basic Hebraic education.[16] Ernestine's questions became increasingly precocious, unconventional, and blasphemous: punishable offenses that her patient and tolerant father hid from the community. The story goes that a five-year-old Ernestine rejected God as a cruel autocrat because he put her father's health at risk with religious requirements that he fast several times per week.[17] Unable to reconcile God's love with her father's poor health, Ernestine was a dutiful, albeit faithless daughter, who performed her responsibilities as an obligation to her parents.

Because of Rabbi Potowski's status, Ernestine associated with many Jewish and non-Jewish supplicants, politicians, students, and locals who constantly surrounded and sought Rabbi Potowski's religious and civic advice.[18] Whoever went to the rabbi was assured of getting his help.[19] These supplicants brought news, information, and ideas from universities in other cities and distant empires. Ernestine was able to follow political developments through the constant conversation in her home and around her father. Ernestine may have looked upon the increasingly insular and superstitious behavior in her community as being backwards, at least in contrast to spreading Enlightenment ideals that focused on knowledge, science, and the rejection of a strict adherence to religious narratives that held most captive.

I grow up in a fundamentalist household with a Christian stepfather who is also the pastor of our church and a high-ranking official in the sect. My parents' religion offers me cultural fluidity, literacy, organizational experience, and public speaking skills. We host guests in our home and travel to new places regularly. I begin to question doctrine, practice, and scripture. These early impertinences are dismissed with confounding, opaque answers, but as I age and my intellect sharpens, my precociousness morphs into a dangerous, heretical mindset. My parents begin to silence me. As my religious doubts grow, my intellect surpasses that of my peers.

I am beaten and coerced into conforming to my faith. When I can no longer accept the violence and hypocrisy, I run away from home at fourteen. By sixteen, I am officially an emancipated minor.

Polish-Jewish folklore tells of the mythical borderlands where only supernatural forces, magic, and collective subterfuge can save the tribe from the constant onslaught of pogroms.[20] In the didactic tales, it is the absence of tribal support that leads to death. Ernestine lives despite estrangement from her people.

A Taste for Victory

Unwilling to forfeit her dowry to a man she did not love and to whom she gave no consent to marry, Ernestine Louise Potowski—a strong-willed teenager with a knot in her stomach—put on her cape, hired a coach, and embarked upon the long trip across Poland to Kalisz, in winter, by herself. It was 1826, and Ernestine intended to sue her father to break the marriage contract he had secretly negotiated.

I have held the same allure since childhood. I am not beautiful. I arouse desire. I wake tigers with my scent. The hungers of men have always found nourishment cradled in my body, with the child's eyes, in my plumpness, in my long fingers, the same as my mother's and grandmother's, La Bruja. It is like this from the beginning. I will never be safe. I have always been devoured alive.

Along the 143 kilometers from Piotrkow,[21] the icy country road meanders through empty vales, dark pine woods, and black pastures. Looking out of the carriage, Ernestine sees poorly garbed peasants in winter rags, their shabby abodes open to the wind, and within them, the raw and hungry faces of their children. When the driver stops to repair the broken wheel, the slant of the sun shows the silhouettes of figures gathering on the edges of darkening fields, looking with bloodlust at her shoes and simple frock as if upon a lamb in a ravine. If she fears the howling as night approaches, she does not relent.[22] Gaunt wolves, the kind that eat solitary women—oppressed beasts, thin and malnourished, hounded and destitute by royal decree—stand at the edge of the coppice, watching the pretty girl as she waits by a fence post, shrouded by the clouds of her own breath. The sky grows grayer, and frigid dew falls on her hair. The rakish figures in the shadows edge closer, soundlessly. Not wishing to relinquish her freedom to the fabled beasts of the night, she hurries the sleigh driver, and they set out again, leaving the wolves behind.

When I run into the woods, I find that it is a jungle, and the wolves are not the only predators to evade. There are tigers and crocodiles and other beasts in my future. My mother teaches me with animalistic blows and sharp words to obey, submit, and rise in silence to an ill-defined worthiness.

The patterns of my mother's brutality will repeat themselves in all of my relationships for many years to come. Only the most violent and vile beasts will attract my notice. They must be able to withstand bitterness, aloofness, and sarcasm. Sex is the only way I will be able to feel and survive. I will intentionally lose my virginity to an older boy from a distant Brooklyn neighborhood, thinking that no one will know. He is not the silent type. It does not matter. He is not sophisticated—has not seduced me into the love affair. I have chosen him because I have absolutely no emotional attachment to him. He believes he is special. I arrange everything. He believes he has persuaded me to love him, to give him my virtue. I let him believe what he wants.

The legal hearing in Kalisz[23] begins as an indulgence by the Polish court officials, who snicker at Ernestine for venturing out of the *shtetl* to fight an injustice through a state system that did not formally recognize Jews as legal citizens.[24] The judge's eyes crinkle with mirth, his expression holding the same pious condescension that her father's did when he announced that Ernestine would marry his good friend, an old man with yellow teeth. Because her father, Rabbi Potowski, was a local official and representative of his community, she was among the few registered Jews,[25] which enabled her suit. What began as patronizing humor and droll entertainment, a good story for the hearth, soon became serious as Ernestine commanded the specifics of her case. Representing herself before a court of men for the first of what would be many times, she proved to be no ordinary young woman. Ernestine Louise Potowski, successful in her lawsuit, returned to her home only to find that her father had married a girl her age. Within a year, Ernestine gifted her inheritance—the house and most of the money from her suit—to her father and the community, which she would leave behind, unknowingly, forever.[26] She kept only enough money to reach Berlin.

When school begins, my sister, who is almost ten, is to walk me to school each morning. But my sister is more concerned with her schoolmates than the smaller version of herself. It is not long before I am recruited, in a perverse twist of fate, to be my sister's protector. My sister hides behind a willful shyness, employing my brave boldness for the duration of our short childhood. I am her shield.

To Prussia and Beyond

She was heir to the world. In 1827, the young, unfettered, seventeen-year-old Ernestine Potowski wanted to experience urban life. Embarking on another remarkable journey, Ernestine set her sights on the frontier of possibility: the Prussian capital. Berlin was the center of power, where freedom and Enlightenment ideas awaited. Or so she thought.

It took only minutes for her blood to boil when she learned, upon arriving at the main Berlin station, of the many prohibitions against Jewish immigrants—most notably, the need for a German sponsor and a commitment to remain for a pre-determined length of a time, sans employment of any kind, as an invited guest of a citizen.[27] Indignant and dissatisfied with the odious ordinances, Ernestine Potowski was unwilling to conform. Not stopping to wallow in the disappointment and shock of what she perceived to be the kingdom's moral decrepitude, she inquired about King Friedrich Wilhelm III's court and headed directly there.[28]

I am lost in poverty, a maze of unescorted children drifting west toward Rivington Street. The school building, away from the housing projects, is our family's ascension into stability. When the children disperse, I hold in my hand an unfamiliar coin, round and too large for my palm.

Ernestine walked, not rushing, in order to take in with all her senses, the city and the topography, even the fashions of the place. At court, Ernestine was the only woman. Sporting a youthful face with calm composure, she was already the object of slights and ridicule. Even so, she met every eye with characteristic boldness and held her place in the order of things, knowing she had as much right as any man to challenge the authority of the king.

King Wilhelm responded with amusement when his page announced a Jewess on the list of petitioners. Intending to mock her and entertain his courtiers at her expense, the king heard her. Practiced in her art, the anti-authoritarian Ernestine Potowski cross-examined the king's notion of justice before laying out her requests. Condescending to her bold questions because he was impressed by her intellect, expressiveness, and forthrightness, he sat on his throne, delighting in her saucy rhetoric. When she finally demanded that he rescind the hateful anti-Jewish policies, he offered her conversion and all its ensuing privileges. She refused, of course, but moved King Wilhelm enough with her persuasive arguments that he granted her "permission to remain in Germany for as long as she wanted and engage in whatever business she desired."[29] She had escaped the prohibitions, but the king failed to abolish the egregious decrees against other Jews. Unable to gain true freedom for oppressed Jews, the small, personal victory caused her to note both her powers and her limitations: on one hand, Ernestine Potowski had twice confronted authority and shifted minds enough to get her needs met; on the other, emancipation for one was hollow,[30] for as she'd later come to articulate, "freedom is not satisfied with half measures."[31]

Establishing herself in a Berlin tenement, Ernestine Potowski exhibited the values of her Jewish upbringing despite renouncing the religious aspects of her culture. In the Jewish tradition, livelihood and self-reliance were woven together.[32] Like any resolute young woman in a big city, she solved problems. The tenement houses were permeated with the "smells of onions and kerosene, herrings and soap, dishwater and rubbish, petroleum and cooking, mold and delicatessen."[33] The resourceful entrepreneur decided that what urban life required was freshness. Ernestine Potowski invented an incense paper, which after burning, eliminated lingering odors and other undesirable smells from the crowded apartment buildings. Along with tutoring, the sale of the incense paper[34] earned Ernestine Potowski her livelihood and permitted her to study as she prepared to travel again.[35]

I bring the enormous coin to my waist and tuck it into the lace-edged pocket on my frilly dress. All day long, I finger the half-dollar. The other hand holds a dazzling bag of candies: ruby Swedish fish, nutty wrapped Mary Janes, my sister's favorite Tootsie Rolls, and sugar-coated rainbow jelly fruits with white rinds. I have wrapped communion wafers and pill-size Sweet Tarts to be prescribed on the playground. The treasures outnumber their value.

First-World Citizen

Considering that even in 2016, most of the world's population will live and die within a fifty-mile radius of their birthplace, Ernestine's peripatetic lifestyle foreshadowed the migration patterns of the carefree or desperate. Open-minded, freethinking, and flexible, she saw possibility and fluidly adapted to various cultures. She acquired languages with unparalleled skill, adding German and French to her repertoire. When she left Berlin two years later, she toured Europe, stopping in major cities to experience life, art, and the people along the way. During a visit to Holland, Ernestine Potowski went before yet another king, this time on someone else's behalf.

Learning from a newspaper account of a woman accused of a crime incurring capital punishment, Ernestine investigated the woman's case. Ernestine defended the wrongfully accused woman, who was too poor to afford counsel. As a result, the woman was pardoned and reunited with her small children.[36] How Ernestine was able to do this is testament to her intellectual acuity. This was Ernestine's innate strength—she a beautiful, brave soul with a distinct battle cry: "The world is my country, and to do good my religion."[37]

When I try to understand my personal history, I am pushed away. A rift opens, a chasm in the deep ocean, a dark and dangerous middle passage. My oldest sister agrees to accompany me to find our father on the island of our birth. I am thirty. Perhaps it is her assumption that I will not find him, but I do. When I make contact, my sister's voice grows icy. She bullies me, telling me she is tired of waiting, that she wants to go to the beach. In the film footage of that day, my sister's eyes are roving; aversion creases her mouth. She is furtive and brusque like a trapped animal. She is afraid. I don't recognize her fear. It goes unnamed. I have not yet learned the names and signs of emoting. I only know words, hasty, sharp ones.

With our father, my sister is small. I have never seen her small, my oldest sister. She is the size of a field mouse. I am listening for words.

My sister does not answer direct questions. Afterwards, she avoids me, cutting me off from communication with my niece for the next fifteen years. When at last she calls, it is to menace me with the news that our sister is on her deathbed. Her words are chosen carefully to slice open the scars on my heart.

As she traveled, she witnessed unrest sweeping through Europe. By June 1830, Ernestine Potowski arrived in Paris, a place that would prove dear to her for all times, and where she was privy to the making of history. Looking onto the balcony of Paris Hotel de Ville, where General Lafayette conveyed the reins of power to Louis Philippe, Ernestine Potowski predicted that the newly crowned king's destiny was as ill-fated as his predecessor's was,[38] nodding to the victories of the just and suggesting she had no patience for tyranny. Later that year, Ernestine made her first attempt to return to Poland, apparently to help liberate the country from Czarist oppression. Rose was reputedly willing to take up arms. She was denied access at the Austrian border.[39]

If she worried and wondered about the fate of her father and the community she left behind, she would soon apply her energies where they would be most effective. She sailed for London, the vanguard city of Enlightenment reform,[40] where she set her sights on social change. Though she understood court processes, it was clear to her that women would need more authority and power if the world were to evolve on her timeline.

I am six. My sister is supposed to hold my hand and walk me to school. My sister drops my hand at the door of the store. I am in the store with a rowdy flock of children, who flutter about the aisles hunting treasures. My sister will drop my hand many more times in the years to come. I learn to expect an empty hand. I learn to count on no one.

The change in my hand is superior to the dollar bill tendered. I am mesmerized. I am six-years old, unused to handling money. I imagine what I will buy tomorrow, how much candy I can have in exchange for my large coin.

One day, the door opens and the other plovers flock out. Only I remain. My feet dangle in the air. My mouth is full of tobacco and barbed spikes. I cannot breathe. The nightmares begin that night.

London Bridges and New York

Miraculously surviving a shipwreck near England in 1830, Ernestine Potowski arrived a cultured and traveled twenty-year-old. She found work tutoring Hebrew and German[41] while she studied English, which she mastered easily. In London, she met her mentor and adoptive father Robert Owen, a well-to-do manufacturer turned social reformer,[42] joining his progressive socialist movement and beginning a life of service in the Owenist tradition.[43] Ernestine helped to found the Association of All Classes and of All Nations,[44] through which, in an auspicious coincidence, Ernestine met her husband, William Ella Rose. Of their courtship, nothing is known. The self-identified atheists married in a civil ceremony and in 1836 sailed for America, where Ernestine entrenched herself in US politics, believing that "human freedom and true democracy are identical."[45]

My mother's intent is to shame and humiliate me, to make me small and yielding, compliant and humble. My mother's model of womanhood is loud, proud, quick to anger. She is a dry alcoholic, lunging at the bottleneck of drama and belligerent confrontation. She will alight upon any target. When I am grown, she will not admit to the beatings and violence. She will defend herself as a good mother who has made sacrifices. I have repaid them all.

The Roses joined with other Owenites in America, where Ernestine sought to replicate the Utopian aspects of her childhood in communal societies. After two tries, they became disillusioned with the various lifestyles in these communities, preferring to live independently in city apartments on the Lower East Side of Manhattan and in Queens. Ernestine Rose explained their decision to Robert Owen: "Some of the other members do not understand the first rudiments of the social science, and the rest are moral cowards though good men and thus become the tools of the more designing."[46] Despite Ernestine's prolonged search for belonging, she was unable to fasten a hold to a people or location, so she drifted, tethered only by William's love and devotion, which gave her all the stability she needed.

Ernestine and William Rose eventually found lasting community and culture in New York as members of the Thomas Paine Celebration, which honored Paine with an annual birthday party,[47] a popular, secular winter holiday.[48] Ernestine was one of the first women to join the men on the floor of the formally segregated hall for public toasting, singing, "Health to the sick; honor to the brave; success to the lover; and freedom to the slave" in 1840.[49] She began to mentor other women in speaking at the annual celebrations, imploring them to "catch a spark of the fire that burned in [Paine's] bosom, when at the sacrifice of home, friends, interest, reputation, liberty, and the risk of life, he devoted himself to the rights of man."[50] Eventually, Ernestine presided over the event as a scheduled annual speaker, lauding Paine for his unswerving integrity, moral courage, and love of human freedom,[51] all qualities that she herself possessed.

To maintain their independence in New York, Ernestine crafted high-quality German cologne water, which she sold at lower prices than imports, to which they were purportedly superior.[52] Along with William's employment as a silversmith, the two were able to sustain themselves in modest comfort from the 1830s until their departure thirty years later. Crafty and ingenious businesspeople, had the Roses chosen to immerse themselves in capitalism, financial stability, and monetary security, they could have easily become millionaires, and yet, they directed most of their earnings to the mission of furthering human progress. During the period, Ernestine was on the road for roughly half the year, while William sustained her public service with his business revenue.

Throughout her years based in New York City, 1836–1869, Ernestine actively toured all over New York State, and later, extensively throughout the country. Because there was no radio or television, and the press seldom captured the content of her speeches, she often gave the same speeches at various locations—veering toward broad humanitarian issues to address as many concerns as possible with a given audience. Rose was also exoticized for her heavy accent and praised for her precise language.

Rose created an incredible buzz. In today's terms, her fame was of Kardashian proportions, with millions of followers on Instagram. She was well known in the US and internationally. The force of her words penetrated the collective conscience. Even those who disagreed with and despised Rose could not engage the topic of woman's rights without first trying to eliminate her from the discourse, a very difficult task because the petite warrior's voice filled halls with the power of truth. She was a formidable opponent.

᷾

Social Agitator
A One-Act Re-enactment of Woman's Rights Activism and Opposition

*(All dialogue is true and taken from various speeches, convention
notes, letters, newspapers, and print publications between 1853-
1869, the period when Ernestine L. Rose was most recognized as
an activist and public speaker.)*[53]

THE CHARACTERS
(In order of appearance)

CHORUS OF PRIESTS, Christian and Protestant
Preachers, Journalists, Elected Officials, Bigots of all
Genders, Sexist Husbands, Authors, and Community
Leaders

QUEEN OF THE PLATFORM, Ernestine L. Rose:
Speeches 1853–1869

WOMEN ALLIES, Susan B. Anthony, Lucretia Mott,
Antoinette L. Blackwell, Lucy Stone, Paula Wright Davis,
and Elizabeth Cady Stanton

༄

A large crowd of over 1,600 people gathers in the
cramped auditorium of Melodean Hall to hear the
so-called "Infidels," advocates for woman's rights.
The activists gather in public venues and in the State
Assembly to move forward the rights of woman. The
belligerent Chorus of Priests stand in the doorways and
aisles, chanting, stomping, and jeering. These detractors
are empowered by a Christian morality and are drawn to
the Queen of the Platform as a person upon whom they
may pour their venom. They interrupt the proceedings.
They grow angry and truculent every time she speaks.
The Queen of the Platform, dressed in black with white
lace ruffles at her collar and wrists, is the only woman
with unbound hair. She remains genial and focused
despite the tirade from the Chorus of Priests.[53]

༄

[*Enter, from the side, Chorus of Priests, carrying Bibles, long forks, and sticks. They push, shove, and jeer as they overcrowd the room. At center stage, behind the podium, stands the Queen of the Platform with her arm raised in an attempt to gain order. The Women Allies sit in calm composure to her left. The lights flicker.*]

QUEEN OF THE PLATFORM: [*Curls bobbing freely as she speaks*] All we need are the right principles to live by, and the rest will take care of itself.

CHORUS OF PRIESTS: [*With contemptuous male gazes*] The woman's presence here is a stretch of folly and a flight of impudence.

QUEEN OF THE PLATFORM: [*To the women of the Woman's Rights Convention*] We must not heed the taunts, ridicule, and stigmas cast upon us. We must remember that we have a crusade before us. We therefore must put on the armor of charity, carry before us the banner of truth, and defend ourselves with the shield of right against the invaders of our liberty. We must claim our rightful inheritance.

CHORUS OF PRIESTS: [*Speaking directly to the Albany State Legislature, while carrying burning crosses*] She is indecent, an unevenly yoked woman who should not be permitted to engage in public speaking. Why is she permitted to agitate the public? Let us use our power to silence her.

QUEEN OF THE PLATFORM: [*Lovingly to the daughters of the Enlightenment, who hold up their infant daughters*] It requires far more true courage and persevering heroism to carry on a moral war than a physical one. It is much easier to take a fortress, composed even of granite, than to storm a citadel of prejudice sanctified by superstition, engrafted by age, and strengthened by habit.

CHORUS OF PRIESTS: [*With scornful aggression and foot stomping*] On the other hand, the view that there will be periodical resurrections of the women's movement reduce the whole affair to ridiculous impotence, making it only an ephemeral phase in the history of mankind.

QUEEN OF THE PLATFORM: [*Gaily, with musical flourishes of the hand, smiling*] Woman's claim for the ballot does not depend on the numbers that demand it or would exercise the right but on precisely the same principles that man claims it for himself. White men are in the minority in this nation. White women, black men, and black women compose the large majority of the nation. It is time we proclaim to the world universal suffrage.

CHORUS OF PRIESTS: As Darwin pointed out, the proper comparison is between the most highly developed individual of two stocks. "If two lists," as Darwin wrote in the *Descent of Man*, "were made of the most eminent men and women in poetry, painting, sculpture, music— comprising compositions and performance, history, science, and philosophy, with half a dozen names under each subject, the two lists would not bear comparison."

QUEEN OF THE PLATFORM: [*Sarcastic, cutting*]Will you tell us that women have no Newtons, Shakespeares, and Byrons?

CHORUS OF PRIESTS: [*Consulting the male canon in the form of books*] The prospects of the movement for intellectual advance on the part of women are not very promising.

QUEEN OF THE PLATFORM: Greater natural powers than even these possessed may have been destroyed in woman for want of proper culture, a just appreciation, reward for merit as an incentive to exertion, and freedom of action, without which the mind becomes cramped and stifled, for it cannot expand under bolts and bars.

CHORUS OF PRIESTS: [*Patting each other on the back*] It is only to that male part of her that she owes her special capacity of whatever importance she may eventually

gain. It is absurd to make comparisons between
the few really intellectual women and one's average
experience of men.

QUEEN OF THE PLATFORM: [*In tears to Susan B.
Anthony and the Women Allies*] I take them by the words
of their mouths. I trust all until their words or acts
declare them false to truth and right.

WOMEN ALLIES: [*Touching the bonnets on their heads*]
I have copied out the Christian hymn to soothe your
soul against your male opponents.

QUEEN OF THE PLATFORM: [*Indignant*] I refuse
to pander to their sensibilities and assimilate to gain
popularity.

WOMEN ALLIES: [*Justifying to one another and the*
CHORUS OF PRIESTS] A white woman here,
a slave holder, says she frequently gets perfectly
disgusted with slavery, that the "licentiousness"
between the white men and the slave women is so
universal and so revolting.

CHORUS OF PRIESTS: [*Congratulating each other*]
She is merely a Polish propagandist.

QUEEN OF THE PLATFORM: [*Aside to* **WOMEN
ALLIES**] No one can tell the hours of anguish I have
suffered, as one after another I have seen, those whom
I had trusted betray falsity of motive as I have been
compelled to place one after another on the list of
panderers to public favor.

WOMEN ALLIES: [*To Ernestine, with passion, in
unison*] I have given you the legitimacy of my name,
class, and religion.

QUEEN OF THE PLATFORM: [*Aside to* **WOMEN
ALLIES**; *the crowd murmurs*] You clique of abolitionists
protect each other's bigotry and make allowances for

unwarranted biases. But to hasten this glorious period, we, my sisters, must not remain idle.

CHORUS OF PRIESTS: [*Holding up their burning crucifixes and Bibles*] But the idea of making an emancipation party, of aiming at a social revolution, must be abandoned.

QUEEN OF THE PLATFORM: I know there is great prejudice against our claim to political rights; childish fears and apprehensions are rife.

CHORUS OF PRIESTS: Away with the whole "women's movement," with its unnaturalness and artificiality and its fundamental errors.

QUEEN OF THE PLATFORM: [*Punctuating the air with a finger*] The Bible tells us that the Earth is flat and stationary, and that the sun moves around the Earth. Copernicus and Galileo *flatly* deny this *flat* assertion and demonstrate by astronomy that the Earth is spherical and revolves around the sun. Though I cannot believe in your God, who you have failed to demonstrate, I believe in man.

CHORUS OF PRIESTS: [*Spitting, stamping, booing, while waving their Bibles*] She is a thousand times below a prostitute.

QUEEN OF THE PLATFORM: [*Raises her hand and steps back from the lectern*] I almost smelt brimstone, genuine Christian brimstone!

CHORUS OF PRIESTS: [*The lights flicker out several times to thunderous shouting*] Universalism is not wholly to our taste, yet it is far better than Judaism.

QUEEN OF THE PLATFORM: [*With an ironic smile*] It is time we consider whether what is wrong in one sex, can be right in the other. I speak for myself. I am loyal only to justice and humanity.

CHORUS OF PRIESTS: [*Hissing, blaring baritones*] Fetch

the tar and feathers.

QUEEN OF THE PLATFORM: [*With a sweeping hand gesture*] I have stood more than this in opposing error, and I can stand this. For what is life without liberty?

What Is Love?

It would be easy to imagine her motivated by every lost cause, but Ernestine was inspired as much by the possibility of happiness and equality. When the contentious issue of divorce was raised in the women's rights movement, Christian women with husbands in positions of authority were deeply divided. Elizabeth Cady Stanton proposed the ten resolutions in the 1860 convention and was instantly opposed by Rev. Antoinette Brown Blackwell, the first ordained Christian woman in the US. It was Brown Blackwell—not a man—who countered with her own resolutions.[54] Susan B. Anthony and Ernestine supported Stanton. Rose, who was convinced that for perfect equality to exist in a union, "love must be free, or it ceases to be love,"[55] concluding, "educate woman, [...] enable her to promote her independence, and she will not be obliged to marry for a home and a subsistence. Give the wife an equal right with the husband in the property acquired after marriage, and it will be a bond of union between them." Failing this, Rose felt, divorce was a most necessary curative.[56]

Later, when other women's rights leaders such as Lucretia Mott favored divorce, it was owing to an unhappy marriage, and personal preference prevailed. Rose, Stanton, and Mott presented their divorce bill before the Albany, New York Judiciary Committee in 1861[57] without Lucy Stone, who waffled on them.[58] But it was solely Ernestine who was motivated by her position on marriage happiness and her unique belief in egalitarian love.[59] "What constitutes marriage? The violation of that, whatever it is, is a sufficient ground for a legal, social, and entire separation between them; and that is divorce."[60] She eventually managed to convince Rev. Antoinette Brown Blackwell of the validity of divorce.[61]

As a woman who waited until her mid-forties to marry the right man, I understand her desire to find the sanctity of bonds forged of free choice. That kind of decision is possible for me because Ernestine made marriage a choice and a matter of free will. Rose's advocacy for divorce as an exit strategy was just a small part of her large vision of human equality.

Civil War Bigotry for All

Not surprising, Ernestine despised slavery, slavers, and bigots. She defined slavery as an evil abomination: "Not to be your own, bodily, mentally, or morally—that is to be a slave."[62] During the Civil War, Rose asked convention participants if a "vile mob, headed by corrupted and treacherous politicians," would be permitted to "trample the dignity, the manhood and the liberties of the North" and "barter away the rights, the progress and the civilization of the free."[63] She was clear that in life, "it is all true or all false; all free or all slave, and as we are not all free, we are all slaves and we are all slaveholders to some extent."[64] Her abhorrence of being complicit in America's practices of human bondage caused Ernestine to resist the lackadaisical response of her peers. She was vocal about wanting Lincoln to crush the Confederates, who stoked her rage and indignity. Her wit and sarcasm cut down her opponents' justifications, and she famously said, "You have openly thrown down the gauntlet to fight for Slavery; we will accept it, and fight for Freedom."[65]

Horace Seaver, a former ally of Rose's and the editor of the *Boston Investigator*,[66] joined in the bigotry, prompting a heated exchange in the press between Rose and Seaver that lasted months.[67] Seaver supported the Confederates,[68] labeling Jews as "untrustworthy" in order to scapegoat them and tap into antisemitism. Ernestine challenged Seaver to maintain lofty, free-thought ideals: "let us, as Infidels, while promoting liberty and spreading useful knowledge, to prevent any sect from getting power, not add to the prejudice already existing towards the Jews, or any other sect."[69] She defended the Jewish people, vowing to protect the downtrodden and to extend the mantle of her protective voice over her people, whose religion she rejected but whose lives she treasured no less than any other sacred human being. Their notorious public clash was predated by an earlier equally famous incident, in which she journeyed into slave country.

It's not clear what drove Ernestine into the heart of hostile slave territory in 1848, where she had a life-threatening encounter with a Southerner, a slaver who explicitly menaced her with "tar and feather," had she been a man. Rose retorted with vigor that she would be giving him a decent day's work—for once—because most slavers were idle good-for-nothings.[70] Speculation that the real reason Rose was in the South was to contact Jewish émigrés settled there— she perhaps longed for connection.[71] It's also possible that she intended to disrupt their complacency and unravel their justifications when she found slave-holding

Jews, proclaiming, "Emancipation from every kind of bondage is my principle. I go for the recognition of answered human rights, without distinction of sect, party, sex, or color."[72] Ernestine understood that "loyal means to be true to one's highest conviction. Justice, like charity, begins at home."[73] From Ernestine's perspective, the liberty of enslaved people was a moral imperative, and slavery a mark against the Constitution.

We are reading Shakespeare with a substitute teacher who does not realize we are supposed to be intellectually inferior to other city kids. Romeo and Juliet *is easy for me, like reading the Bible. I want to play every part. I raise my hand again and again. Later, some girls will lock me in a heavy steel desk, which they push against a wall. I stay there all night until my mother opens the dark school and finds me. Nearly suffocated by my own exhalations, I am broken, weeping, hot in my play oven. I have not been taught to defend myself.*

Ernestine stood at the vanguard of the human rights movement in every way. Rose admonished supporters at rallies: "Freedom and slavery cannot live in harmony; the one must destroy the other."[74] She declared, "We have one great advantage over physical war, for the breaks and inroads we make on the stronghold of conservatism, ignorance, and error can never again be repaired; a breach once made goes on widening of itself, every stone helps to undermine the foundation until the whole super structure will crumble at our feet."[75]

Using her primary roles as advocate, agitator, and spokeswoman, Ernestine even printed copies of her speeches and distributed them free of charge, cross-pollinating complex social issues in the process. Rose criticized the use of religion in political debates, asserting, "Whatever good you would do out of fear of punishment, or hope of reward hereafter, the Atheist would do simply because *it is good.*"[76] She didn't give a hoot what was said about her, so long as she could perform the duties of converting hearts and minds. Her restlessness grew with each injustice she witnessed.

Suffrage, Deferred

Her spirits never flagged, even when she gathered only five signatures on her 1836 marriage-rights petition.[77] Each time Rose heard the word "no," she transmuted the fear she saw in the women's eyes into fuel for the necessary work of reform, viewing their emotions as their need for a champion. Ernestine rightly believed that the "ballot-box is the focus of all other rights, it is the pivot upon which all others hang; the legal rights are embraced in it, for if once possessed of the right to the ballot-box, to self-representation, she will see to it that the laws shall be just, and protect her person and her property, as well as that of man."[78] The ballot remained elusive.

Ernestine worked closely with Elizabeth Cady Stanton, Susan B. Anthony, Lucretia Mott, Antoinette Blackwell, and Lucy Stone from the 1840s through the 1860s on numerous married women's concerns.[79] Years of unpaid, unsolicited work by Ernestine and her growing brigade of women warriors yielded a first, if short-lived, victory in the woman's rights struggle: in 1860, the New York State Legislature passed the *Act Concerning the Rights and Liabilities of Husband and Wife*,[80] giving married women access to courts, parental custody, and salary and inheritance rights—everything they wanted, except suffrage.[81] Although this was a great achievement, one hundred years later, echoes of Rose's stance on suffrage could be heard from great activists such as Dr. Martin Luther King, Jr., who continued to insist that the long wait for equality needed to end.

Strongly aligned with black Americans, she welcomed opportunities to join their two struggles.[82] Believing that after the war, women would be granted the vote, Ernestine proposed to dissolve the woman's convention in favor of supporting the enormously disenfranchised black community,[83] preferring to strive toward abolition rather than prioritize—at least temporarily—the concerns of white women. Her resolution was adopted by the organization only *after* she took the podium, where she maintained that "we have proclaimed to the world universal suffrage; but it is universal suffrage with a vengeance attached to it."[84] There was widespread disappointment when they learned that the 1860 Legislative Act had been secretly overturned after the Civil War began,[85] and again in 1870, when only black men were granted the vote.[86]

After a decade as a principal leader of the Woman's Rights Conventions, Rose had what I can only describe as a dissociative episode during the 1869 conference. Disappointed with the insidious biases internalized in the hearts of her allies, she finally gave up the fight to dismantle their oppressive sentiments—she stopped fighting Elizabeth Cady Stanton's bigotry,[87] avoided correcting Susan B. Anthony's stereotyping,[88] and ceased to correct Paula Wright Davis's racism.[89] She withdrew into herself and away from the rancor in the suffrage debate, which pitted white women against the interests of black Americans. Instead, a preoccupied and uncharacteristically unfo-cused Ernestine turned to old measures of reform, speaking on pay equity. Such was the force of her will and the strength of her campaign that when she did so, her disengagement unmoored the movement and unglued the women in the struggle, halting the work of woman's suffrage for another fifty years until they were able to reestablish a unified women's movement.

Written on the Body

Taking time from her hectic touring schedule in 1855 to attend the annual Thomas Paine gala, Ernestine, who then traveled nearly six months out of the year, instructed her allies on self-care: "I have interrupted my journey for the pleasure of being with you this evening; for when the heart and head are severely taxed, they require social recreation to restore a healthy equilibrium to the system."[90] She was exhausted and needed the company of friends.

> *The body is a map of our emotions, our history writ in scars and markings. Not surprising, the years of enduring the hostile racial climate begins to show on my face and body. My autonomic nervous system goes haywire. Skin lesions appear; tests reveal, literally, "nothing." The disease has no cure.*
>
> *For a teacher, physical ailments can have psychological tolls. The residual impact of the poisoned environment as it manifests in my body persists with terrifying intensity. The damage crosses over the psychic barrier, weakening my immune system and resulting in a bout of shingles, one of the most painful physical, neurological autoimmune illnesses the body can produce. The price of my professional life is evident on my formerly vigorous body: only a full retreat from the academy is possible.*

Travel during the mid-nineteenth century was difficult: stagecoaches were uncomfortable, infrastructure deficient, and weather in various re-gions unpredictable, making it almost impossible to prepare for long trips. As early as 1844, Ernestine experienced health complications. In a letter to Robert Owen, the Roses mentioned that they were considering moving for health reasons: "My health since you left us has not been good. I had several severe attacks of depression of mind."[91] The next year, William wrote to Owen of Rose's persistent poor health: "My Dear Ernestine was very low with the remittent of Brain fever [...] she is very feeble and great care has to be taken with her."[92] Ernestine contracted malaria during her travels and suffered from the associated fevers and weakness. She also had at least two miscarriages,[93] which were disappointing and draining in their own right. These glimpses into her private sanctity reveal that she suffered a good deal over the losses of her parents, unborn children, and country.[94, 95]

Rose attracted the malice of the masses, who, drawn to the venues by the thrill of violence, tried to censor her, especially as her notoriety grew. Surveying the crowd before attempting to speak once more, Ernestine stood proud and unwavering behind the lectern. Fatigued and exasperated by the third interruption of an unruly mob,[96] Ernestine uncommonly deviated from her topic to focus on the behavior of the audience. She aged in that moment.

Her slight frame, imposing in her righteous authority, became tiny, mortal flesh, as she admitted, "My friends, there was once a time when I had a voice strong enough to speak against all opposition, and be heard, but that time is past."[97] She spoke of the challenges to her health: "My constitution has been somewhat broken, and mainly broken in the great conflict against error. I had hoped that whatever our opponents might think of my opinions, they would behave like gentlemen."[98] At last, exhausted to near ruin and unable to deflect the contempt and aggression of her opponents, in 1856, she begged a "furlough, to gather fresh strength for the glorious battle of freedom."[99]

The body is also the seat of lineage and genealogy. I carry my ancestral history with me. The seed of my father's alcoholism sprouts. I drink whiskey in the middle of the night in an attempt to numb the searing pain that sweeps through my body at nightfall, rendering me unable to sleep, think, or write. The alcohol has little effect. My vitality, joy, and spontaneity ebb ever further. My days darken into despair and loneliness.

In 1869, the Roses at last sailed for England and a much-needed retirement. Susan B. Anthony threw the Roses a huge farewell bash and raised a donation that was a welcome gift after her three decades of volunteer work.[100] There were few other moments of appreciation for Ernestine's work. She sought no rewards save the transformation of society and was driven by her conscience.

The Heart of the Matter

Though Ernestine rejected religion, she lived by a creed of human kindness. Much evidence exists that Ernestine upheld Jewish cultural values, honoring the traditions of her forebearers. Most significantly, she practiced the Jewish tradition of *Tzedakah*, which is Hebrew for the acts that we call "charity" in English—giving aid, assistance, and money to the poor and needy or to worthy causes.[101] However, the nature of Tzedakah is very different from the idea of charity, which suggests benevolence and generosity, a magnanimous act by the wealthy and powerful for the benefit of the poor and needy. The root and connotation of Tzedakah means righteousness, justice, and fairness. In Judaism, giving to the poor is not a generous or magnanimous act; it is the simple performance of a duty, an act of justice due to the poor. Through a lifetime of activism in which Ernestine advocated pro bono for human rights causes, she selflessly performed Tzedakah daily. She did so "in spite of hardships, for it was not easy to travel at that time as now, and the expense, as I never made a charge or took up a Collection, I look back to that time when a stranger and alone, I went from place to place, in high-ways and by-ways, did the work and paid my bills with great pleasure and satisfaction."[102] In this context, the world's children became her children, especially when the Roses couldn't have their own. The deep, abiding love in her—for the country and the world—became the repository for her strong emotions. Rose's entire life was her Tzedakah to humanity.

These pains are not separate. Though they had been neatly stacked and stored away from each other, I can no longer compartmentalize the sensations that reside in me if I am to heal and move forward, as my spiritual teacher tells me, into wholeness. The more I keep each part of myself segregated in manageable pieces, accessible to feeling and acceptance at the distant time of some ordained day, the more each part breaks through its confinement into the body, where it asks, "Now?"

The connectivity of the bodies: emotions, physical, psychological, and spiritual, make themselves known. There is no turning back, no looking away, and no ignoring the sensations, feelings, and emotions.

Rose was uncompromising in seeking to destroy stagnant social structures like sexism and racism. "As gold is purified and refined when passed through the fiery furnace, so does Truth come out clearer and more beautiful from under severe criticism."[103] Urging women to participate in their own liberation, she insisted, "She must untie [ignorance and superstition] with the sharp points of reason, dissolve the links by the light of knowledge, and thus, bursting the unholy fetters, she must claim her rights equal with man, and then indeed will she be a woman."[104] Ernestine shattered the ideologies in a shock of sound, using her voice as a powerful thunderbolt hitting the shield of truth. These were her gifts.

Kindred Spirits

A soul in pain, she was sick on and off for years, never fully recovering from any illness before taking up the Woman's Rights vanguard again. No doubt the bond of love and friendship that Ernestine and William shared sustained her through difficult periods and healed her spirit. For their six months of vacation in 1856, the pair stayed away from controversy, traveling throughout Europe as tourists, visiting England, France, Germany, and Italy.[105] Ernestine, long estranged from loved ones, believed that "those who feel it, can tell the trials and sufferings of those who, for the cause of Freedom—the cause of Truth—have to sacrifice home, wealth, friends, all that makes life desirable, and become strangers and wanderers in foreign lands."[106] Her tremendous obstinacy and independence notwithstanding, she yielded to her heart: the Roses attempted to enter Poland, presumably to see Ernestine's father. They were denied admission.[107] She must have grieved the displacement from her homeland and news of growing pogroms and antisemitism.

Arriving as an infant in my mother's arms in 1971, my family was a full decade in advance of the main influx of Dominicans, which began in the 1980s. As one of the only visibly black, yet Spanish-speaking people in the Lower East Side community where we lived, we stood out from the lively mix of Jewish, Chinese, African American, and Puerto Rican neighbors, who were well established by the time we arrived. The sounds of the markets, their languages, and customs were part of the elaborate fiber of the culture from which we were the suspect curiosities, outsiders in the concrete forest where food grew in cans and chickens bred under the Williamsburg Bridge. We were the Platanos—black wetbacks—outsiders no one wanted to play with.

I was wounded by criticism, alienation, and ostracism. I wanted to be included, befriended, and have my presence noted. Eventually, I would find my soul mate.

At the start of her retirement years, she and William traveled together and were often recognized and well received in Europe, having reputations as activists in the US. They attended the World Exposition in Paris in 1878, a luxury of pure joy for the couple.[108] Until her death in 1882, she took yearly trips to therapeutic spas, where the pains in her joints were eased in the hot springs of Europe. Activists sometimes burn out from prolonged struggles. This was her way of taking care of herself, nurturing her soul and body. In this way, Ernestine modeled the self-care needed to survive difficult, demanding times and stress, although ostracism seldom bothered Ernestine. For her, life was not about making friends, being popular, or even being remembered.

Deep Footprints

Ernestine's path was a lonely one, to be sure—a true warrior, she traversed the harsh political landscape for the sake of others. She admirably transcended adversity and the countless self-imposed—and externally projected—limitations of her time. In the end, Rose's contemporaries remembered her with a tender fondness that bordered on adoration. Her supporters, some from surprising quarters, esteemed her highly, evidence of her sweeping impact on society. New York Rabbi Jonas Bondi bid her farewell in a front-page homage in *The Hebrew Leader*, an important Jewish newspaper:

> *Among all the advocates of human freedom and moral and social progress, who have labored in this country for the last twenty-five or thirty years, none have exhibited more constancy, devotion, sacrifice, earnestness and ability, than Ernestine L. Rose, and but for the fact that such genuine reformers are never suitably appreciated in their day and generation, she would now be the most popular, as she has long been the best female lecturer in the United States.*[109]

Kind words spoken within one's lifetime must be gratifying. However, I sincerely believe history owes a good deal more to this audacious warrior, a woman whose legacy broke the hard ground of ideology for the seeds of true justice to root. I have little doubt that if she were alive today, she would be involved in the continued struggles for women's pay equity, poor and homeless rights, and would be a powerful force in the Black Lives Matter movement, among other worthy causes. When Ernestine L. Rose saw injustice—wherever she saw injustice—she used her power to expose it. She found solutions. She worked to remedy each wrong.

Ernestine L. Rose spent the duration of her life striving for the highest possible rights for women and to obtain universal suffrage, which she recognized as the key to power. She was utterly devoted to justice, and considering that Ernestine, a perennial non-citizen, did not benefit from the policies she helped institute, she was entirely virtuous. Ernestine asked the world to reflect on the budding women's movements, holding unequivocally to women's capacity for intellectual engagement at every level, given the resources, support, and education afforded to men:

> Compare her present position in society with the one she occupied forty years ago, when I undertook to emancipate her from not only barbarous laws, but from what was even worse, a barbarous public opinion. No one can appreciate the wonderful change in the social and moral condition of woman, except by looking back and comparing the past with the present.[110]

Ernestine Rose's principles were based on purely humanist egalitarianism and a complete rejection of any repressive ideologies that limited individual potential and progress. She looked for deep connections that would unite people of various origins. If she could not win them over with humanitarian appeals, she pounded them with her logic and knowledge. Few could defeat Rose in debate. Without her own staunch atheism, she would not have pushed through the barriers that prohibited women from daring to think of themselves as independent human beings. In her work for the full inclusion and recognition of women in government, the judiciary, and education, she elevated the discourse that expanded our democracy to its current apex. As a society, we realized part of her dream when Shirley Chisholm ran for president in 1972.[111]

Today, we take many of our rights for granted, seldom acknowledging the lengthy battles of indefatigable women like Ernestine Louise Rose, who despite poor health, estrangement from her ancestral land, family, and the Jewish people, and several encounters with civil war, never succumbed to hopelessness. In contrast to our contemporary societal infection of apathy, Rose used her considerable oratorical skills and her financial acumen to lobby for and defend important issues in public spheres where most people, but especially women, dared not go. Rose's determination to bring attention to how unequal pay for women, who were relegated to menial professions and barred from many educational institutions, translated into a lifetime of inadequate wages has merit even today.[112] Rose foresaw many nuanced facets of contemporary women's issues in the nineteenth century, which established her as a courageous freethinker and a visionary revolutionary.

Sadly, for today's young women, by the late 1860s, revisionists were already erasing Ernestine's legacy from history books. They have largely succeeded, owing to hegemonic Christian values that hold her birth as a Jewish woman and her self-identification as an atheist suspect, both of which appear sufficient to overshadow her unfailing integrity, astonishing intellectual capacity, and commitment to democracy. Even some of her closest friends attempted to rewrite her life, omitting her identity as a women's rights advocate when eulogizing her.[113] Had Ernestine Rose been a white, Christian woman, the world would know her name as well as the two famous women whom Rose personally mentored: Elizabeth Cady Stanton and Susan B. Anthony.[114] We take for granted the controversial right to divorce that was raised by Stanton in 1863 at the Woman's Rights Convention,[115] which was so contentious that Stanton had only two supporters in attendance that day: Rose and Anthony. It was Rose's off-the-cuff speech to the delegation arguing the merits of divorce as the key to freedom, love, and happiness that turned the tide.[116] Shamefully, too many Americans don't know that Ernestine is the primary benefactor of women's abilities to cash their own paychecks, retain custody of children after divorce, and inherit or retain property after the death of a spouse. That's the kind of troublemaker Ernestine was.

Rose was faithful and transcendent to her last day on Earth, refusing to subjugate the rights of one oppressed group for another's. She raised women's issues at abolitionist conventions, advocated the abolition of slavery at women's gatherings, and challenged authority wherever necessary. Rose's bottomless fount of compassion was replenished and renewed by her faithful husband, William Ella Rose, and the exhilarating force of a community of mountain-movers who worked to improve the lives of those most in need. Unlike those who in public were grandly open-minded but privately bigoted, Rose held no duplicity of character. Militant in stance and diction, she named and exposed all manner of bigotry, aiming always to the highest possible evolution of human advancement and economic stability for all. She spread the doctrine of liberty in the nation through

media and public speaking and sowed the seeds of lasting change while receiving relatively little credit for her policy changes and consciousness-rais-
ing. She did all of this while maintaining principled perspectives, which were
often unpopular.

She was a kind and faithful mentor to the women around her. I believe
that had Ernestine and I met, we would have become instant friends. In the
contemporary struggles of people's movements for justice and democracy,
she'd stand with those of us in need of a champion. I imagine she would express dismay for feminists who don't embrace pluralism in their personal and
professional lives, something she found troubling in her contemporaries. For
now, I look to Ernestine as a teacher and ancestral guide who steers my moral
compass. I feel she bestows her powers of moral courage and bravery upon
me, her brown daughter of lineage, as I work toward my own liberation and
to foster peace and justice in society. Rose was humble in her estimation of
herself, had no ulterior motives to her altruism, and certainly did not indulge
in self-gratification. She was one for all. In the performance of her duties, Ernestine L. Rose was a perfect rose in bloom. With each breath, she wanted to
do right and do *good,* and she did both. It is my turn now. Ernestine is smiling
at me from the photograph on my desk. I can hear her egging me on, tenderly
chiding me: "Success to our cause and love to the Friends devoted to it."[117]

---

*Dedicated to my sister-muse Adrienne Cacitti and my husband, Hal, without whose
love and support I would not have written from my heart.*

Up from the Rubbish Heap:
The Persistence of Julie D'Aubigny

By Caitlin Grace McDonnell

*A*s a kid, I aspired to be part of the Funny Face Club, a group of rebellious neighborhood kids who rejected the cliques of jocks and girly girls, instead opting to play in the streets and root through the trash for hidden treasures. My older sister, an androgynous kid before androgyny ruled, was one of the founders. She didn't take me under her wing, but she let me tag along some of the time when they hid in the graveyard or dumpster dived. One day, I spied something red and white and pink on the side of the heap outside the church of St. Thomas Aquinas. It was a doll with eyes that shut halfway when you laid her down, dark and curly hair, and red lips. I knew in my heart that I'd scored and walked all the way home, alone and with her tucked under my arm. My mom wanted me to clean her, but I liked her the way she was, seeped in the interesting scent of disregard. What else has history tossed away?

Fierce women have always been with us. Julie D'Aubigny was born in 1673. Her father, Gaston D'Aubigny, was a secretary to Count D'Armagnac, who was the Master of the Horse for King Louis XIV. After an early childhood at the Tuileries Palace, where her father worked in the riding school, she was raised in the stables of the castle of Versailles. Her father decided she would learn the same skills as his sons had, dressed her as a boy, and taught her fencing, at which she excelled from a young age. Atypically for the time, he also made sure she was educated like his sons; because they were raised among royalty, she became one of the most learned teenagers in France. She was said to be beautiful with thick auburn hair and blue eyes, and her beauty caught the attention of the lecherous and entitled Count D'Armagnac. They became lovers when she was just a young teen. She was married off (by her father or by the Count, depending on the source) to Monsieur Maupin, a tax collector who lived overseas.[1] Mostly absent, he made an ideal husband for D'Aubigny, as he contributed financially to the life she was able to live on her own terms.

⌒

I am proud to come from a clan of women who also strive to have meaningful and purposeful lives. I am the middle sister of three grown and unmarried women, all of us artists and teachers. We live close to the bone and stay true to our ideals, sometimes at great cost. My mother divorced my father after years of an unhappy, abusive marriage. My sisters and I watched closely as she pulled herself together and created a new life on her own terms. It wasn't easy; at one point, she told me vehemently, "Never get married. Never merge your money with anyone's." (She doesn't remember this. Who knows? Maybe I dreamt it?) In any case, my mom, like most mothers, became both hero and cautionary tale. My eight-year-old daughter, who recently stood up voluntarily in front of hundreds of women, men, and children to talk about gender inequality, seems to have inherited my mother's fierce independent streak.

I was attracted to D'Aubigny's story in part because of its parallels to another woman who excelled at fencing and lived life how she wanted: my maternal great-grandmother, Eleanor Baldwin Cass, who was, like D'Aubigny, a redhead. What I've always known about her is that she was the first female fencer performing in vaudeville, and that she wrote *The Book of Fencing*. The other details of her life I've gleaned from family gatherings. At one holiday dinner, for example, my cousin, her wife, and my lesbian sister all clinked glasses with a wink after sharing their theory about her sexual preferences.

Eleanor's marriage was arranged and not a happy one for her. She eventually lived on her own in the former Prince George Hotel in New York City. I asked my aunt, a sister in the Focolare Movement, which is an inter-

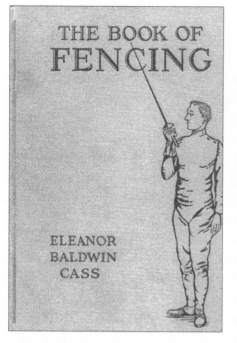

national organization founded in Italy with ties to Christianity and Roman Catholicism, about her memories of her grandmother. She said Eleanor lived a colorful life. She was a very good friend of Cardinal Spellman, trained Errol Flynn in fencing, and performed on Broadway and for the Queen of England. Looking through old press archives reveals her to be a minor celebrity of her time. One paper did a whole story on how much she loved to play with her children.[2] When I speculated about her sexuality, my aunt denied that she could possibly be a lesbian. "She was a strong Catholic," she said, as if that precluded lesbianism. "What else do you want to know? She lived a good life, way ahead of her time. She did what she wanted. She was not easy."

It is impossible for me to write anything about fierce and disregarded women at this moment without connecting it to the fervor with which I promoted the woman who ran for president of the United States of America in 2016. Hillary Rodham Clinton, the first viable female candidate for the American presidency, wound up losing, at least in part, because sexism runs far deeper than any of us had fully realized. Initially, I had suspicions about her, along with a vague distaste for her, although I couldn't name the origin (other than her husband). The more I read and interrogated my own resistance, the more convinced I became that she was the victim of two or three decades of unfair smears to her character from the right—and, it's becoming clear, Russian bots. She had been visible in politics for a long time, and that worked against her, because politicians change their minds, and they make compromises. I'm now convinced that she would never have been a candidate had she not made the compromises she did, and I'm awed by her resilience. I defended her in both the primaries and the general election with the fervor of a twelve-year-old girl woken out of a dream to defend her mother against her father's raised fist. I lost friends and warded off potential suitors. Do not fuck with a twelve-year-old girl. It is my firm belief that Hillary's place in history will be significant.

❧

The black-and-white photograph of Eleanor from the front pages of her book is the antithesis to John Berger's description of photographed women existing purely for the male gaze. According to Berger, the photographed woman is "offering up her femininity as the surveyed [...\ to the surveyor/owner."[3] By contrast, Eleanor stands strong, just right of center, and is flanked by two beautiful men. They are on a Persian rug with a black background. The men are her sons, Edward and Leo, who hold their swords with the tips to the ground. She holds hers loosely in the left hand, with two fingers from the right wound around the blade. Her sword bends slightly. Her head tilts slightly to the right. Her eyes look serious, knowing, haughty, bored, tough, and authoritarian. Her hair is short, asymmetrical, and lightly curled; I imagine it's reddish, maybe a color like mine. She wears

little makeup except dark lipstick on her thin lips. Her jawline is androgynous, her physique masked by her clothing. We cannot see the shape of her breasts through the stiff white blouse, which also covers her neck. She wears a dark, pleated skirt that falls below her knees, stockings, and Mary-Jane-like flats. Her feet, like those of her sons, are in a slight lunge position: the right faces forward, and the left turns out. Her calves, shapely and strong, offer a glimpse of femininity. Leo's arm touches hers conspiratorially, while Edward stands slightly behind

Courtesy of Charlotte Crosby Studio.
EDWARD B. CASS,   LEO. J. CASS.
ELEANOR BALDWIN CASS.

her. He is all in white and holds his sword with his right hand only, and his helmet is tucked under his arm. Leo is the most ladylike of the three, with his full lips, vulnerable eyes, and right hand that holds the top of the sword as he leans on it as if to pose. He looks straight at the camera, while she and Edward look slightly to the right.[4]

As I write this, my daughter is next door at Jiu Jitsu. Her eight-year-old body is lean and strong. She is learning to defend herself with focus and grace. According to Berger:

> *To be born a woman is to be born, within an allotted and confined space, into the keeping of men. The social presence of women has developed as a result of their ingenuity in living under such tutelage within such a limited space. But this has been at the cost of a woman's self being split into two. A woman must continually watch herself. She is almost continually accompanied by her own image of herself. Whilst she is walking across a room or whilst she is weeping at the death of her father, she can scarcely avoid envisaging herself walking or weeping. From earliest childhood she has been taught and persuaded to survey herself continually."*[5]

My daughter, like my grandmother, is learning to embody her body rather than only survey it for an external gaze. This is what I hope she can carry with her through adolescence. The photograph of my grandmother, strong and straightforward, gives me hope that the generational chain of her spirited DNA remains unbroken for her granddaughter.

Back in the 1680s in France, Julie D'Aubigny was a restless adolescent. She grew tired of D'Armagnac and took up with a fencing master and outlaw named Seranne. They traveled around Marseille, performing at fairs and taverns. She began singing with the Opera de Marseille and discovered she had an uncanny talent for it—which, along with her good looks, intelligence, and charisma, made her a natural performer. She had quite a following, especially among her own gender—we might regard her as the Taylor Swift or Lady Gaga of the 1600s.

One young woman, whose name is unknown, saw her perform and became quite taken with her. Julie claimed she was tired of men and returned the girl's affections. The girl's parents disapproved and sent her away to a convent, but unsurprisingly, Julie followed. It seems they were intoxicated by their love for each other against all odds. They became outrageous outlaws together—they stole the body of a deceased nun, put the corpse in the girl's bed as a stand-in, then burned the convent to the ground. They were sentenced to death by fire to fit the punishment to their crimes, but escaped the law for three months before the girl's parents took her home and left Julie on her own.[6]

I like to imagine those three months, because when a girl loves a girl, she is the most dangerous creature to men, knowing through all her bones that she has no use for them. For those months, the women were free and had what they most wanted: each other. They were on the run, hiding in forests, killing game, maybe tricking a man for a drink at a tavern. They had bodies that fit together like commas to come back to, deep in a cave between the trees. They had everything and nowhere to go. But Julie had a sword and several more stories to live before her end.

ᴗ

I've never practiced fencing myself, but more than one person I've been in relationship with has accused me of being drawn to argument. That accusation used to cause a defensive reflex in me, but I've decided it's time to embrace it. As a kid, I looked forward to debates at school. I still remember the enthusiasm with which I prepared for my debate with my sixth-grade crush. We were going to argue whether "if someone kills someone [...] the government [should] be allowed to kill them." (My central argument was that two wrongs don't make a right.) When I teach college students to write argumentative essays, I often tell them to think of shadowboxing: "You must anticipate what the counter-argument will be and be ready to refute it." My recent online dating profile says that I enjoy "sparring"—from Old English *sporran*, "to strike out"—because I believe that a healthy argument doesn't need to put a relationship in jeopardy. Like the title of Sarah Schulman's book says, *Conflict Does Not Equal Abuse*,[7] in fact, it might teach us about ourselves. Like those who engage in kink, couldn't we say that good debaters enjoy fighting, as long as they know the parameters? The opening of part two of *The Book of Fencing* includes a Lefauhtere epigraph that speaks to this dance of power: "Hold your foil as if you had a little bird in your hand, firmly enough to prevent its escaping, yet not so firmly so to crush it."[8]

My great-grandmother, Eleanor, also makes interesting points in *The Book of Fencing* about the origins of swordplay, something that came about paradoxically, as the result of firearms. "When a commoner armed with a *calivar* or *demi-haque* could shoot an expensive suit of armor and its noble wearer full of holes at a hundred feet, even the most conservative began to realize that spring had come and it was time to shed their iron overcoats."[9] The middle classes created fighting guilds to teach townspeople how to protect themselves.

A letter to "Mr. Cass" from Lord Desborough, the president of the Salle Bertrand fencing club, included in the introduction to *The Book of Fencing*, states:

> *[F]encing was a conversation with the sword, and to make the conversation interesting each of the controversialists had to be well educated in the art of argument. No conversation could take place unless your opponent understood the language. If he merely parried carte and sixte, it was just like talking to a man who could only say "yes" and "no" whereas if he understood the language of the sword he could reply to your attach and counter-ripostes with every sort of argument and variation, which adds intensely to the interest of an argument with the foil.*[10]

Alone and on the run from the law, Julie continued to wander the countryside dressed as a man—or, as some biographers claim, dressed simply in the clothes in which she felt comfortable.[11] One day in her wanderings, she literally bumped into young nobleman Comte d'Albert. Not realizing she was female, he challenged her to a duel. She beat him but nursed him back to health, and the two either became close friends or the singular loves of each other's lives, according to different accounts. I love this story and like to envision a genderless intimacy growing out of sparring with someone who makes a worthy opponent. At the opening of *The Book of Fencing*, there is a poem called "The Woman with The Foil," which was written by Edwin Markham in 1929 for Eleanor and which suggests a similar kind of male–female camaraderie. He writes in celebration of her freedom from "pots and pans" and from being a "butterfly to fashion." It ends, "Stand forth, O woman, free of pains and pallor— / Stand forth under the great sky, / And teach men how to greatly live in valor, And how to greatly die."[12]

Julie D'Aubigny was well armed with swords and books—the skills her father made sure she acquired growing up—but she also was served by her art (singing and performing), and she used her charisma and sexual appeal to open doors. After leaving D'Albert, she took up with Gabriel Thevenard, who was also a singer. The two auditioned for the opera in Paris. She knew she would need her crimes to be forgiven if she wanted to be on the stage, so she coaxed her former lover, Count D'Armagnac, to get her pardoned by Louis XIV. She became an opera star at age seventeen—that's right, all of this happened before she was seventeen—and became known as La Maupin. She appeared in all of the opera's major productions from 1690 to 1694 and was adored by the public.[13]

When I asked family about my great-grandmother, I was told to get in touch with Victoria Cass, my great-aunt, a writer and a scholar of Chinese culture. She is the author, notably, of *Dangerous Women: Warriors, Grannies and Geishas of the Ming*[14] and other books, and she has a lot of knowledge about Eleanor Baldwin Cass. She did not confirm my cousin and sister's suspicions about Eleanor's sexual proclivities, but did speak of rumors associated with Prince Van Alen, who left $100,000 to his "little fencing instructress" when he died in London. Victoria also pointed me to newspaper archives that contain an abundance of articles about Eleanor. According to those archives, Eleanor was also an instructor to the Duchesses of Manchester and Marlborough, "Conseulo Vanderbilt," and many others.[15] It is unclear whether she ever knew about La Maupin, but Eleanor was a woman who had opinions about other female fencers. "The American woman is a better fencer than her European sister," she told the *Honolulu Advertiser* on June 22, 1924. "She has more vitality and pep. Her life is established on a different basis. Even in France, for centuries a dueling country, the Frenchwoman, lazy at sports, is seldom expert with the foil."

If there was truth in Eleanor's criticism, clearly D'Aubigny was an exception. Throughout her opera career, her skills with swords continued to influence the operatic drama that was her life. In Paris, at the height of her singing career, she attended a ball dressed as a man and kissed a young woman on the dance floor. Three different noblemen were offended and challenged her to duel. She told each of them she would meet him outside, fought all of them at once, and beat them all. She fled to Brussels, where she became the lover of the Elector of Bavaria. After she dramatically stabbed herself on stage with a real dagger, the elector had enough of her and offered her 40,000 francs to leave him alone. She threw the coins at the feet of his emissary and left for Madrid. There, she worked briefly as a maid to a Countess Marino. The arrangement ended when Julie secretly and mischievously dressed the countess's hair with radishes to make her look foolish and then took off to return to Paris.[16]

⁓

Although Eleanor, like La Maupin, did not delight in marriage, she did find immense joy in motherhood. In fact, the playfulness that she enjoyed with her children gave her a second childhood. In a profile in the *Boston Sun* dated March 20, 1921, she is quoted as saying, "A woman should be a child as long as she can! She should have two youths—the one her own, the other with her children." And later, "I'm no spring chicken, but I'm not ready to be laid on the shelf—not yet. I play with my boys. I turn cartwheels, somersaults and flips. And I'm just as happy and merry and active as I've ever been."[17] I share this delight in the play associated with motherhood. I do cartwheels at the beach with my daughter and ride the Brooklyn Flyer at Coney Island. My daughter's sense of wonder reawakens my own, and I like to think that this rejection of traditionally prescribed parenting roles is another fierce, inherited trait.

I've wasted a fair amount of time over the years wondering what went wrong in my family of origin that sometimes makes it difficult for me to have a relationship. An uncle who had a bit too much to drink once told my sister that all the women in his family were both passionately independent and angry about it at the same time. "They need something from men but resent it at the same time." I see his point, and it no longer brings up shame. At this moment in our nation's history, it is most abundantly clear that women are damned if they do and damned if they don't.

Therefore, I've decided to stop pathologizing my evident ambivalence about participating in heteronormative coupledom. The stories of D'Aubigny and of my great-grandmother inspire me. In their own ways, and each armed with a sword, they lived their lives according to their own inner compasses, not society's dictates.

Like many stories of historical women, La Maupin's has missing pieces. We know her mostly through her love affairs and crimes. She did not take kindly to rejection. It is said that when her opera co-star Fanchon Moreau did not return her affections, she attempted suicide at age twenty-five.

She also made it her mission to protect other women from the unwanted advances of men. In 1703, D'Aubigny fell in love once last time, with Madame la Marquise de Florensac, who was known as the "most beautiful woman in France."[18] Florensac had been stalked by the Dauphin in Paris and left for Brussels to escape him. The two women are said to have lived together in bliss in Brussels until de Florensac died of a fever. In her grief, D'Aubigny entered a convent, where she died at the age of thirty-three. In the words of one biographer, she was "destroyed by an inclination to do evil in the sight of her God and a fixed intention not to," after which, he claims, "her body was cast upon the rubbish heap."[19]

But her bravery cannot be so easily disregarded. She was immortalized in *Mademoiselle Maupin,* a fictionalization by Theophile Gautier (1835).[20] Kelly Gardiner's generous online research for her 2015 novel *Goddess* was an invaluable source here.[21] There was a 2004 La Maupin movie,[22] and there was a successful Kickstarter campaign online for a NYC Fresh Fruit production of *La Maupin* in 2017.[23] One could say she lives on in the blockbuster movie of the summer of 2017, *Wonder Woman.* Like the doll in the dumpster and the stories of my great grandmother and her *Book of Fencing,* she will be discovered and dusted off by women throughout the ages. We need the inspiration of female vitality so fearlessly lived more than ever.

For my Mom, my daughter, and all the moms and daughters

The Blazing Worlds of Margaret Cavendish

By Robyn Kraft

he first time I went to a comic book store, I was twelve. This was the mid-nineties, before the superhero movie market opened up to appeal more to women. I was the only female in the store, and I had no real idea what I was doing, only that I wanted to read some *X-Men* comic books, having been introduced to the animated television series. I was offered plenty of help in finding what I was looking for. The man behind the counter at the time was probably in his mid-twenties, but early on, it was unsettling to realize his disproportionate eagerness to assist me. I was treated as an oddity, more so when I went in with my best friend, also female. We were the best-tended-to customers in the store, every time we went. (Twenty years later, that same man flits around the edges of my group of friends and still makes himself overly familiar with me, despite the fact that I've never expressed an interest in him, and he first knew me when I was, again, only twelve years old.)

Comic books have become more mainstream and are even on the brink of garnering acceptance as a literary genre. The most recent time I went into a comic book store, I was an adult, and I knew that I was looking for the newest bound volume of *Saga*. Again, at a different store, with a different employee, I was offered help three different times, and I knew instinctively not to drift too close or show too much interest in the items behind the counter, or I'd inevitably be engaged in needless conversation. Still, I couldn't resist checking out the selection of playing dice, even when I knew there would be repercussions in the form of unwanted attention. This is a choice that I have to make in certain spaces—I must decide what I'm willing to put up with in order to be there authentically and see what I want to see. Yet, I haven't found a way to navigate this. I know I am not alone in this struggle, and the recent calling out of misogyny with the #MeToo movement going viral bears this out.[1]

For posterity, in the hope that someday such movements will not be necessary, #MeToo was a hashtag used by women to share their common experiences of living in a world in which they are treated as objects instead of full human beings. It succeeded in bringing the daily struggles of women to the forefront of conversation and opening the eyes of well-meaning men who hadn't realized just what their female-bodied friends and loved ones went through by simply navigating in the world. The movement caused enough of a stir that the "silence-breakers," or the women who were credited with starting the movement, won the *Time Magazine* Person of the Year award for 2017.[2]

What these experiences imply is that men see these spaces as belonging to them, and that any woman who wanders in is not only a rarity but also someone they can usher into their world and subsequently impose their expert mansplaining. It seems that from the male perspective, we are by default blank slates that need to be written with their wisdom. All women in these male-identified spaces are there for purposes of being chatted up, to serve as distracting ornamentation. The perception is not that women are there because they have a legitimate interest in the culture on offer, nor will they ever have more accurate knowledge about any items there than the man who is explaining it to them, whether he was asked for the information or not.

Although I have a lot of women in my circle of friends who enjoy comics, graphic novels, and other geeky paraphernalia sold at comic stores and science fiction conventions, it's the men I know who become regulars at these places. Women tend to only go in groups, with other women, or with a man to lend them legitimacy and protection from unwelcome advances. Not surprisingly, it was a genre convention at which my friend, who had taken time to dress herself attractively for her own pleasure, was accosted by a man who had never met her before, who asked for a hug because she "looked cold." He then requested that she be his "con-girlfriend," so he could have some arm candy to elevate his cachet among his peers. In his mind, she wasn't there for her own edification but only to get attention from men, who were supposedly the only ones "genuinely" interested in the convention. If she were there because she was a nerd, too, she would have been dressed in a frumpy and unattractive way, which would mark her as a member of the same outcast construct in wider society, as mocked and undesired as the men in these spaces perceive themselves to be. The common joke is that attractive women only attend conventions to benefit nerdy men who will fawn over them and possibly make it worthwhile by making a lot of money in the future.

It is here, at this juncture of alienation and performance, that we find Margaret Cavendish, a writer who had varied interests that were deemed unseemly for her sex, including such issues as animal rights. Her poem titled "The Hunting of the Hare" takes the perspective of the titular animal and its fear during a hunt, offering a shocking perspective on a popular recreation at the time, especially among the nobility. [3] An avowed royalist during a time when that could cost you your land, if not your life, she was not shy about political commentary, philosophy, and science, which she frequently wrote about together in several of her books of "observations" and "philosophies." All of this happened long before the first comic book store was imagined, and before women made any real strides into the field of science.

Cavendish's name is better known these days than it was even a few decades ago, thanks to efforts of literary scholars to allow women their due place in literary history. Nevertheless, a brief biography: she was born in 1623 in England as the youngest of eight children. When she was still young, her father died, and her mother had to run the household, defaulting to an example of "female independence and administrative competence." [4] This presents an image of a strong-female-led home. Cavendish's family were staunch royalists during the English Civil War in which King Charles I eventually lost his life, and in consequence, they lost much of their remaining lands and wealth. In 1643, Cavendish asked leave of her mother to join the exiled Queen Henrietta Maria in Paris, and there, she met her future husband. In 1644, Margaret married William Cavendish, the Duke of Newcastle. He was thirty years her senior and had been previously married, but all evidence suggests—sometimes in florid prose from Cavendish herself—that their union was happy. William and his brother, Charles, were well-educated men and kept company with thinkers and scholars at the time, including Thomas Hobbes and Descartes. In this atmosphere, Cavendish was exposed to thoughts and conversations to which many women did not have access, and this spurred her writing.

William supported Margaret, providing her with capital to write and publish her voluminous body of work, even after they lost their estate and social stature in 1649 with the overthrow of the monarchy. Much of Margaret's focus remained on reclaiming her husband's estate. In fact, it was while petitioning for recompense from 1651 to 1653 that she began writing, and from that point on, she never stopped: "The sheer quantity and variety of Cavendish's published work was extremely marked amongst women writers of the seventeenth century, and unprecedented amongst earlier English women writers."[5]

She published her first two books, *Poems and Fancies,* and *Philosophical Fancies,* in 1653 using her own name, something that was unusual at the time for women writers, who often hid behind pseudonyms. She wrote in various genres on a number of topics, including poetry, plays, philosophical treatises, memoirs, and novels, allowing her own interests to justify her writing rather than catering to popular tastes or seeking any praise from her contemporaries. Early in her writing career, she even wrote a brief memoir of her own life, recognizing that she would be unlikely to be understood by her contemporaries but hoping to be known and recognized for her foresight by future readers. Indeed, much of her writing was met with a chilly reception. As her 1994 edition editor Kate Lilley points out, "The spectacle of Cavendish as a writing woman has disturbed commentators is clear. Her writings have suffered a similar resistance, leading generations of commentators to suggest that paraphrase is as much as, or more than, her work requires."[6]

History leads one to believe that Cavendish didn't really care what other people thought about her. She was known as an eccentric and an exhibitionist, on paper and in person, and had a habit of doing what she wanted to do, no matter how others perceived her. Interestingly, she did not think of herself in the same light and often claimed modesty and shyness in appearance, even when responding to the gossip about her clothing. Samuel Pepys once noted, of an outfit that she wore to court, that she was "in antique dress. [...] There is as much expectation of her coming to court, so that people may see her, as if it were the Queen of Sheba."[7] In her memoir, she explains, "I took great delight in attiring, fine dressing, and fashions, especially such fashions as I did invent myself, not taking that pleasure in such fashions as was invented by others. Also I did dislike any should follow my fashions, for I always took delight in a singularity, even in accouterments of habits," which does more to reinforce the idea of her fashionable exhibitionism than to discourage it. Her prolific and varied writing—and her ambition to be known for it—she would proudly accept upon herself. She was fascinated by science in particular, and in her *Reflections on Science and Philosophy*, she describes how she "continued her attempt to insert herself into a masculine public sphere, particularly through the discourse of the new science."[8] During Cavendish's lifetime, there were advancements in technology, including the invention of microscopes and telescopes, which expanded human understanding of the world, something that interested her greatly.

There is a well-known anecdote about Cavendish using her husband's name and rank to gain access where she wasn't wanted. The Royal Academy was known for being a place for the most enlightened, or at least the wealthiest men of the time to gather and learn by discussing science and philosophy. At one point, against the wishes of the men in the group, Cavendish attended a scientific demonstration. She was the first woman ever to gain entry. She was dressed outlandishly, and she was impossible to ignore. Reportedly, she briefly viewed the demonstration, airily dismissed it with mild disinterest, and then departed in a swirl of skirts. How she actually responded is unknown, given that the men recounting the tale weren't inclined to favorably view a woman who had invaded their private space. By her own account, she was shy, and she framed her discomfort in crowds as a form of social anxiety. Possibly, it was not a lack of interest in the demonstration but an overwhelming feeling of being unwanted that caused her to make her retreat.

Despite not being welcomed to formally study science, Cavendish was undeterred. In a world that would not allow her to participate, she responded by creating her own universe, which she could both rule and play an active part in. Her most well-known work is *The Blazing World*. In a world created by her own imagination, science worked however she thought it should, and she states quite clearly in the preface, that "there is but one truth in nature, and all those that hit not this truth, do err [...] But fictions are an issue of man's fancy, framed in his own mind, according as he pleases."[9] It is interesting to note that she refers to a writer—herself—with masculine pronouns.

She was proud of her writing and her reasoning, and she hoped to be remembered for it. Early in her writing career, she wrote a memoir of herself and her life in order to make herself understood—not to her contemporaries who mocked her, but for the future generations she felt would better understand her work, thus granting herself immortality as an author. "But I fear my ambition inclines to vain-glory, for I am very ambitious," she writes, "yet 'tis neither for beauty, wit, titles, wealth, or power, but as they are steps to raise me to Fame's tower, which is to live by remembrance in after-ages."[10]

Although Cavendish was bold and forward, she was not known as a champion of other women who sought to write. She believed that her interest in science elevated her above other women. Because it was a traditionally male-dominated field, the subtext was that she also thought men were superior—or at least that their interests were. In her memoir, she wrote of women:

> For the truth is, our sex doth nothing but jostle for the pre-eminence of words (I mean not for speaking well, but speaking much) as they do for the pre-eminence of place, words rushing against words, thwarting and crossing each other [...] But if our sex would but well consider, and rationally ponder, they will perceive and find, that it is neither words nor place that can advance them, but worth and merit.[11]

Worth and merit come from speaking less and reasoning more on the sciences or participating in masculine discourse, as Cavendish, who thought to offer this advice in writing, does. However, she also groups herself with women, as if to absolve herself of any contradictions or inaccuracies in her reasoning, or perhaps as a subtle jab at men who think women cannot reason like men can:

> I have heard, that some should say my wit seemed as if it would overpower my brain, especially when it works upon philosophical opinions. I am obliged to them for judging my wit stronger than my brain: but I should be sorry that they should think my wit stronger than my reason: but I must tell them that my brain is stronger than my wit, and my reason as strong as the effeminate sex requires.[12]

The Blazing World, although it is superficially hard to classify, is often given as one of the earliest examples of science fiction. It presents a Utopian world founded on scientific ideas, and though no one would call the science presented tenable, that's what makes it fiction. This was hardly the first time in literary history that women were at the vanguard of a new development in literature. A woman likely wrote the first novel, although there is some debate about whether it was *The Pillow Book* by Sei Shonagon or *The Tale of Genji* by Murasaki Shikibu.[13] When constrained by society, women use their minds to escape and create, and they have long used written language to do so.

This is not to suggest that novels are the exclusive domain of women. Many readers don't question the omnipresence of a male protagonist who, upon entering a new world, time, or situation, is suddenly heroic, saving everyone and everything. Only the male lead can cast the right magic spell, pull the sword from the stone, or use his scientific ability or martial prowess to save the day. In genre fiction, readers are so conditioned to identify with male heroes that it's notable when a book has a female protagonist instead. When geek-identified men are bullied for their interests and go on to write eponymous heroic stories, they win awards. If women compete for awards for writing similar stories, they are ignored—or, worse, face threats and harassment.

One need only look to the 2015 Hugo Awards, where a group of white male authors, frustrated at the increase in diverse authors winning awards the previous year, attempted to gather followers to weight the ballots to hand wins to more white, male authors.[14] The backlash against these men, the "sad puppies" and the "rabid puppies," was striking, despite their claim that they feared the awards were being given at the behest of "social justice warriors" rather than for quality fiction.[15] Women writers, writers of color, and queer authors are increasingly being recognized for their work, despite the best efforts of those trying to maintain a dwindling status quo.

"Mainstream society" has decided that "nerds" are outcasts who are socially awkward, can't get dates, and are almost always men. How many jokes revolve around self-deprecating humor from a man in a science field about his inability to get a date? This is also a major plot point in a very popular sitcom, too. In CBS's long-running *The Big Bang Theory,* nerds are male and can't get women to take an interest in them. Historically, however, the economic elite were the ones who were at liberty to indulge in traditionally "nerdy" interests, such as the Royal Society. Women were not welcome in the Royal Society because it was thought that they were not intellectually compatible with the society's agenda. This manner of gate-keeping, based on a perception of male-nerd-intellectual superiority, merged with social isolation and rejection, persists to this day, making women feel uncomfortable and marginalized in STEM fields—or, on a cultural level, in comic book stores. Although people of both genders are now playing video and board games, watching superhero movies, and reading comics, it doesn't appear to disable the conceit of being a misunderstood outcast genius, which is a central part of the male nerd identity.

Additionally, the construct that treats women as outliers instead of as accepted participants doesn't limit itself to incidental circumstances, and the gatekeepers aren't always men. One summer, I was fortunate enough to get an internship for a writing center at a well-established creative and artistic enclave in New York. The woman who sponsored the internship was very friendly and welcoming, with one caveat: there was a young man on an overlapping internship, and she doted on him and his writing. We were both poets, and although I did the bulk of the work as he ran around and seduced the journalism interns, he was the one she gushed about, and he was the one she kept in touch with, even sending him home with a copy of a book she'd written and self-published. He was not impressed with her writing but seemed otherwise used to being gushed over by an older woman. Although he seemed to think it odd that I didn't also get a copy of the book, he never once questioned why that discrepancy occurred, though I was there for a full summer, and he was only there for two weeks. It made me feel confused, hurt, and angry—and sparked a lot of new writing from me as I attempted to prove my place.

Margaret Cavendish wrote a story in which her extremely wise, beautiful, powerful and insightful empress commands and impresses order upon one world and saves another. "*The Blazing World* combines a narrative of the effortless rise of a woman to absolute power, with a narrative of the liberty of the female soul and the emancipatory possibilities of Utopian speculation and writing specifically for women."[16] If this summary is startling, try changing the pronoun and see if it sounds like most fiction.

A brief summary of the novel will make this clear. A sailing ship abducts the empress, who is never given a proper name, for her extraordinary beauty. The ship holding her captive goes off course and somehow manages to reach the North Pole, where it enters a new world, the Blazing World, which contains a new star-scape in the sky and new kinds of creatures. The woman, who is the only survivor, is rescued by the animal–man hybrid of this new world and taken to their emperor, who immediately recognizes her true superiority and marries her. He then vanishes from the narrative while the empress begins her reign of reason and science. She begins by speaking to all of the natives and learning how their world is laid out and how it runs, expounding upon science and reason and ordering everything efficiently.

After a time, she gets lonely, and her soul leaves her body to search for a companion soul by entering her original world and happening upon none other than the duchess of Newcastle. The stand-in for the author meets the author and brings her spirit back to the Blazing World to live in her body with her other self, where she will help the empress by utilizing Cavendish's writing skills. They visit frequently. The empress even visits the duchess in her body and forms a profound platonic relationship with the duke of Newcastle, and their three souls live together in deepest harmony. However, word reaches the empress that there is a threat to the kingdom of her origin, and she brings to her original world an army of fish- and bird-men to defend her shores from invaders, triumphing in a literal blaze of ultimate glory. No hero of speculative fiction could have a more magnificent homecoming, arriving transcendent and elevated above his formerly misunderstood and invisible status.

This novel is a wish-fulfillment fantasy at the most blatant level, and it earned censure from contemporaries, literary critics, fellow writers (Virginia Woolf, notably, was not a fan, despite the fact that it was Woolf's writing on Cavendish that brought the duchess back to the public eye in the first place), and even contemporary academics, who tend to focus more on Cavendish's life and impact than on the quality of her work. After all, we're taught to look the other way in the face of wish-fulfillment novels—particularly when they're packaged as genre fiction, which is only now starting to gain a foothold in academic circles as a valid source of study, and especially when they fulfill *feminine* wishes.

Consider the comparative response between the genres of mystery versus romance. Both genres lean heavily on tropes, formulas, and serialization, but more people readily admit to being mystery fans than romance fans. One major difference is the intended audience, and the other is the gender most frequently found behind the keyboard. Fantasies written by and for women tend to be looked at as ridiculous, though fantasies written about men going out and saving humankind against a galaxy of evil aliens are considered good entertainment and possibly a reflection of the human condition. Less profound thought and agency is granted to the feminine genre, although most romance novels are about a woman finding a man to treat her with respect, compassion, desire, and love—something that can happen in the mundane world off the page. Nevertheless, romantic fiction is perceived as silly and trite in contrast to the sci-fi fantasy of a man wielding a sword made of energy to kill goblins, which is a phallic allegory at best. As Kameron Hurley, a modern writer of rather dark and gritty science fiction put it, "This type of writing, because it is written by women, is considered somehow deviant or disorderly."[17]

It is notable that the story of a strong woman rising to ultimate power is set in a Utopian setting. Who could imagine such a thing, especially at the time the novel was written, happening in the real world? Cavendish is quite candid about it in her foreword to the novel, where she directly addresses her reader. The quotation is long, but gives a brilliant insight into the woman herself, and the impulse behind the novel:

> *I am not covetous, but as ambitious as ever any of my sex was, is, or can be; which makes, that though I cannot be Henry the Fifth, or Charles the Second, yet I endeavor to be Margaret the First; and although I have neither power, time nor occasion to conquer the world as Alexander and Caesar did; yet rather than not to be mistress of one [...] I have made a world of my own: for which nobody, I hope, will blame me, since it is in every one's power to do the like.[18]*

As I write this, I contemplate how utterly different my life has become from what it was one year ago. At the time, I was very unhappily married to a controlling and angry man who left me shaking and terrified. I felt like I was squatting in my house and could lose it to him at any time. I didn't have a job to defend myself. I had to hope I didn't get seriously ill because I couldn't afford insurance. I was more depressed and anxious than I have ever been in my life. And I was full of story ideas for fantasy worlds where I could escape and realign the world to benefit the weak and frightened, enabling them to become permanently strong and powerful. Now, I own my home, have a full-time job, a settled divorce case, a partner who loves and supports me and makes me feel secure and safe. I have some power to shape my own life the way I want it to be. But I don't feel compelled to write anymore. The words that used to thrum through my veins have never been so silent, because I'm expending my energy now to create my three-dimensional life the way I want it to be. As Cavendish remarked, it is within everyone's power to create their own world as they see fit, be it on paper or in reality.

Intriguingly, Cavendish hadn't shown all that much interest in writing until her husband lost his estate in the revolution. She began her writing while in England, petitioning to have his estate returned to him, and never stopped. It was when her life was at the most difficult in the supposed "real world" that she turned to creating fiction to escape into a world she could control. Her quotation above indicates that she found great satisfaction in that power, and yet, she comprehended its limitations. A wise and compassionate woman with omniscient powers ruled her utopia. When she wished to learn science, she demanded it be explained to her, and when she wished to take her people into battle to end a war in her home of origin, she manifested the outcome that she desired. Beyond the fact that the inhabitants of the Blazing World were animal–man hybrids, the most astounding and unrealistic thing might be the unchallenged power immediately granted to the empress.

Women have added incentive to write about worlds that don't quite resemble our own. When one's world is constrained by lack of power, autonomy, and options, sometimes, the only way to escape is to create a world where that doesn't matter. A contemporary book in which women cause all the trouble and chaos but also power all of the solutions is *The Stars are Legion* by Kameron Hurley. In this book, the world ships that populate the vast universe of the story are peopled entirely by women. There isn't a man to be seen, let alone a male savior to come in and save the women from themselves. The reviews are more positive than one might expect, but there are some critics who complain about how hard it is to suspend disbelief to read about a world in which there are no men at all.

Despite women being involved in sci-fi from its inception and making significant contributions, men still dominate the worlds of fantasy and science-fiction writing. It is within these genres—and at the conventions dedicated to them—where women frequently complain of feeling marginalized, sexualized, and simply unwelcome and uncomfortable. Stories of gender-related issues at literary conventions abound, including an absence of all-women panels, dominantly male headliners, women writers assigned token status if included on a panel, and so on. The most blatant and frankly creepy stories stem from genre conventions where stories of sexual harassment and assault seem to come up frequently. Men write genre fiction for the same reason that women do, because they lack power in the real world. So, they create new ones in which similarly situated men—(i.e., physically smaller, less conventionally masculine, and peer-marginalized)—become magically heroic by virtue of an overlooked special quality or power and end up saving the world. By extension, these heroes get all the women that they want, as men throughout history frequently have.

Just consider the number of young girls married off to wealthy older men, whether royal or merchant, throughout history, to see this long running precedent. If men are used to writing, reading, and imagining themselves living in worlds in which women are prizes to be won for their own benefit, it is unremarkable after they achieve some celebrity for their writing that they subsequently believe that women at conventions are also prizes that are won by their notoriety. And in such male-dominated spaces as comic book stores, they aren't used to seeing women at all. A woman wearing a comic book T-shirt will be grilled by men on minute details of the comic as they police whether she deserves to wear the shirt, something to which they don't subject their fellow brethren.

This can sometimes backfire, as when Natalie Portman wore a T-shirt in *Star Wars* font proclaiming "Stop Wars." Internet heckler @kleptomaniantic said, "The picture of that stupid fucking hipster chick in a starwars shirt needs to stop she probably hasn't even seen all the movies [sic]." Internet denizens incredulously asked him if he was joking, given that Portman acted in three of the *Star Wars* movies, but most women have to constantly prove their right to exist in these spaces.

If women want to be in a space fully under our own power and initiative, where we don't have to contemplate what we will have to give up or what we are willing to tolerate to be there, and where we are not subject to the arbitrary rules that men have set for us, then we have to create that space for ourselves. Women have been doing it since they began writing novels, and despite mockery—Dorothy Osborne, a contemporary of Cavendish, wrote, "Sure the poore woman is a little distracted. She could never bee so rediculous else, as to venture at writeing book's and in verse too" [sic][19]—we persist. And one day, we can sincerely hope that the worlds we write about won't be necessary anymore, because we will have the rights and freedoms that presently can only be found in genre fiction.

Cavendish died in 1673, and it can't be said that she reinvented the way science was understood or literature was written by women in those fields. But she did blaze new trails of her own, creating a world in which a woman ruled all, supreme and wise, and she showed nothing but grace, understanding, and responsiveness to the inhabitants of the new world she found herself occupying. She bestowed forgiveness to the world she had been taken from by the roughness of men who thought her nothing but a beautiful prize. Centuries later, we are still waiting for this utopia to become something more than fiction, but at least we can read, and write, and get some glimpses of what such a future might look like. 🌿

For my soulmate, who always supports me and
actually likes listening to my research.

Radiant Identity: Chicaba Herstories

By Chicava HoneyChild

A queen because she ruled over herself,
and because she ruled over herself,
still a queen...[1]

Our Meeting, My Naming

When I decided to become a burlesque dancer, I named myself after a nun. Not just any nun, but a nun who'd been through something—Chicaba, Sister Teresa Juliana of Santo Domingo. Born free to royal lineage in Africa, abducted into slavery, and taken to Spain, she died in a convent for fallen women. Although venerated after 268 years, she still awaits sainthood. She was an extraordinary woman whose life reads as a swirl of hagiography and slave narrative.[2]

I first learned about Chicaba in Ivan Van Setima's book, *African Presence in Early Europe*, which I read in college. In a few sentences, a world opened up to me, and my heart opened to a woman I had never conceived existed: a black nun in eighteenth-century Spain. I held her name in my mind over the years, thinking that, one day, I would name my daughter—or perhaps a cat—Chicaba. When coming up with a burlesque name, I knew I wanted something with depth and lasting meaning, as opposed to a cheeky name or one with blatant sexual overtones. "Cherry Chocolate" was not going to do it. When I remembered Chicaba, I felt like I'd struck gold. And I had.

As I have become Chicava the Second to her Chicaba the First, she has gone from being an exotic name to a woman whose life I contemplate deeply and whose publicized narrative I am suspect of. But allow me to introduce ourselves.

Chicaba the First

Chicaba was born into the Ewe tribe in the Gold Coast of Africa, the collective of countries now called Benin, Togo, and Ghana. Chicaba is both a title and a name, meaning "golden child," "she who brings the gold," or "she who enlightens the people." She was born to bring forth the transcendental gold in those she touches. "Golden child" referred to the precious metal, the sun and, on the sacred level, to the Christened, the awakened Christ consciousness, and the higher consciousness within all beings.

The Ewe trace their prehistoric origins to an area in modern-day Japan.[3] From there, they migrated to the East African continent to the area known as Khemet, which is now collectively known as Egypt, Sudan, and Ethiopia. The Ewe people then moved southwest across the continent to the Gold Coast.[4]

The source text of Chicaba's life, *Compendio de la Vida Ejemplar de la Venerable Madre Sor Teresa Juliana de Santo Domingo* [Compendium of the Exempla-

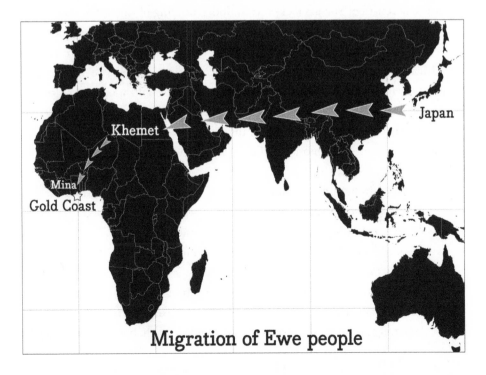

Migration of Ewe people

ry Life of the Venerable Mother Sister Teresa Juliana de Santo Domingo], was written by Father Juan Carlos Miguel de Paniagua, and it begs the reader to buy the slave trope—a happy and pious slave/nun/healer/servant. He referred to her people as worshipers of Lucifer. In Catholicism and Christian theology, Lucifer has oft been conflated with Satan—but Lucifer actually refers to the morning star, and this star is the planet Venus. Visually, Venus orbits the sun within Earth's orbit; and, given the time of year and one's location on Earth, it is either the first or last visible celestial body of the night. This synchronizes with a primary concept of Ewe cosmogony, that the supreme deity encompass-es the sky. The Ewe name for the creator is Mawu-Sogbo Lisa, which means "that which is greater than man:" the vastness of the sky, and along with it, constant change.[5] Chicaba was born into a culture of people who oriented themselves cosmologically—through the heavens—and intimately connected themselves to the sky, the Earth, and the sea, on the continuum of universal life and their places within it.

The Ewe people carried their cosmogony in their migration from Khemet to Mina. It is important to note here that Eurocentric scholars are quick to conflate the Ewe, Igbo, and Yoruba traditions to expand their points of view about Chicaba's spiritual life. To cast Chicaba's Ewe culture as derived from or a syncretism of Yoruba lacks a vital understanding of who is the shaper and not the shaped. As outlined in *The Story of the Ancient Ewe Language,* there is a very clear lineage of understanding the carrying of Khemetic culture to West Africa. Eurocentric scholars miss this out of erroneous belief that the people of modern day *Egypt* are in any way related to the civilization and culture of people who built the pyramids, the Khemetic people. *Egypt* and *Egyptology* are constructs of racism used to detach the African people from whom and what they come from—the most prolific works and wonders that humankind has ever created.

Chicaba, in her life as a slave to Teresa Juliana, was a Spanish house Ne-gress, and she was granted her freedom to join a nunnery only after the death of her owner. She was a faith healer who bestowed miracle healing on the downtrodden people to whom she gave her life in service. Today, we might classify her miracles as reiki or another energetic healing modality. For Chi-caba, this power was cloaked in Christianity. In eighteenth-century Catholic Spain, these gifts were credited to Jesus, who was using her as a vessel.

Attaching her spirit to a stripper is a fitting afterlife hobby for a woman who spent the predominant part of her life at a convent for fallen women, healing prostitutes and outcasts during the Spanish Inquisition. Imagine the stories of foul horrors endured by sex workers of the 1700s. Chicaba was a yoni (womb) healer who energetically healed the psyches and bodies of women who became commodities to survive. She restored the sacred and the sensual in women of the 1800s.

Piety

Slave owners taught Christian piety in order to use it as a weapon of behavior modification. It was a critical tool for crushing the minds, hearts, and consciousness of the enslaved. Piety is the first ingredient in the making of a saint and the breaking of a slave. Piety, or the performance of it, is essential to adapt to the trials and conditions of captivity, the means by which the oppressive culture vindicates itself as a savior of those "damned" to slavery. The repercussions reverberate to this day through generations of African-American Christianity.

The reality of Chicaba's life was grossly at odds with eighteenth-century Catholic Spain. Adapting mentally, physically, and psychically was imperative to her—and every slave's—survival. There was no psychological concept of well-being or acknowledgment of the reality of post-traumatic slave syndrome. My desire is to feel into Chicaba's heart as opposed to presenting the story as a way of fulfilling the agenda of Catholic sainthood. In telling her story through that lens, I aim to highlight the conflicting demands pulling on her from the time she was abducted to her post-mortal path to sainthood.

The path to sainthood has changed since Chicaba's passing, but the essence of it is this:

> *Servant of God*: In this stage, the faith of the subject
> and their servant's works are inspected.

> *Venerable/Heroic in Virtue*: The servant must
> be seen as fulfilling the virtues of faith, hope, and
> charity, and "the cardinal virtues of prudence, justice,
> fortitude and temperance, to a heroic degree."

> *Beatification/Blessed*: This stage requires that
> at least one proven miracle was performed by the
> servant; after their death, the miracle is usually
> a medical one, such as spontaneous healing. The

direct communication with God, or "beatific vision," is
confirmed. Once beatified, the Venerable title advances
to "Blessed." The servant is believed to be "worthy"
of residing in heaven and is then able to intervene on
the behalf of those who pray to them for aid. They are
also given an official day of celebration in their resident
parish.

Sainthood: Canonization requires the confirmation that
at least two proven miracles were performed after the
servant's passing. The servant is given an official feast
day, churches can be built in their name, and they can be
openly celebrated.[6]

Chicaba's petition for sainthood has remained in the limbo of "venerable"
since she was declared such in 2006.[7] Beatification gives permission for the
servant to act as an intercessor for those who pray to her. Chicaba's body was
exhumed by local townspeople and robbed for relics; this might be part of the
cause for her venerable status to be in limbo. For Catholics, this indicates that a
cult around her had arisen.[8] In the petitioning process, this concern about cult
formation is grounds for denial of sainthood.

It is important to note—and to keep in mind throughout the story—that the
only surviving primary source on Chicaba's life is derived from an oral history
given to Father Juan Carlos Miguel de Paniagua when she was around sixty
years old, long after she was enslaved by a culture she'd been learning to survive
in since she was ten years old. Trauma, memory, and politics greatly color the
narrative she offered Father Juan Carlos. His objective was to record Chicaba's hagiography with the goal of attaining her sainthood—not necessarily to
faithfully transcribe her actual thoughts, even if she were actually comfortable
enough to share honestly with him. We might think of him as a PR agent who
would spin his client's story to influence the Vatican to grant her sainthood. The
argument for sainthood has to be so strong that the text will stand the test of
time—there existed a waiting period of at least five years after Chicaba's death,
coupled with the unknowable factor of how long Father Juan Carlos would be
alive to speak on her behalf.

Chicava the Second

Chicava HoneyChild. That's me. The double entendre was inadvertent...

Golden Child, Honey Child. I came up with the name before knowing the meaning of Chicaba. HoneyChild is a southern phrase used as a term of endearment and sometimes applied to *loose* women. HoneyChild was a popular term in the 1970s, and I wanted to hear it in popular vernacular again. I remember hearing the phrase on *Sanford & Son* and *The Flip Wilson Show* and then echoed by my aunts and uncles. Older men often say to me, "You know what that means, don't cha, baby?" It's that sweet, dripping hotness of Pam Grier or my Aunt Barbara to which I'm giving my unique embodiment. These names together root me in both the African and the African American while expressing the integration of my spiritual and sensual beings.

I became Chicava during a time of profound spiritual growth. I was living in Los Angeles and engrossed in my spiritual community, Agape International, a trans-denominational community based in Culver City. My dance practice was blossoming as a member of the dance ensemble, Movement of Agape. After an Episcopalian upbringing, I had finally found a soul home with space for all my facets and fascinations—the metaphysical, quantum physics, and the roots of Khemetic culture. I realize I needed the sensual empowerment of burlesque right at that moment, because dating in LA sucked, especially in contrast to my New York life, and being one of thousands of no-name actors didn't help. My beauty needed affirmation and celebration. Pursuing an acting career in LA involved a variety of psychological strategies to meet white, normative expectations. The portrayals of black people and the psychological maneuvering required of black actors are well documented in such films as *Hollywood Shuffle*, which echo the pious slave narrative.

The work I've had to do on my psyche, my worth, and that of those I teach and entertain demands a way to celebrate with self-determined sovereignty. Self-determination is the precedent to self-actualization. Beyond the realms of political, economic, social, and sexual equality is a soulful need for fulfillment and actualization. From this place of self-ownership, a woman is in a much better position to make choices that take advantage of the work of the feminist movement. I am interested in the spiritual evolution of women through the creation of processes, practices, and experiences that assist in their physical, emotional, mental and spiritual integration. Those that lead us back to the core of ourselves and are nestled in the source of all creation.

Feminine sovereignty is my prime directive, both as it relates to developing it within myself and to creating a working method for the next level of feminism, which is based on spiritual teachings like the Science of Mind movement (SOM), the channeled teachings of Germane,[9] Taoist sacred sexuality and tantric practices, women's studies, and feminist movements. From the SOM perspective, as we develop from a state of victim consciousness to creator consciousness, our ability to recognize that we are physically transforming our world expands and shifts our reality. The teachings of Germane on sovereignty discerns rights from privileges and civil from common law. Women's studies and the waves of feminist movements provide a point of departure for this larger work, and the study of sacred sexuality, physicality, and energy places that work in women's bodies.

Thus, Chicava the stripper channels Chicaba the nun.

Daddy's Girls

My father got in trouble that night. My mother was fuming as we sat in the CU Boulder ballroom watching him deliver a speech. I felt special, though. I wasn't quite sure what a Mohegan was, other than an American Indian, and I didn't know what it meant to be the last one. I just knew my daddy made reference to me when he said, "And there's my last Mohegan." Everyone in the room looked at me. I wasn't hard to spot. I was the only black kid in the room, and by then, at six or so, I had come to enjoy being Boulder-famous as the mayor's daughter. In the car, my mother angrily criticized him for making such a comment in front of white people—she didn't care what his intentions were. I understood it differently, though. For me, it was about the pride he took in knowing that somehow, in my way, I would carry his vision forward for another generation as a surviving Mohegan.

At his funeral, his dear friend recounted a story of him seeing me off to college while she was at the house for a meeting with him. He said to her, "Everyone deserves someone in their life who thinks they are perfect, [and] for me that's Roslyn, my baby girl—she thinks I am perfect."

In my imagination, the bond Chicaba had with her father was like what my father and I shared. However, Chicaba's father would never see his baby girl grow into womanhood. Born in 1676 in the Gold Coast of Africa—the land now called Ghana—she was like the mayor's kid as the daughter of an Ewe tribal King in Mina, West Africa. She didn't remember her father's name, I suspect, because she never called him by it, but she did remember her mother's, Abar, and her brothers, Juanchipiter, Ensu, and Joaquin.[10]

Chicaba, the golden child, was the baby of the family, and she was considered to be a radiant gift to her family and community. Her gifts of reflection and spiritual connection were recognized early on, so much so that it aroused the envy of her brothers. She told Father Juan Carlos that she quelled her brothers' jealousy by telling them that she knew life had something different in store for her, and that she would not usurp their ascension to the throne.

Chicaba had a propensity for wandering off on her own to commune spiritually and play with her imaginary friends. On one of these wandering, she reported seeing the Blessed Mary and baby Jesus in the sky, and following this vision, she determined that she was to marry Him. This imagery would have been far removed from that which aligned with her cultural upbringing, and had she not expressed it, she would have been vulnerable to the Portuguese and Catholic missionaries, who by then, around 1685, would have made their presence known on the shores of her people.

Her abduction into slavery around age nine was foreshadowed in the weeks before, when her father's enemies kidnapped her. The kidnappers might have attempted to sell her off to slave traders as an act of aggression against her father. Her father's army successfully brought her back to safety. Once back at the village, she was watched vigilantly by her mother for four days. On the fifth day, she wandered off on her own and was captured by Portuguese slavers and taken from her homeland.[11] In her hagiography, it is recorded as a fateful and exciting event whereby "white and perky young" man of light *uplifted* Chicaba onto the ship, a shockingly distorted perspective of kidnapping and enslavement.[12]

Chicaba's Middle Passage

Chicaba became one of 600,000 Africans abducted into slavery by Portuguese slavers between 1675 and 1700—one of 24,000 human beings taken from the west coast of Africa and their loved ones each year.[13] Her middle passage was not the arduous length of three to six months, as was the case for Africans kidnapped to the Americas. She was taken to the island of Sao Tomé, off West Africa, where she was baptized as Teresa in a mass christening of newly captured West African people. Then, an eight- to ten-day voyage to Seville ensued, which forced her into a horror story that she would come to associate with all Protestants. She was likely raped, suffered from dehydration, disease, and abuse to the point where she attempted to throw herself overboard to a certain death rather than face the unknown before her.[14] She was stopped short of carrying out her leap overboard by the return of the vision of Blessed Mary and Jesus, which provided her with faith that all would be well.

Life with the Marquis and Marquesa

There are varying accounts of how she came to the house of Antonio Sebastián de Toledo and his wife Juliana Teresa, the marquis and the marquesa of Mancera, once she arrived in Spain. By one account, Portuguese slave traders thought her jewelry and attire signified noble status in her community, so she was gifted to King Charles II. The gifting of kidnapped Africans of royal lineage to European royalty was common practice among the ruthless, conniving thieves who made humanity their commodity. King Charles presented her to the Marquesa Juliana Teresa Portocarrero of Mancera, who additionally baptized Chicaba as Teresa Juliana.[15] By another account, she was purchased solely by the marquesa, who was the duchess of Arcos prior to becoming the second wife of the marquis.[16]

The marquis had been viceroy of Mexico and during his tenure there, and the savant Juana Inés de la Cruz lived in his court as a lady-in-waiting to his first wife, Vicereine Leonor Carreto. Dubbed the "tenth muse," Juana was celebrated for her brilliant writing, her religious devotion, and the breadth of her scientific knowledge. At age seventeen, the marquis had her "tested" by theologians, scientists, poets, and others, an action that was on par with a modern-day visit from the Mensa Society or ESP experts to meet a gifted child whose acclaim has spread. Her success at these trials increased her fame, which continues to this day.[17]

Though the marquis showed some ambivalence about slavery, he did not share the same confidence in Chicaba that his wife did. He thought her to be unstable and possibly fraudulent. I take this to signal that he was probably a racist who believed that Africans were inferior, so he was not moved by Chicaba's radiance or gifts. Thus, he required Chicaba to face different tests of verification then those of Juana of Mexico. Chicaba was subjected to inquisition, tied in restraints, and exorcised. The evaluation committee of Chicaba's trials included Protestants. The costumes of the era distinguished people based on their countries and religious affiliations, and the Protestants were Portuguese. She remembered their distinct dress and customs, and their presence triggered terrifying memories of what had happened to her in the hands of the Portuguese Protestant slavers during her middle passage. She pleaded that they be kept away from her. Her reaction supports the assertion that she was likely raped during her voyage from Ewe village to Portugal. By some miracle, she survived her inquisition and the injustice to her humanity and spirit and remained in the house of the marquis and marquesa of Mancera.

Marquis Mancera was inclined to seek the advice of leading men to define the ultimate nature of the skills of their "adopted." So he did in Mexico with Juana Ines, and later, so he did with Teresa Juliana, but here the similarities end. The "evaluation committee" could not be more different: for the Mexican will be a committee of excellence, and for the African, an inquisitorial committee. His thin margin of confidence about the kindly nature of the black disappears as soon as Teresa shows signs of mental instability.[18] The marquesa appears to have been against slavery generally, although was not by definition an abolitionist, given that the term has uniquely nineteenth-century-American connotations and context. She felt a great affection for Chicaba. and recognizing her as a bright and spiritual child, she invested her time in Chicaba's education, teaching her to read and write, as well as showing her the manners of courtly women and the ways of a Catholic woman. Chicaba's spirituality would continue to develop, and her keepers would accept her piety, while she endured a life of double consciousness, as defined by W.E.B Dubois in *The Souls of Black Folk*.[19]

> *As a member of the retinue of this religious aristocratic household,*
> *the young slave habituated herself to the piousness of her mistress*
> *and developed an intense spiritual life that in time became her key*
> *to freedom.*[20]

From what I perceive of Chicaba's nature, those open to her gifts experienced a great peace and an abiding connection to the Holy Spirit (from a Catholic purview) in her presence. They recognized her profound level of spiritual development. Had it been Marquesa Juliana's choice, Chicaba would have joined them at every meal, as she saw her as more of a daughter than a servant. She became Chicaba's spiritual director, which included daily prayers together and the reading of scripture. The marquesa inherently knew that Chicaba was more attuned and spiritually advanced than she was, and Chicaba soon became her spiritual counselor. In addition to overseeing her education, Juliana allowed Chicaba private time for spiritual devotion and contemplation. Juliana used her authority to grant Chicaba her freedom upon her death.

The favors bestowed on Chicaba by Juliana were deeply resented by the rest of the servants in the house. Her seventeen years in the house of Mancera were comprised of much spiritual contemplation, but they were punctuated with attacks by house staff and slaves. Her studies and her time with her confessors were routinely interrupted. The housekeeper was especially filled with jealousy and loathing, routinely beating her. Attempts were made to poison Chicaba. At one point, a Muslim slave from Turkey came to the house, and the girl refused pressure to convert to Christianity. Though the Turk was gravely ill, she attempted to stab Chicaba. Soon after the unsuccessful attempt on Chicaba's life, the girl died, and it was Chicaba to whom she made confession and conversion to Catholicism before passing over.

One of the worst offenses was committed at the fountain of Retiro. Retiro, now a public park in Madrid, at the time was reserved for the king's court. Chicaba and other servants were in the park for the day when she mysteriously fell into the fountain. Although the record suggests that she was unable to swim, it's also possible that she could not swim in the roughly fifteen or twenty pounds of soaking-wet clothes that would have constituted her eighteenth-century garments. The girls from the house ran from the fountain in a fright. A gentleman observed them fleeing, and after checking to see what the disturbance was all about, he retrieved Chicaba from the water. In a legendary version, it's said that the devil entered the spirit of one of her fellows and knocked her into the water, as opposed to an actual person trying to drown her. Her rescuer was a mythic man of light (i.e., white). He pulled Chicaba from the fountain before immediately disappearing, and she emerged from the plunge completely dry.[21] Catholicism is colorful.

A Marriage Proposal: The Chance to Go Home

The transatlantic slave trade had not yet hit the height of its despicable rapacity when Chicaba was abducted. By 1700, when Chicaba was twenty-four years old, the number of African people savagely abducted into slavery would escalate from 24,000 a year to 60,000. Indeed, her family and the ways of the Ewe people were devastated as the years passed. I'm sure that each day, she prayed for her family and her people, wondering about their fates. In this year came a day that answered the questions tormenting her mind about the circumstances of her family and community.

In France, an Ewe slave, who was seen as exceptional in the same way that Chicaba was—for his royal African lineage—lived in the court of Louis XIV. His slave name was Juan Francisco, and he was Chicaba's uncle. He'd heard of the Ewe princess in the house of Marquis Mancera and was quite certain it was Chicaba. Juan Francisco negotiated his freedom and a guarantee of passage back to Mina in exchange for becoming France's cohort in the region, becoming their native on the ground. He set his mind to bringing Chicaba home with him as his bride and queen. According to Baltasar Fra Molinero, "it seemed in France's best interests that Juan Francisco be returned to his court, [and] he in turn would corroborate with the French, their ships, merchants, ensuring expansion of the kingdom's interest."[22]

A joyous reunion ensued when Juan Francisco entered the house of Mancera—the two had found each other after so many years of tumult. Juan Francisco told Chicaba of her family's fate: her father, mother, and brothers, and most of her community had indeed converted to Christianity before their deaths. By what means they met their demise was not clear. It's not hard to guess, however, because slavers were dismantling a culture, which required the murder of leaders as the European colonialists gained ascendancy and domination over the people and land. The people she loved and the way of life from which she had been cleaved had come to a brutal end.

The Marquis's position in Spain's monarchy allowed him close ties with Louis XIV's court. Aware of the advantages the Protestant Dutch and British kingdoms had as slavers, and the progress of their enterprises in the new land of America, he agreed to the marriage plans crafted by Juan Francisco and Louis XIV's court. The marquis welcomed Chicaba's marriage to her uncle and their return to Mina, despotically attentive to the fact that the political union would link Spanish and French interests in the region. Thankfully, the Marquesa Juliana had some control in affairs of Chicaba. I believe she advocated for Chicaba's sovereignty to make this decision of her own counsel. Chicaba took three days to contemplate the marriage proposal and subsequent reunion with her homeland. She'd been informed that her family was dead and was being advised of the destruction of the life into which she had been born, so she was understandably wary of returning. Aware of her trepidation before her time of contemplation ended, Juan Francisco attempted to kidnap Chicaba and take her back to Mina against her will, but the plan was thwarted. This trauma solidified Chicaba's resolve to marry the white man of her vision, now known to her as (white) Jesus, and to become a nun.

When she reflected on her life, she confided to Father Paniagua that she remained torn by her decision to not return home with Juan Francisco. Though her life in the Mancera house was filled with treachery, the uncertainty of Juan Francisco's scheme was daunting. Heartbreak would have greeted her in Mina, which had been ravaged by slavers. She would have become a tool, a despot for the French monarchy and their malevolence. Staying, I believe, was a wise and measured decision.

Racism and Refusal: Becoming a Nun

Teresa Juliana (Chicaba) is now my maid and slave, I set her free, promising fifty ducats a year for her expenses. [22]

—Juliana Teresa Portocarrero, Marquesa of Mancera

The marquesa placed a knight, Diego Gamarra, in charge of the search to find a convent for Chicaba. Racism prevailed many times, and she was refused entry into numerous convents. One convent was willing to accept her were it not for the protestations of a noblewoman cloistered there: "LA NEGRA HERE OVER MY DEAD BODY."[23] Hurt and humiliated by the three years of constant rejections, Diego assured her "that [her] wishes [would] be fulfilled."

Finally, Diego traveled to Salamanca and met with the mother of a house of Dominican Sisters of the Third Order. The Third Order of the Catholic convents is made up of lay and ordained women who are committed to living a simple life, professing of sins, and wearing the habit. It is hierarchically far below the nuns of the Second Order, which is comprised of cloistered nuns affiliated with men: the priests, friars, and monks of the First Order.[24] The Dominican's values emphasized being in the community, having an intimate and personal relationship with Jesus Christ, and being open to mystical experiences. It's possible these values syncretized with the remaining beliefs of her African childhood in ways known only to Chicaba's heart.

The Dominican Sisters of the Third Order of Saint Mary Magdalene in Salamanca, founded in 1548, focused on converting and cloistering "regretful fallen women" and prostitutes. Perhaps the *Magdalene* name was not coincidental.[26] On November 9, 1703, the bishop of Salamanca, Francisco Calderon de la Barca, "with some repugnance for the matter" was bestowed with Chicaba's fate by the marquesa's butler, D. Andrés Bárcena.[27] The bishop was in it for the money, and this is clearly recorded, "being of big utility of the community and increase of the revenues of the above mentioned convent."[28] Her dowry was substantial enough to make her acceptance worth their while, but the wealth she brought to Convent of Santa Mary Magdalene did not grant her status of the bishop's gratitude. Bishop Calderon showed his disdain by admitting Chicaba only as a tertiary and servant. By denying her entry as a novice, she was also denied a mentor in her religious life and studies. Eight months into her residency at Mary Magdalene, Bishop Calderon acquiesced and initiated Chicaba into the novitiate.

On June 29, 1704, she finally married the white man of her visions by taking her vows. The ceremony was marked by a mystical experience; although only she could see them, spirits of recently deceased nuns joined the chorus of the living to celebrate her.[29] She knew they were different from the others because she saw no hypocrisy in their expressions. In addition to her interactions with beings on the other side, she reportedly had profound energetic healing talents and the ability to levitate. It's worth pondering whether these are veiled accounts of Chicaba encountering ancestors or spirit archetypes from her homeland. This is a part of her spirituality that she would have kept to herself, especially after having sustained inquisition and exorcism as a child in the house of Marquis and Marquesa Mancera.

Chicaba's so-called freedom in the convent was wretched and definitively harsher than the conditions of her life as a slave in the Mancera house. Lower than the laywomen of the convent, she was not allowed to eat in the dining hall, sleep in the dormitory, or be admitted to the choir. She slept in the infirmary, where she cared for prostitutes and the sick and downtrodden people of the community. The only surviving poem written by her uses the framework of a polygamist marriage to Christ as a metaphor for the inequities of racism she endured at the convent. This poem, as a complaint of a Christian woman from Africa, exposed the idea of individual marriage to

Christ as absurd, rejected the social division of labor in her convent, and most importantly, asserted her right as a bride of Christ to pray and contemplate like the other nuns could. She wanted a world where all people shared equally in spiritual communion and physical labor.[30]

> *Oh Jesus, where are you gone?*
> *I cannot stand a moment Without seeing you.*
> *Oh, Jesus of my soul,*
> *Where are you gone?*
> *It seems you are not coming back*
> *And you are lost.*
> *Oh, Jesus, what shall I say?*
> *If you go out with other women,*
> *What shall I do?*
> *I will wail, I will cry,*
> *'Till I see God,*
> *and if not, if not,*
> *I will die of love.*

In these desolate moments, she found a new love—not that of Jesus Christ but of the people she served. She would come to be known as Teresa, Sister Juliana of Santo Domingo, Bold of Penance. She had a special place in her heart for the marginalized. The power of her prayer brought miraculous healing to those she looked after. Not only did her dowry keep the house of Mary Magdalene afloat, so too did the offerings she received. Chicaba was the money-maker in a convent created for hookers, and she paid many a sister's fees to the church. Through her generosity and compassion, the community she served uplifted her—she was no longer disgraced or dismissed for her ethnicity. For Chicaba, "each exclusion and insult is followed by a mystic episode in which God or one of His saints to exalt her above all the other nuns, in contrast to the humiliation received."[31]

Marketing a Saint

On the night of December 6, 1748, at the age of seventy-two, Chicaba shuffled off the mortal coil and died of palsy, which today we would probably call a stroke. She was quietly buried, and few people attended the ceremony.

When news of her passing spread through Salamanca, a great mourning took over the town. Her tomb was raided, and her personal belongings became relics: rosaries were pulled apart, her clothes were shredded, her papers were scattered—everything Chicaba had touched became immensely valuable. Whether in response to her fame or in praise for how she gave of herself, the convent of Saint Mary Magdalene commissioned two portraits of Chicaba for veneration.

She spent her last days recounting her life to Father Paniagua, who would write her funeral oration and subsequent hagiography in pursuit of her sainthood. Their objectives in the recording of her life are contradictory—Paniagua's marketing of Chicaba's life emphasizes the trope of a slave's piety along with the Vatican's demand that her enslavement be viewed as a measure of divine providence. Chicaba desired to be worthy of veneration through her African humanity, not in spite of it. I believe Chicaba's spiritual richness and depth is rooted in her cultural background. Father Paniagua's hagiography is the last-remaining, authenticated source document of Chicaba's life, and it is a hybrid of her memories and his fashioning of her story to prove her worthiness for sainthood. Hers is a personal story of syncretism, and the deific energies of her birth culture were deeply embedded in it. However, she kept them to herself at psychological cost and veiled the tales of her life and mystical experiences to be acceptable to those who had power over her.

Identity: What it all Means

Positive racial identity, much like the concept of well-being, is a fairly modern idea to the descendants of slaves. Believing that one's captor and oppressors are superior is a nearly unavoidable byproduct of slavery. If Godliness is measured in might and force, those with the most weapons and the most means would seem to be closer to God and therefore more beloved. This distortion positioned the slave traders, their enablers, and their customers to alter the destiny of trillions of people and generations of families over the course of 600 years, and it set the warped religious, moral, cultural, and societal standards that we are just beginning to question and reject. Acquiescing to these beliefs placed the enslaved in a self-perpetuating quandary of being lesser human beings in need of salvation from their barbaric ways.

The journey of Chicaba's life restores each of us: I restore her each time her name is spoken in the arenas of joy, sexiness, theater, and women's healing. She restores my ability to generate joy and faith in fulfilling my responsibility to share my gifts and teachings. She bequeathed her name to an ecdysiast, a creature that transforms like a caterpillar blossoming into a butterfly, a snake reviving each time she sloughs off an old skin to inhabit a new one. As a part of global re-knowing of her name and story, my perspective of Chicaba's life flies in the face of many an academic, nun, or devotee of Catholicism. And it should. I, as an artist, mystic, and keeper of the old traditions, have the freedom to speak of her life as a channel and as I intuit it.

Chicaba the First and I, Chicava the Second, offer the dichotomy of a nun and a stripper who need each other. Chicaba and Chicava are both real-life fictions—real because we are actual women, and fiction because both of us exist as lore—one as history told by another's pen and the other existing in fragments of time on a stage. Facing trauma, madness, and bending through time, Chicaba broke my heart and gave me dance. I am a tale that spins itself, a living legend of the stories told by my body and those to whom I pass the torch. I am seeking safety, intellectual freedom, sexual and creative expansion, and most of all, sovereignty over the creation that is myself. I hope I bring her spirit joy, not just as an individual woman but as the against-all-odds perpetual joy of the African woman.

What is piety on this shambolic path?[32] For the abducted, raped, renamed, enslaved, stabbed, beaten, nearly drowned, socially shunned, and forced to live among the infirm? Perhaps true piety is rejoicing in the fantastical orchestration of your very existence. The simple gratitude of being in a story of survival and subjection to a Eurocentric rendition of a savior in whose name Chicaba was trapped—which stole her mother, her father, her brothers, her community, and her identity—in order to save her. Is piety being able to give love when it has eluded you?

And yet, still not beatified. Why should the Vatican further rule over Chicaba in her afterlife to decide whether her transcendent spirit makes a proper guide? They are not worthy of her. 🪶

> *Here lies the chaste, the pure, the innocent and mortified one; in her soul a*
> *dove, if in her body black; black, but beautiful; born a queen, died a slave,*
> *but instead of a slave, a queen, and a queen because she ruled over herself,*
> *and because she ruled over herself, still a queen...*[33]

CAST OF CHARACTERS
(So many similar names)

CHICABA, SOR TERESA JULIANA OF SANTO DOMINGO, referred to as Chicaba

CHICAVA HONEYCHILD, author, referred to as Chicava

THE MARQUESA JULIANA TERESA, referred to as Juliana or the marquesa

THE MARQUIS OF MANCERA, referred to as the Marquis

JUAN FRANSISCO, Chicaba's uncle, referred to as Juan Francisco

FATHER JUAN CARLOS MIGUEL DE PANIGUA, Chicaba's biographer, referred to as Father Paniagua or Paniagua

---

To every woman that had to forsake the Goddess to survive the patriarchy.

Under the Cover of Breeches and Bayonet: The Story of Deborah Sampson

By Jessie Serfilippi

Deborah Sampson paces the length of her room in Middleborough, Massachusetts. She stops in front of her bed and stares down at the array of clothing gathered there. Today, she is trying on male clothing for the first time.

She tugs on linen stockings and breeches that hug her thighs in an unfamiliar way. She buttons the waistcoat that she spun and sewed herself and marvels at the way it fits atop her bound breasts. She slips the linen coat over her arms and admires its flare over her hips. She laces her brown leather shoes. She takes a few steps, amazed at how much easier it is to walk without a petticoat. She grabs a worn straw hat off her bed and places it on cropped, brown locks, adjusting it so a shadow falls over her face, partially obscuring her Roman nose and sharp jawline.

She opens the door and steps out into the crisp night air, hoping it will ease the apprehension that has gnawed at her all morning. She juts out her chin with the confidence she's seen men wear throughout her young life—the type that says "I belong here. I have nothing to fear."

Just as her nerves start to subside, she notices another figure walking on the path. She catches sight of his face in the moonlight and sucks in a sharp breath. The man is her neighbor, William Bennett. They pass each other, sharing only a nod, but Deborah swears a hint of recognition flashes through his eyes. She darts into the woods, the need to escape detection propelling her forward. She doesn't feel the branches and brambles as they scratch her. She doesn't worry about where she's going. She just goes.

When she finally stops, she realizes that she has no idea where she is. Although she'd rather run off and never return to Middleborough again, she needs to know if her disguise will pass muster in the daylight. Her nervousness heightens as she gets closer to town, which is much busier now that the sun has risen.

As she passes a sea of familiar faces, she waits for someone to point at her, to reveal her true identity. But she makes it back to her room undetected. Once she's safely behind closed doors, the truth dawns on her: the neighbor had not recognized her.

Deborah Sampson has just pulled off her first masquerade.

⌁

*D*eborah Sampson was born on December 17, 1760 in Plympton, Massachusetts, not far from Boston. Born three years before the end of the French and Indian War, Deborah came of age during a time of disdain over British taxes and the British occupation of Boston, and when farmers, merchants, and schoolteachers turned into militiamen. If regular folks could be soldiers, why not a headstrong Massachusetts girl?

Although Deborah still remains relatively unknown to most Americans, it's not for lack of attempts at telling her story. Her original biographer, Herman Mann (1771–1833), interviewed Deborah for the first version of *The Female Review: Life of Deborah Sampson, the Female Soldier of the War of Revolution*, and published it with her approval in 1797. He also wrote the address she used during her later orations and sought her permission to publish a revised version of the biography in the 1820s.[1] She agreed, but only under the circumstance that it not be published until after her death, suggesting that she was not entirely pleased with her portrayal in the biography.[2] It's not difficult to understand why she might have been unhappy with Mann's biography: it has falsehoods in the telling—most glaringly that she fought at the Battle of Yorktown—in order to sensationalize her story.

These fabrications have been perpetuated in many nineteenth- and twentieth-century retellings of her life. It wasn't until Alfred F. Young (1925–2012) published *Masquerade: The Life and Times of Deborah Sampson, Continental Soldier* in 2004 that the many myths Mann started at the close of the eighteenth century were corrected through thorough research. Because of its return to primary sources, it is Young's book that has brought me closer to her true story and served as my go-to guide through Deborah's life.

༶

A TV show called *Liberty's Kids* first introduced a nine-year-old me to Deborah Sampson. I was enamored by this program. Every afternoon I rushed off the bus, grabbed a snack, and plopped down on the floor in front of the TV, setting the channel to 11. I quivered with excitement as I waited for the familiar theme song—a very 2000s combination of R&B, country, and rap—to start.

An animated series about the American Revolution that aired on PBS from September of 2002 to April of 2003, *Liberty's Kids* follows two fictional teenage reporters, Sarah and James, who write for Benjamin Franklin's Philadelphia-based *Pennsylvania Gazette*, and a French youth, Henri. Made up of forty episodes, each about twenty minutes in length, the series covers both familiar and forgotten figures of the Revolutionary Period. Episode 34, "Deborah Samson: Soldier of the Revolution," tells the story of its namesake.[3]

Voiced by Whoopi Goldberg, Deborah Sampson is shown in her Massachusetts light infantry uniform with her light brown hair cut short. She has tan skin, and lively blue eyes. She enters the episode by rescuing Sarah, who is traveling through the area in a horse-drawn carriage, from Tory gunfire. Deborah explains that Tories still occupy parts of New York and aid the British by attacking American troops when and where they least expect it. Although the episode compresses events that spanned Deborah's nearly two years of service into a few days, it manages to stay mostly true to her story.

This young woman risked her life in search of agency. She was exactly the kind of woman I idolized as a child—someone who fought for what she believed in despite the social barriers placed upon her. She also fit the dictionary definition of deliverance as someone who sought liberation in many different ways. Deborah Sampson didn't wait to be rescued. She brought about her own deliverance.

༶

Deborah Sampson was born into a family that had been in Massachusetts since the Pilgrims landed on Plymouth Rock. Although she was descended from original Plymouth Pilgrims and a former governor of Massachusetts, any wealth her family once had was long gone by the time she was born.[4] Deborah's father tried to support his family through farming, but he was unable to turn a profit.[5] By the time she was five years old, her father had vanished. She was told he was lost at sea while working on a ship, but he'd actually run away to Maine, where he started a new family.[6]

Unable to support her children on her own, Deborah's mother had no choice but to send them to live with relatives, which Alfred Young, Deborah's primary modern biographer, describes as the "eighteenth-century way in New England of providing for dependent children."[7] Deborah was shuffled through the homes of different relatives and neighbors until the age of ten, when she began the next chapter of her life: indentured servitude.

Around 1770, Deborah was indentured to Jeremiah and Susannah Thomas, heads of a well-known family in Middleborough.[8] Working on the Thomases' farm brought stability to her young life and insured she'd have food, clothing, and shelter for as long as she was with the family. Deborah also got to spend time around other children, since the Thomas family was huge. She picked up a wide array of domestic skills, such as weaving, sewing, and yarn spinning, and helped around the Thomases' farm, where she learned about livestock care, planting, and harvesting.[9]

Bound to the Thomas family until she was eighteen,[10] not only did she live in a society that ranked girls and women as second-class citizens, but she also lost all of what little freedom she had prior to indentured servitude. This included the freedom to do the one thing she most wanted: go to school.

Thanks to the cousin who'd cared for Deborah in her youth, she could already read and write, and that was more than enough of an education as far as Jeremiah Thomas, who did not believe in educating girls, was concerned.[11] She requested permission to attend school with the Thomas boys, but Jeremiah ignored her pleas.[12] But even as a young girl, Deborah's well of inner strength was astoundingly deep. Denied the right to physically attend school, she convinced the Thomas boys to lend her their schoolbooks and spent her precious free time reading and learning everything she possibly could.[13]

Her persistence paid off. At nineteen, Deborah was chosen by the town board to serve as a teacher in Middleborough, Massachusetts.[14] The following year, she continued in this position in the nearby town of Sharon.[15] Teaching wasn't considered much of a career at the time, but it certainly wasn't the only thing Deborah did. She was also a weaver—a job which, like teaching, both men and women performed.[16]

She continued as a teacher and weaver until 1781, when the twenty-one-year-old decided that she wanted more from life. She was what was known as a "masterless woman," meaning that she had no husband or father to answer to;[17] she could do exactly as she pleased. Deborah knew what she wanted: more freedom. And she also knew, masterless or not, that she was not going to find it as a woman.

That is why on May 23, 1782, Deborah Sampson stood in front of the enlistment register holding a quill dipped in gleaming black ink.[18] With a scratch of the pen across the parchment, Robert Shurtliff was born.

In 1782, it wasn't all that difficult to get into the Continental Army, which was running low on draftees.[19] Morale had dropped because the war was in its seventh year, and Massachusetts had to resort to a draft in order to get enough recruits. The bar for entry was at an all-time low: there was no physical exam and no need to provide any identifying information.[20] Deborah joined fifty or so men, who also signed three-year enlistment contracts, and who, under the command of Captain Eliphalet Thorp, marched from Worcester to West Point.[21] During this march, she first glimpsed the Hudson River Valley, where she would spend the majority of her time as Robert Shurtliff.

Although the American victory at Yorktown in 1781 was the last major battle of the war, there was still a lot of fighting happening in the Southern colonies and in what is known today as New York's Westchester County but was then known as "neutral ground." Stuck between American-held Albany and British-occupied New York City, neutral ground was a lawless land. It was so dangerous that many of the occupants fled years before Deborah's regiment arrived on the scene, and those who remained could trust no one. They were subjected to roves of Tory raiders, referred to as cowboys, who roamed the forests and pillaged the farms and homes scattered throughout the region. They stole crops, livestock, and whatever other goods and valuables they could get their hands on. Patriots—or skinners, as they were called—were no better. Food was scarce. In this lawless land, there were few qualms about plundering the enemy, or anyone thought to be the enemy.

Robert Shurtliff and the rest of his regiment, a group of roughly twenty men, follow two Dutch boys to a cave, where Tory cowboys have stashed stores of food. Robert, accustomed to the thick darkness that envelops the Hudson Valley at nightfall, moves through it confidently, but he is mindful of keeping his steps as soft as possible. Amid a chorus of crickets, katydids, and peepers hidden throughout the swampland, he and his compatriots squat in the cool dampness of the cave and feast on the bacon, cheese, and honey they find there.

He has just finished off a slab of cheese when the crack of a gun and the shouts of the men stationed on guard cut through the night. He races to the entrance of the cave, where he can make out the shadows of men riding on horseback, the silhouettes of their bayoneted guns prompting him to ready and fire his own. He fires, reloads, fires. He watches as men fall from horseback and dashes toward an unmounted horse, climbs atop him, and chases the enemy out of the area.

Something drips down his forehead, and a sharp pain throbs in his shoulder as he clears the area of attackers. It is then that he touches a dirtied hand to his forehead and feels a warm liquid. Blood. He sucks in a quick breath as he places a hand on his shoulder and feels blood rushing from a small hole carved by a lead bullet lodged deep in his flesh.

Deborah Sampson reaches for her pistol. Death is more honorable than discovery, she reminds herself. But something stops her. By the light of campfire later that night, with the bullet still embedded in her shoulder, she pours alcohol into the wound. The agony and sting, she decides, are worth it, so long as she can continue to fight.

ᶜ

There is still much debate over where on her body Deborah was shot, or if she was shot at all. Popular theory claims she was shot in the thigh, but this seems to have been born from Mann's need to sensationalize Deborah's injury by placing it close to her groin.[22] If she was, in fact, shot anywhere, the likely place would be her shoulder. It's where she claimed to have been shot in the first draft of Mann's biography—the one with the fewest embellishments—and those who knew her never recalled her walking with a limp.[23] Some believe she might not have been injured at all, but as Alfred Young says, "we might find out if her grave in Sharon [Massachusetts] were opened. But this is a ghoulish, unnecessary prospect. It really does not matter."[24]

Even if she wasn't injured, *why* would she make up an injury? Is it proof that she fought? Did she put herself in danger just to feel free, to live without the societal confines of womanhood for nearly two years? Is it something undeniable, to which she can point and say, "This happened to me?" If she made it up, I understand. Evidence of a hard-fought battle—not a literal battle, but a cultural one—is rewarding. It's part of the reason why I write: to say, "This is proof of my suffering and my ability to overcome it," even if only momentarily. Whether in the form of a bullet embedded in a body or stories written late into the night, they serve the same function: tangible proof of deliverance.

⸎

Hamilton: An American Musical transformed my idea of deliverance. When I first got the album, I listened to the first act on repeat until I'd memorized it. It wasn't until a month later that I listened to the second act, which is when Hamilton's feat of deliverance comes into play.

Anyone who has listened to *Hamilton* can tell you that it is not just a musical. It's a way to connect with historical figures who are often made boring and stiff by school textbooks. It's a bridge between America's past and present. It redefines what it means to be an American citizen through an inclusiveness that, now, after seeing it masterfully done, seems so instinctual that it makes previous attempts at telling the founders' stories look dull. There is something overwhelmingly genuine about the way it portrays distant historical figures as living, breathing people—and the way it does this best is through song.

One of the most humanizing songs of the musical, and the one that focuses on the idea of deliverance, is "Hurricane." The song is performed when Hamilton's life begins to crumble. Metaphorically, he is in the eye of a hurricane as he recounts all of the traumas and difficulties he lived through and overcame as a boy and young man. He recalls how his writing talent moved him forward in life: a letter he wrote got him out of the Caribbean and to the American mainland; he captured Washington's attention during the American Revolution through his essays; and his love letters wooed his wife, Eliza, when they were courting. He lists these moments while trying to convince himself that writing the Reynolds Pamphlet is a good idea (it isn't).

It is these two lines in particular that changed my life: "And when my prayers to God were met with indifference / I picked up a pen, I wrote my own deliverance." When I heard these words, I was left speechless. All I could think was, "Yes, yes, yes." My own view of writing was revolutionized. My view of myself as a writer, as a person, was forever altered. It was the moment I realized that I didn't have to wait for anyone to save me. I hadn't been waiting. In fact, I'd been writing my way out the entire time.

I am constantly writing my own deliverance.

꙰

Robert Shurtliff sits on the floor of a dusty attic that is stuffy and hot during the day and drafty and cold at night. Richard Snow, his fellow light infantryman, lies a few feet away from him, sweating and shivering with fever.

The drunken guffaws of Tory cowboys drift up through the floorboards from the kitchen below, where the man of the house, Abraham Van Tassel, is gathered with his fellow raiders. Robert takes a calming breath. When he'd been stationed here to care for Richard Snow, Van Tassel had posed as a patriot, but as soon as he was alone with the two men, he shoved them in the attic, providing no food or medical care for Richard. Robert often fantasizes about what he would do to Van Tassel if he had him alone for just one moment.

Footsteps echo up the stairs. Robert clutches his gun, knuckles white from fear. He's outnumbered, and he knows it. If the Tories decide to rough him and Richard up, there's little he can do to stop them. But that doesn't mean he won't fight.

The footsteps stop at the top of the stairs, and the door slowly swings open.

"I brought you some food."

Robert nearly cries with relief as Mary Van Tassel, Abraham's teenage daughter, shuffles into the room carrying a worn tray filled with food and drink. "It is not much, but I hope it is of some aid."

"Mary," Robert says, waiting for the girl to look him in the eyes. "Thank you."

A blush rises to Mary's face as she nods in response, and she quickly takes her leave. Robert smiles as he listens to her soft footsteps retreat down the stairs, the image of her gentle round face lingering in his mind.

He already can't wait to see her again.

꙰

We cannot prove whether the preceding moment did or did not happen. However, it is known that Robert Shurtliff and Richard Snow stayed in the Van Tassel house until Richard succumbed to his fever.[25] It is very likely that Abraham Van Tassel's daughter took an interest in the young soldiers and helped them by secretly bringing them food and water.[26] And we know that after Richard's death, Deborah was angry. The Van Tassels, save for Mary, treated the two soldiers with no respect.[27] They had not provided anything beyond the most rudimentary shelter to them. If it weren't for Mary, who knows if they would have any gotten sustenance.

Unknown factors enter here. According to Herman Mann, Deborah asked to lead a raid on the Van Tassel house.[28] She strategically wanted to surround the home on a night when Tory cowboys were gathered there after a night of plundering so she could take the Tories hostage.[29] Her commander was reluctant, but eventually gave in and allowed Deborah to recruit a small group of men from her regiment.[30] Once she had her men, they set out for the Van Tassel homestead. But how would she know when the Tory cowboys would be there? That's where Mary Van Tassel and more suppositions come in.

According to Mann, before Robert left the Van Tassel homestead after Richard's death, he and Mary had a heart-to-heart.[31] They sat in Mary's room, sipped some wine, and even shared a kiss before Mary's mother called for her.[32] This relationship is key to the raid Deborah planned, for when she returned to the area with a small group of men a few weeks later, it was Mary she turned to for help. In Mann's telling of this story, Mary's role was essential to the success of the raid.

Mary was hesitant to aid Robert at first.[33] She was a patriot, but she still worried for her father's safety. Robert told Mary this was in her father's best interest because the war was nearly over, and it wouldn't be good for him or the family to remain loyalists after America was formally given its freedom.[34] Mary said she would help Robert under the condition that her father wouldn't be harmed.[35] Robert agreed and left her with the promise that he would return soon.

⁓

Deborah returns with men in the blue uniforms of the light infantry flanking her. She finds Mary in secret and confers with her before she returns to her men, who wait under the cover of wild bushes on the outskirts of the Van Tassel property. Deborah instructs them to stay hidden until she signals otherwise. Now, all they can do is lie in wait for the rumble of distant hoof beats, for the Tory cowboys to return from their latest raid.

The shouts of men soon fill the air. They get louder as the low thunder of horses on the run gets closer. Deborah sees Mary waiting by the stable and watches for the brass flash of the key that the girl is to leave under a nearby rock, ready for Deborah to find so her men can steal the Tories' horses. Once Mary's first task is done, she follows

the raiders inside, and Deborah pictures Mary serving them grog, watching them grow more and more intoxicated before she filches their guns and slips the flints out of them, rendering them useless. Nearly an hour passes before Mary appears in the window and gives Robert the signal.

Deborah waves to her men and instructs them to stay low as they creep out of the bushes and toward the house. Once they are within a stone's throw of the front porch, she motions for them to stand. She loads a bullet into her gun and aims it toward a distant star. At the sound, the cowboys stumble out of the house, shock and confusion on their drunken faces.

"Surrender, and nobody will be hurt!" Deborah shouts.

After a moment's hesitation, they surrender. Abraham Van Tassel is so grateful when he is not taken prisoner that he offers to feed the troops. Deborah accepts his offer, then spends the night camped on their property before heading back downstate to their main encampment with the Tory prisoners, forever taking her leave of Mary Van Tassel.

⚜

I need to say this now: as much as I want to believe that the quasi-relationship and the raid happened, I cannot. The documentation, namely Mann's retelling, is far too unreliable. If we had Deborah's original account of the story, it would be more believable, but we don't. History relies on primary documents, and this incident lacks them.

But that doesn't change how badly I want to believe it—especially the flirtation between Deborah and Mary—and how crushed I was when, despite all of my research, I found little to actually support its happening. There is a certain power in seeing people throughout history who are like you. There's a certain power in being able to point to someone who did something great and say, "She is like me. She loves like I do, and she is still strong. She is still important. She is still a worthy person."

I never learned about LGBTQ people in history class. As a student, there was a certain emptiness that made its home in my chest, an emptiness that comes from being left out of the narrative of human history. I often wonder if learning about gay or bisexual historical figures would have helped me accept my sexuality sooner, and if it could do the same for other children.

Not once in school was a historical figure anything but straight. At my conservative, Catholic high school, the only time we ever talked about being

gay was when we discussed AIDS or going to Hell. I felt dirty and wrong for loving other girls. I felt like a sin personified. I loathed myself. I spent nights crying, silently begging God to *please* make me different. I would have done anything to change that part of myself.

That is the damage that erasure causes.

I'm still a work in progress. Six years after graduation, I'm still undoing the devastation the erasure and negative messages inflicted on my self-worth. The more I came to accept my sexuality, the stronger my need to see myself in popular narratives grew. I devoured young adult books with LGBTQ main characters. I watched any show with the slightest hint of representation. Then, I turned to something I'd loved since my *Liberty's Kids* days: history.

Thanks to the internet, I found theories about Washington and Lafayette sharing more than "brotherly love." I learned that some of my favorite poets, like Elizabeth Bishop and Emily Dickinson, were not straight. When *Hamilton* came out, I learned about John Laurens and the overwhelming evidence that points to his being gay. I nearly cried when I discovered the romance-laden letters between Laurens and Hamilton.

Eventually, I learned that Deborah Sampson, too, was not as straight like I'd believed she was throughout my childhood. The excitement that coursed through me was indescribable. If she had a place in the narrative, if she'd done such amazing things, then I could, too. But there was one issue: the truth of her story was tangled up in many falsehoods. Someone would have to comb through them and determine fact from fiction. I decided I would be the one to untangle it. I would write my own deliverance, and through it, I would help others find themselves in the pages of history.

But this newfound empowerment doesn't change the lack of actual historical evidence to conclusively state that Deborah Sampson was gay or bisexual. In many of these cases, that is the problem. There is no conclusive evidence. It was extremely uncommon and dangerous for someone in the eighteenth century to explicitly write that they loved someone of the same gender. Instead of giving up my search, though, I realized I had to look from a different angle. Even if I can't definitively state that it happened, that doesn't mean the supposed raid and innocent affair between Robert and Mary aren't worth discussion and speculation. Mann—and Deborah—still decided to tell the story, after all. Why?

It's easier to figure out Mann's motive: he loved to dramatize everything. He thought these various exaggerations made the memoir stronger, when in

reality, it made it harder to believe. As he revised the book in the 1820s, the idea of chaste but romantic relationships between women was becoming more idealized, which would explain why he embellished that aspect of the story in subsequent drafts, although it is important to note that this relationship between Deborah and Mary is included in the original 1790s version of the biography, too.[36]

The most interesting question is this: why would Deborah allow the story to be told? If it didn't happen, did she like the idea of it happening? Is it based on a less risqué truth? Did Deborah pine for Mary but know that even if Mary returned her feelings, there was no way they could be together? Did Deborah decide to live in the moment and follow Mary's lead? Although these questions may hold some of the answers, before drawing any conclusions, we must consider Mary's story.

Mary married within a year or so of the raid and had a son, but by the time her son was born, she was already living apart from her new husband, which was an uncommon occurrence during the period.[37] We only know this because, in a letter, her brother referred to his sister living at home with their parents again, and because there is mention of Mary in her father's will, which decreed that she was to receive land and be allowed to live out the rest of her life in the house—not something a father would do if his daughter was happily and securely married.[38]

There are many reasons Mary might have divorced her husband after so little time in the marriage. Maybe he was abusive. Maybe he was unfaithful. Maybe he'd kept some awful secret from her that she couldn't reconcile. Maybe Mary didn't like men. Maybe she couldn't stop thinking about that handsome soldier, Robert, who'd been at her house not so long ago. Maybe she somehow knew Deborah's secret and wanted her anyway. The truth eludes us.

Very little else is known of Mary's life. Even her burial site and whether she lived out the rest of her days on the Van Tassel property is a mystery; the property has been lost to time and development, and documents about women were rarely kept. But we can have our theories. We can let our minds run wild with possibilities. We can say, "Maybe."

⚘

With the help of Google Maps, my dad and I drive to the very spot that the

Van Tassels and other locals called "Collerbarack." The outskirts of the area have been converted into a four-lane highway lined with a BJ's, a Dunkin' Donuts, and a Nissan dealership. We turn off of the highway and onto Old Crompond Road. It's a tight, winding country road. There are houses, but they're set apart from each other, swallowed by greenery and built around the town's water reservoir. In the woods near the water, there are scores of rowboats locked together or tied to trees. There are quaint stone walls around nearly all of the properties and many creeks and reservoir tributaries, marked as such with little signs.

We pass a house that has a blue historical marker sign in front of it, declaring that it was built in 1730. Not too far from the house, we happen upon a Baptist church with an old cemetery adjacent to it. Although the church was built in the early 1800s, the cemetery dates to the time Deborah was in the area.

We get out of the car and walk among the graves. Dead leaves, turned to mush by many layers of snow, threaten my footing. I find the grave of a boy who died at the age of fourteen during the war. I stand in front of his grave for a few moments and think about what his short life—and untimely death—might have been like.

This brings me back to Deborah, who I realize could have walked the very grounds I was standing on. Did she and her men pass through the cemetery, then much smaller, with legible and sparse headstones and no church nearby? Did she see the house I drove past? Did Tory cowboys raid it, or did a Tory live there? I imagine her leather boots caked in mud, dead leaves stuck to their soles. I imagine her filling her canteen in some of the many creeks. I imagine her walking through the cemetery, one of the graves freshly dug.

I creep over the colorless leaves and picture Deborah doing the same, rifle in her hand, her ears attuned to bird calls and the scampering of squirrels and chipmunks, always waiting to discern the footfall of friend from that of foe. I imagine her waiting in the dark for Mary, for the Tory cowboys to return from their raid.

Now that I have been there, now that I have seen and walked what is left of the land as she knew it, I have a new appreciation for how isolated and how risky her missions in neutral ground were. I have a new appreciation for her fortitude, her bravery.

⸎

Deborah Sampson is losing consciousness. She shakes and glistens with the fever

that has gripped her and countless other soldiers and civilians in Philadelphia. She is so weak, so unresponsive, that she is nearly taken for dead, and only a strength-zapping twitch saves her from being carted to the mass grave, filled with victims of the fever. With all of the life left in her, she prays she will not be discovered. She holds onto that hope as tightly as she can as she finally succumbs to the darkness that now blankets her mind.

It's not clear exactly what type of fever Deborah contracted. There was a measles outbreak at the time, as well as one of smallpox, which she most likely didn't have, because there are no mentions of her skin being marred by the pox.[39] Whatever type of illness she caught, it incapacitated her. She was brought to the army hospital and placed in a bunk with two other men of her rank, both of whom died.[40] She was nearly taken for dead, and it was her rally to give some sign of life that caught the attention of the ward matron, who called over the doctor, Dr. Barnabas Binney, to examine the young patient.[41]

The moment of discovery was upon her. Unconscious, she was powerless to stop Dr. Binney from checking her pulse, only to be puzzled by the thick layer between her shirt and skin. She was unaware as he ripped off her shirt and cut through the bindings that had kept her secret concealed for nearly two years. She was lost in the grips of illness as the doctor gasped in surprise then quickly concealed her chest once again.[42]

He took her home with him and personally oversaw her recovery, addressing her as Robert and allowing her to wear Robert's clothing the entire time. She was still unaware that her secret had been discovered.[43] It remains unclear if she ever knew her secret had been discovered while she was under his care.

Once recovered, Deborah made her way back to West Point, where her commanding officer, General Paterson, had since returned. With her she carried a letter from Dr. Binney—the letter that would reveal her true identity.

After nearly two years of avoiding this very situation, the moment of her discovery dawned upon Deborah. How, exactly, it occurred is a mystery. All that can be safely inferred is that Deborah was scared for her honor and life. In the past, when she was wounded in the shoulder, she viewed taking her own life as more honorable than discovery would be. No matter how her true gender was made known to her commanding officer, one fact is known about their interview: it led to Deborah Sampson's honorable discharge from the Continental Army.

On October 25, 1783, Robert Shurtliff once again became Deborah Sampson when he was released from the army at West Point by General Henry Knox.[44] Deborah Sampson had not only helped her fellow countrymen win the larger war, but just as importantly, she'd achieved something more personal: deliverance.

But deliverance doesn't always last.

⁓

Deborah returned home in the later days of November 1783. She moved to Stoughton, Massachusetts and lived with her aunt and uncle on their farm.[45] While there, she kept up her disguise, this time taking on the name of her recently married brother, Ephraim.[46] She undoubtedly helped with farm work during her time there, but she also had some fun, it seems. As Herman Mann says, "Her uncle being a compassionate man, often reprehended her for her freedom with the girls of his villa."[47] Not much is known about this time in Deborah's life, but it seems to have been a period of transition between army life and married life, a time when she may have romantically pursued women. This echoes back to her supposed affair with Mary, the Dutch girl from Collerbarack, and once again leaves us with more questions than answers, but that's okay.

Who she truly loved, we'll never know. As badly as I want to assume she was like me, I can't. As hopeful as I was that I could uncover the truth, I couldn't. Maybe her story—and the holes that exist in it—can be a reminder that we cannot erase differences from history. We *should not* erase our differences from history.

⁓

On October 14, 1784, Deborah Sampson and Benjamin Gannet, a local farmer's son, posted their intent to marry with the town clerk.[48] They married on April 7, 1785. There was what Young describes as "a very long time" between their engagement and marriage, the average being a few weeks to a few months at the most, not half a year.[49] There's also the fact that she gave birth to their first child, Earl, on November 8, 1785, making him what was referred to at the time as an "early baby."[50] Young points out that Deborah wasn't "a passive person who accepted what life dealt her," but instead took her time "calculating her options."[51] He also ponders if the wait between engagement and marriage is an indication of her reluctance to marry Benjamin, or maybe a reluctance to marry at all.[52]

Based on some later occurrences, it seems as if their marriage was one of mutual necessity rather than love. Incidents that suggest this include Benjamin joining the church that had shunned Deborah after her transgression,[53] and his attempt at killing a willow tree she planted by placing rocks under it.[54] Deborah's sentiments toward Benjamin may best be seen through the lack thereof. She wrote often of her children in her travel journal but never, not once, of her husband, even when she thought she might be dying, which suggests that he was not close to her heart.

Once they were married, they did their best to build a stable life together, but fortune was not on their side. The land the newlywed couple lived on had been over-farmed, making it difficult to produce enough crops to turn a profit, and Benjamin wasn't the wisest investor.[55] Even though they were still struggling financially, they had three children together and adopted a fourth.

Deborah's life of adventure could have stopped there. She could have returned entirely to the domestic sphere and raised her children, never again going off on anything like the adventures that had filled her life as a soldier. But Deborah wasn't the type to sit still. Her breeches and bayonet may have been retired, but she was about to engage in an entirely new type of fight.

࿇

Deborah Sampson Gannett watches her husband come in from another unsuccessful day of farming, head hung low, dirt smeared across his tanned face, brow furrowed in anger. She places her youngest child, Susannah, at the dining table and watches as her other three follow their father in from the field. Their cheeks are rosy, their faces smiling, eyes bright. She worries about how she will provide for them for what feels like the hundredth time that day. There is no doubt in her mind that her husband has continuously failed at doing so—whether because of the poor land, his lacking business skills, or a combination of the two, she does not know. All she knows is they need money, and she has no issue being the one who makes it.

࿇

Deborah decided to petition for a disability pension. In 1792, nearly ten years after her service, the Massachusetts State Legislature gave her back-pay for her service in the Massachusetts Fourth Regiment.[56] She was given 34£ in back-pay, with interest starting from the time she was discharged in 1783.[57] Although this was not an unimportant sum of money, it was still not enough to provide for her family or even to adequately supplement what she and her husband made from farming and from her occasional teaching job. So, in 1797, she took her petition to Congress.

In November of that year, Deborah traveled from her home in Massachusetts to New York City to seek help with her case.[58] She had a long list of tasks ahead of her if she was to successfully win her pension. According to Young, a soldier had to endure the following:

> Assemble affidavits from all the following: his officers, or an army surgeon, testifying to the onset of his disability during the war; three "reputable" freeholders in the town in which he lived who could describe the degree to which he had been disabled; two witnesses, to verify the disability at the time of his application; and two physicians who examined him.[59]

This process required a lot of time, effort, and money. Not only would the soldier have to pay to have two doctors examine him, but he also would most likely need a lawyer to handle his case and properly submit the overwhelming amount of paperwork to the federal judge.

Deborah did not go through all of these steps when petitioning for disability pay. Forever a woman of action, she instead sought the help of the renowned and influential poet and writer, Philip Freneau. He not only wrote and published an ode to her in his paper, *The Time Piece and Literary Companion*, on December 4, 1797, but he also authored her petition and publicly supported her campaign.[60] Even with Freneau's help, Deborah's petition got caught in the political warfare of Congress and ultimately failed. For the next few years, it seemed as if Deborah had given up her fight and resigned to her fate as an impoverished former soldier. However, in 1802, that all changed.

⁓

Deborah Gannett sits in the audience of the Federal Street Theatre in Boston, a crowd of genteel ladies and gentlemen surrounding her. The theatre company has just finished that night's performance of The Will, or a School for Daughters *to thunderous applause. Someone climbs the stage and begins to introduce the next performance. Deborah's stomach lurches just a bit.*

"The celebrated Mrs. Gannett is here with us tonight," the announcer says.

Deborah feels herself stand, although she doesn't remember giving her legs the command to do so. She slowly ascends the stage; the audience's claps and cheers echo around her. She has been practicing all week with the theatre company, but still finds herself somewhat nervous. But an emotion stronger than nervousness also builds within her. When she reaches the center of the stage and turns to face the crowd, that emotion explodes into a smile across her face. Excitement, *she thinks as she takes a deep breath, ready to begin.* Excitement.

From March of 1802 to April of 1803, Deborah Sampson Gannett once again made history by becoming the first woman to travel the United States on a lecture series, the lectures centering around her war experience. Her oration was written by Herman Mann, adapted from the biography he'd written on her, but with fewer details and mentions of popular local war heroes added in at each location.

She visited multiple stops in Massachusetts, Rhode Island, and New York during her year of travel. She kicked off the tour with four back-to-back performances in Boston's Federal Street Theatre and traveled on to Providence, Rhode Island.[61] She returned home to Sharon, Massachusetts for a month, and then set out again. She performed in five Massachusetts towns—Holden, Worcester, Brookfield, Springfield, and Northampton—before venturing to New York. There, she performed twice in Albany, near my home, as well as in Schenectady and Ballston. She returned to Albany for a bit then went on to Hudson and Catskill in southern New York before heading west into what was still the New York frontier to the town of Lisle to visit her former commanding officer, General Paterson. It was a dangerous, lonesome journey that often required her to ride in the back of wagons and sleep in shifty taverns until she reached Paterson, and she was in ill health throughout the trip.[62] But she did it, and eventually, she returned to Albany for some time before traveling to New York City, where she gave her final performance.

She traveled all that distance unaccompanied, which was a rarity for a woman. She also endured many hardships and mainly physical illnesses such as toothaches, dysentery, and fevers, which kept her bedridden for days at a time. Deborah chronicled her tour stops in a journal, which has been digitized by the Boston Public Library with the help of the Sharon Public Library. Written in sparse, short entries, her journal is mostly concerned with finances, but it still offers insight into what she did and how she felt during her tour.

Before she set out on the post-Boston leg of her tour, she wrote that her heart was "filled with pain when I Realized parting with my three Dear Children and other friends. I may say four Dear children—my Dear Little Susann Shepperd, which I took at five days old at her Mother's death."[63] Throughout her journey, she missed her children, often lamenting the distance between her and them, but still never expressed regret at the separation from her husband.

She also kept meticulous records of her expenditures during her tour. Most of her expenses were travel-related, but there was an exception: clothing. Specifically, she went on a shopping spree in Albany both times she was there, and she kept a record of each item she bought and how much it cost, so I know that she bought a handkerchief for 1£ and a cloak and trimming for 6.39£. During another visit to Albany, she bought even more clothing but didn't record the cost: "1 pair of Silk Gloves, 1 Silk Shall [sic], 1 pair Moroco Shoes, 1 Neck Hankerchieff [sic]" some lace, thread, and silk.[64]

I took a drive into downtown Albany to map out where, exactly, Deborah Gannett walked. While she was there, she stayed with a family on Green Street, which was then a neighborhood for working-class families referred to as "Cheapside."[65] These days, Green Street is a one-way street that's home to an upscale French-American restaurant, La Serre, nestled among tall buildings that face one of Albany's main streets, State Street. It's also where the Green & Hudson Municipal Parking Garage, complete with a post office hidden within its brick mass, is. After that, it looks dystopian, lined with faded parking lots, grass coming through cracks in the sidewalk, which is littered with outdated parking meters. It winds under some of Albany's many overpasses, more and more parking lots popping up on either side as cars whiz by overhead before it ends, turning into another street.

Needless to say, Deborah's Albany was different. There were the older Dutch houses—brick in the front with stepped roofs, wooden on the sides, crammed close together—that were slowly disappearing in favor of larger, box-shaped homes made of wood, which were also built in tight quarters. The streets were cobblestone or dirt. She likely didn't have to go far to shop given that it was State Street Hill, the main street off of the one where she stayed, where the business district was located. None of those buildings still stand.

The building where she spoke has also been demolished. She spoke in the city courthouse, better known as city hall. It was located only a few blocks down from Green Street on what is now Broadway but was then Court Street, and the Hudson River was visible and nearer than it is today. Now, the current building, the SUNY Plaza, blocks the river from view, and its shorelines have long since receded due to urban development and industrialization. All that remains of the old city hall is a plaque describing the brick building that once stood there and served as Albany's most important government landmark. Next to that is an old, engraved white stone, although the words are so weathered that next to it is another plaque with the words legibly translated on it. It's a stone marking the very spot— the front steps of city hall—from which the Declaration of Independence was read in July of 1776. Deborah certainly saw this spot and maybe even paused to smile at it before she continued inside to give her oration.

Across the street from where city hall once stood is now a slew of brick office buildings for sale, Broadway Plaza Liquor, Coulson's News Center, and a CDTA bus stop. What stood there, if anything, in Deborah's day, I do not know. But I do know that her speeches in Albany went very well. For the first time since Boston, she gave her oration more than once in the same city.

What is so amazing about this time in her life isn't just that Deborah traveled all over the northern states on her own, handling her own finances while she was at it, but that she traveled giving lectures in a time when women speaking in public was not only uncommon but frowned upon. She gave lectures and had large, enthusiastic turnouts. She may not have won her first pension battle with Congress, but her lecture circuit motivated her to once again unshackle herself from social norms in order to make money for her family, and it also gave her the opportunity to travel.

This is the definition of deliverance—taking ambitious steps toward liberation. First, she'd picked up a gun and disguised herself as a man to take her life into her own hands, unfettered by husband or children. Twenty years later, she continued to seek deliverance and achieved it, this time while dressed as a woman, as a wife and a mother, against the tenets of her time. Deborah Sampson Gannett accomplished deliverance on her own terms, and she didn't stop there.

The older Deborah got, the more time she spent unwell, which she blamed on the injuries she'd received during the war.[66] This, along with changes in the procedures disabled veterans were forced to undertake in order to secure their pensions and the Gannett's increasingly distressing financial situation, compelled Deborah to once again file for her pension. Until 1821, she spent most of her time fighting for her pension.

Although Congress had new laws in place that were supposed to make it easier for disabled veterans to get their pensions, they were still reluctant to award them. Often, veterans were forced to endure long delays before receiving them, which is what happened in Deborah's case.[67] Finally, on March 11, 1805, Deborah was placed on the pension list.[68] In addition to the pension she was already receiving from Massachusetts, she received $4 a month (worth about $74 in 2016) and a retroactive sum from the date she originally applied to Congress in 1803.[69] She did not stop there. She kept campaigning Congress for all of the money she was due, claiming she had as much right to it as any male veteran. She did this for years until, on March 31, 1820, Congress turned her down for the final time.[70]

Deborah Sampson Gannett died on April 29, 1827. She was buried in Rock Ridge Cemetery in Sharon, Massachusetts. There is no record of any memorial or religious rites held for her. Alfred Young speculates that her gravestone wasn't even placed at her grave until the 1850s or 60s, when enough funds were procured.[71] It was not until years later—exactly when remains a mystery—that her military service was added to her gravestone.[72] On its back is engraved:

DEBORAH, SAMPSON, GANNETT
ROBERT SHURTLIFF
The Female Soldier, Service 1781 to 1783.

Although the inscription makes the mistaken claim that she fought an entire year earlier than she actually did, it is a beautiful tribute to her. Although, after learning so much about her life, I tend to believe her time as a soldier is just one facet of her story.

As George Washington asks in the final song of *Hamilton: An American Mu-*

sical, "When you're gone, who remembers your name? Who keeps your flame? Who tells your story?" Hamilton's wife Eliza tells his story. Who tells Deborah's? Herman Mann attempted to tell her story but expressed so many falsehoods that to this day, we are still struggling to ascertain fact from fiction. Alfred Young dedicated years of his life to Deborah's story, eventually producing a meticulously researched book about her life and legacy. *Liberty's Kids* told her story in a simple but compelling way, introducing a young audience to this remarkable woman. Why should I tell her story?

As they sing in the *Liberty's Kids* theme song, I have looked at her life "through my own eyes." I have placed myself in her shoes. I have walked the same grounds she did as a young soldier, and I have imagined her pain, fear, and victories. She fought for deliverance in her own way. She looked within herself for deliverance instead of waiting for someone else to lift her up, and she found it. This is what I admire most about her story. This is what we have in common. Deborah Sampson made her own way in a world that did its best to hold her back, to make her conform to the restrictive norms of the late eighteenth and early nineteenth centuries. Her whole life was spent fighting, but because of her fight, she was able to live unapologetically as herself.

Through her fight, she created her own deliverance.

To Barbara O'Brien, who fostered my love of writing, and to all of the women of the past whose stories we'll never know.

Zabel Yessayan: DISAPPEARANCE

Rose-Poisoning: Beauty, Violence, and the Unknown History of Zabel Yessayan

By Nancy Agabian

abel Yessayan was from Bolis, which is what my great-grandparents, Levon and Mari Biberjian, would have called their native city in Armenian. In English, they would have called it Constantinople, a term my mother still uses today, though most of the rest of the world now calls it Istanbul. My mother learned how to speak Armenian by listening carefully to her grandparents, but they rarely spoke of their lives in the city with vanishing names.

So, when I first read Zabel Yessayan's memoir of her early life, titled *The Gardens of Silihdar*, I felt I was learning my great-grandparents' history by proxy, given that they were of the same generation as the author. The orchard of quince, pear, and apple trees that they lovingly tended in their backyard in Cranston, Rhode Island, as described to me by my mother, seems to have been some version of the gardens of Constantinople as depicted by Zabel:

> *I remember spring mornings when those groves—The Gardens of Silihdar—were transformed into a paradise filled with fiery roses in bloom...*

I remember how the wisteria tumbled down the trellis and, like a luxurious cape, masked the gloom of the houses that had fallen into disrepair. Sunlight filtered through the leafy trees and created fleeting patterns on the ground. The cool breeze passed over people and plants like a caress and made young branches sway playfully...[1]

As I read her words carefully, I see Zabel's young life at the same time that I imagine the superimposed imprint of a time and place lived by my great-grandparents. In between those two images, like figures on glass slides that have aged and faded, there is a great deal of mystery. I feel if I can know Zabel, then I will learn more of who Levon and Mari were, which will open up a world into knowing my mother.

But the journey for me to find Zabel as a writer and as a woman has been long, winding, and continuing, for there were Armenians who saved her, wars that ravaged her, and political forces that decided that she shouldn't exist. Shunned and betrayed, her voice brutally suppressed, she senselessly, silently, and violently disappeared.

1.

Twice in her life, Zabel Yessayan was targeted for elimination. The first time, her name appeared on a list of around 250 people to be arrested and deported to their deaths. She was noted as the only woman on the list. Born in 1878, she lived in Constantinople, where she became a writer. At the time that her name was placed on the blacklist in 1915, she had published poems, stories, and a novel. She had lived in Paris, studied at the Sorbonne, and was married with two children. Notably, she had written a book witnessing countless mothers who had lost their minds after seeing their children killed during the massacres of Armenians in 1909.

Zabel lived in Constantinople during a time when the Ottoman Empire was receding, losing territory, and being pressured from within and without to make change. Armenians were a minority in their native land and had long been Christian subjects of an Islamic state; as pressures shifted, and Armenians sought greater human rights and autonomy, they were blamed and targeted with violence, first massacred by Sultan Abdul Hamid II from 1894–96, then scapegoated by counterrevolutionary forces and massacred again in 1909. These eruptions of violence were a precursor to the genocide of 1915, which was a systematic attempt to annihilate them, spearheaded by the Young Turk regime, which was seeking to create a nation of "Turkey for the Turks." Under the cover of World War I, 1.5 million Armenians were killed.[2]

On the evening of April 24, 1915, Ottoman officials came to Zabel's home to arrest her, but she was at a friend's house. She soon received word that she was wanted, and she went into hiding, disguising herself as a Turkish woman and finding refuge for two months in a hospital[3]. Most of the 250 people listed with Zabel were killed. They were intellectuals and community leaders who were considered the "head" of the Armenian population within the Ottoman Empire. In the days, weeks, and months following their deaths, "the body" was eliminated: the soldiers in the army were stripped of their weapons and assassinated, and the women, children, and elderly were marched through the desert to die. Historians have estimated that two million Armenians were in the region before the genocide, and 1.5 million of them died as a direct result of it. In what is now considered Turkey, there were roughly 20 million people. For numerical context, imagine if people of Irish ancestry in the US were targeted by the government for elimination, and 75 percent of their population perished as a result.

From the hospital, Zabel assumed the identity of a Greek seamstress and made her escape to Bulgaria; she then sought to help refugees of the genocide in Tbilisi, Yerevan, Baku, and all around the Middle East. She recorded survivors' testimonies, but she never wrote about her experiences escaping the genocide. She eventually settled in Paris and never went back to Constantinople.

The books Zabel wrote before the genocide expressed her nationalist politics: she advocated for her people and for Armenian autonomy within the Ottoman Empire. But her politics shifted considerably after the genocide, and she wrote books considered to be Soviet propaganda, believing that Soviet Armenia was the only hope for the survival of Armenian people and culture. Eventually, she was invited to live in the Soviet Socialist Republic of Armenia in 1932. The following year, she moved from Paris to Yerevan.

In 1937, Zabel was targeted for elimination a second time. The Stalinist purges were underway when officials showed up at her door. This time, she was home, and she was arrested as "an enemy of the people."[4] During her imprisonment, she was constantly transferred from prison to prison. The last letter her family received from her was in 1942 from Baku. No one knows what happened to her: she simply disappeared. Zabel was a larger-than-life figure, charming and beautiful, outspoken and daring. But after her disappearance, collective memory of her disappeared, too. In the Armenian diaspora, her work wasn't read because of its Soviet-socialist leanings, and she was forgotten. Because of her previous nationalist politics, her work wasn't published in Soviet Armenia, and she became unknown. It's likely that because she was a woman and because she was Armenian, the world hasn't known enough about her to remember.

2.

Sometimes I think that I don't exist.

It happens when people don't see or hear or sense me. An acquaintance will be walking down the street in my neighborhood in Queens, and their eyes will pass through me, not recognizing anyone in their path; I'll say hello, and they'll just keep walking by. Or I'll be on the subway and a stranger will plop themselves into the space next to mine, pressing the air out of my lungs and edging me over two inches. In these moments, I tell myself: It's because you don't exist.

As much as I remind myself that such thoughts are ridiculous, the feelings emerge again and again. Out in the world, I am small, I am a woman, and I am brown.[5] I have lived long enough among the unspoken messages transmitting through people's body language and attitudes to know that small brown women, for most people, simply do not exist.

Even more indicative of my non-existence is the fact that I am Armenian. In the world, Armenians number only eight million, a puny figure compared to 1.3 billion Han Chinese and not very respectable next to 106 million French folks, among other less-threatened ethnicities. Western Armenian, the language of my family and the tongue that Zabel Yessayan read, wrote, and spoke, is on the list of the world's endangered languages. Surely, if you belong to a people, culture, and language that are disappearing, then your existence is somehow compromised. You live in a state of less existence.

It seems my mania is not so unique. Recently, an Armenian author wrote to me in an email, "Please note that all Armenian writers have been ignored and forgotten." Yet, in the Armenian literary community, there is a widespread impulse to save one another, to see one another, to remember one another. There are countless Armenian anthologies, translations, databases, readings, and exhibitions[6] for which the main criterion for inclusion is Armenian identity. Such collection and preservation seems to have roots in defying those who sought to eliminate us, a duty now passed on through culture.

So I simultaneously wonder if I will always exist; although our resources are limited, there will likely be an Armenian who will save, collect, and remember my words. Perhaps the distinction needs to be made, then, that I feel like I exist when I'm in an Armenian space, and I feel like I don't exist when I am everywhere else in the world.

But this would deny that I had to escape the Armenian space of my family and community to come of age. Although my family was loving while I was growing up, I felt constricted in my identity as Armenian, as if some essential part of me couldn't exist. In our diasporic communities, the need to procreate as a way to survive the genocide was transformed through subsequent generations into familial pressure to conform to hetero-patriarchal standards. This likely was an attempt to bury residual shame from being nearly decimated as a people, community, and culture. For a time, I had to break away from my Armenian self in order to express my identity as a bisexual, feminist woman. However, so much of how I have been shaped as a person—including my feelings of lesser existence—is the result of the upbringing of my Armenian-American family. At the heart of that family is my mother.

3.

Of all the marginalized groups that exist in the world, women are the most prominent: we make up roughly half the population. Humanity is in a perpetual state of existing and non-existing: letting some people up will keep others down. In countries all over the world, women are vulnerable; at risk of suffering violence from the hands of loved ones during peacetime; and during wartime, treated like land, raped and scorched to the ground.

As a young woman coming of age, I sought to discover how genocide had impacted my family. Curious about cultural silences surrounding issues of the female body, I read history books about the Armenian genocide, conducted oral history interviews with aunts and uncles, compiled family trees, and found records at Ellis Island and Ancestry.com to see ourselves existing and to fill in the gaps left by what history inflicted upon the women in my family.[7] There is one large gap that I haven't been able to fill at all.

Ironically, I know more about my three grandparents who were born in the Ottoman Empire (and who escaped the genocide) than I do of my mother's mother, Vivian, who was born in Providence, Rhode Island. Her parents arranged her marriage to my grandfather, John, but when financial pressures during the depression caused John to lose their small home, the couple separated. As a single mother with two young children, Vivian moved into a flat one floor below her parents in their triple-decker house in Cranston, Rhode Island. A nonsmoker, she somehow contracted lung cancer and died in 1952 at the age of forty-seven. Because Vivian died well before I was born, and because my mother never learned her grandparents' stories of Constantinople before they died, I am hoping that Zabel's writing can fill the gap of cultural knowledge of my mother's family history.

Zabel's work was first introduced to me in a course called "literature and Catastrophe" taught by Marc Nichanian at Columbia University, in which we read a brief excerpt of her book titled, *In the Ruins*. I later taught the passage in a writing workshop for women in Armenia, only to discover that very few women had heard of Zabel. Lara Aharonian, the director of the women's resource center where we held the workshop, and Talin Suciyan, a journalist from Istanbul, were among the few who had already read and studied her work. They soon set out to explore Yessayan's legacy and created a documentary on the process, *Finding Zabel Yessayan*, which was completed in 2009. Two years later, the film was screened in Watertown, Massachusetts and viewed by members of the Armenian International Women's Association, who were then inspired to publish English translations of her work. Three books came out in 2014 and 2016: *The Gardens of Silihdar, In the Ruins*, and *My Soul in Exile*.

I take some pride in being part of the chain that is bringing Zabel to readers of English, and I hope to a wider audience. But there is a bittersweet quality to the timing: my reading of these books, which connect me to my mother's history, coincides with the erosion of my mother's memory.

4.

At first, she would repeat something that I had just said. For example, if I said to my parents, "I don't want to go to the store now because I have to meet a friend in a few minutes," my mother would parrot, "She has to meet a friend in a few minutes."

Then she progressed to not remembering something that I had just told her. For the last ten years of my life, I always chalked this up to her not listening. But the time in between her forgetting what I said was getting shorter, to the point where if she asked me a question, such as when the early bird dinner special ended, and I answered, "six p.m.," two minutes later she'd ask, "What time do the early birds end?" Over the past year, I got into the habit of prodding her: "I just answered that. Do you remember what I said?" And she would stop for a moment, close her eyes, and say, "Six p.m." She usually could answer when prompted, so I attributed her repetitive questions to the fact that she had always been extroverted and chatty.

But Christmas week was particularly difficult. My mother has anxiety around the holidays because her mother died around that time. She began to have trouble remembering not only what she'd just asked but also shared familial history. When we went to lunch at Gregg's, a favorite spot because of their rich cakes, Mom said, "We won't tell Ken [my brother] we came here. He'll get jealous."

A moment later, she asked, "Has Ken ever come to Gregg's with us?" I looked at her across the booth, her face framed by the halo of her black beret, her big brown eyes bewildered. My father and I did our best to prompt her: "Ken couldn't be jealous if he'd never been here, could he?"

The next day, she and I were watching a travel show about the Swiss Alps when she told me, "Nancy, I think we could see the mountains in Switzerland from Armenia."

Mom traveled to Armenia in 1998 and again in 2007. She had also visited Switzerland on a separate occasion, probably in the intervening years. Mistaking mountains across miles was a different kind of memory blip, and it worried me.

"Think about that," I said. "Are Armenia and Switzerland anywhere near each other?"

She paused for a moment, and her voice lowered. "No, that's not right," she said, still staring at the TV.

I asked if she remembered the name of the famous mountain in Armenia. She was silent. *Ararat*, I thought, the mountain that we gazed upon together when we visited Yerevan, though it is located over the border in Turkey. Ararat, of which Armenians are so proud, easily recognizable the world over as Noah's Ark's resting place. Ararat, a name that every Armenian knows. We continued to watch the show as the host gleefully ate some Swiss cheese.

I felt a sad, ironic sense of loss. My mother was a schoolteacher for a few years before she became a mother. She then volunteered as a docent at a local art museum and served on the board of our town's arts council. At the end of my high school career, she created her own job coordinating art events for the public school system in our Boston suburb. She was also the parent in charge of our family—her word was the law. My mother showed her care for me mostly through her strict rules governing my education and physical health. Though it was problematic for me, I find what I miss most is her controlling nature and the strong grasp of facts and emotions that she wielded in any argument.

Coming of age during the 1950s, my mother grew up during a particularly repressive time for women in American history, and when the second wave of feminism gained momentum, she latched onto it and brought me with her. My mother then talked herself into existence, and I received her story: her mother died when she was just nineteen; she felt pressured to marry at a young age; and my father was unsympathetic to her needs for self-determination. She would take me away from home on trips to art museums around the suburbs of Boston, complaining in depth about her life with my father.

I wouldn't realize this was inappropriate until I was deep into therapy in my mid-twenties, as it made me feel responsible for her and took away chances at my own development. In a sense, I was raised by a teenager; my mother didn't have the benefit of continuing her relationship with her mother through her young adulthood. I was subjected to her lobbying efforts whenever my will conflicted with hers—she pulled out every reason why I shouldn't have fun with friends. I eventually learned that my grandmother was hurt in a car accident when my mother was with her friends, having fun. Vivian thought my mother needed a ride home from the movies, so she made my uncle drive in the rain to find her, and they were hit by another car along the way. The injuries Vivian sustained were attributed by her doctor to be the cause of the lung cancer that later took her life at the age of forty-seven.

As significant as it is, there is more to my mother's history than this loss. A question has always tugged at me: who was my mother before the trauma of losing her mother? Who was her family, and how did they shape her? What were the forces of love and pain that she absorbed and passed on to me? They are a mystery, given that she was never one to open up when I asked questions as a confused and lost teenager and young adult. She kept a tight lid on her past, and it clearly haunted her. But she also didn't have a whole lot of time with her family to find out their history. Her grandparents died not long after her mother did.

When I returned to visit my parents the following month, I decided to read to my mother from Zabel Yessayan's *The Gardens of Silihdar*, hoping it would spark memories from a time before she was a mother. There I was, reading a memoir of a girl born around the same time her grandparents were A girl living in the same city that her grandparents fled, Constantinople. We believed they were escaping the pogroms in 1895, termed the "Hamidian massacres" after the despotic sultan at the time. I sat on the couch by the bay window with Mom across the living room in her chair, the pearly, opalescent Oriental rug and the glow of warm lamplight between us. By turns, she was listening, dozing, and gazing about with a curious, faraway expression.

I read to her a passage early in the book when the young Zabel is at home, sick, watching a snowball fight unfold in the street from her spot by the window. Her family members are concerned that she'll catch a draft that will worsen her illness, so they ask her Aunt Youghaper to put young Zabel to bed. As part of their bedtime ritual, her aunt sings, "The City of Ani sits and cries / There is no one to say, don't cry don't cry." Thus causes so much sadness and hopelessness in Zabel that she pretends to sleep so that her aunt will stop. When Aunt Youghaper retires for the night, Zabel views the shadows of the room and imagines that they are cast by a woman named Ani, slumped over herself, crying.

On the day of the snowball fight, Zabel somehow manages to evade bedtime, and she watches as the boys attack a Jewish tinsmith with snowballs, causing him to drop all his wares and fall to the ground in despair. Zabel now sees this figure as the city of Ani, and she yells out in anguish about the injustice. Her grandmother tells her not to be upset, claiming that he's a Jew, so he gets what he deserves for what his people did to Christ, "atoning for that sin."[8] When she's a bit older, Zabel brings up the issue with her father:

> *"Is it true that the Jews are bad people?" I asked my dad, whose opinion had already become the most definitive in my mind.*
> *"My darling, there is no such thing as a bad group of people. There are good people and there are bad people," he said calmly, his eyes gleaming.*
> *"What about the Turks?" I asked.*

"It's the same for the Turks."[9]

The chapter ends. It seems clear that Zabel was ahead of her time in expressing such egalitarian views just twenty years after the genocide.

"What do you think?" I asked my mother.

"What's the city of Ani?" she asked.

I couldn't believe she didn't know. The ancient city of Ani is often spoken about in Armenian circles, both because it is a historical treasure but also because it's an item of political dispute; its ruins are located in Eastern Turkey, where it has been defaced and left to decay, and its Armenian history has been unacknowledged by the Turkish government until very recently. Along with lectures on these subjects, over the years, my parents had attended presentations about Armenian pilgrimages to Turkey, which often included visits to Ani.

I told my mother that the city dates from around the tenth century and was called "the city of 1,001 churches." One could visit Ani's ruins in Eastern Turkey, though they haven't always been easy to access because of the political situation.

"It's still there, but people don't live there?" she asked. She didn't understand the timespan, the millennium gone by.

"No, it's like the city of Pompeii. A natural disaster or some other shift caused people to leave."

"What happened to the people there?" she asked.

I didn't know what to say. Sadly, I questioned what my mother was really confused about. If the city of Ani sits and cries, who are the people who left her? Her children? Did my mother wonder where her children went? Where her grandparents went? I wondered where her memory went.

5.

As I read the works of Zabel Yessayan that have been newly translated into English, I hope to discover something about my mother's memory. I also expect that I'll figure something out about Zabel as my mother's memory wanes, shifts, and changes. In any case, I suspect I will learn about myself. It's not every day that I am able to read the work of a person born in another century whose identity bears the outlines of my own—woman, writer, Armenian.

6.

Reading *The Gardens of Silihdar*, I discover and admire Zabel's fiery spirit. She grows up among an extended family of middle-class weavers, her maternal aunts and uncles under one roof, working together to create their wares. Each family member has a distinct personality, from the aunt who strolls down the hill to the poor neighborhood to socialize with people the rest of her family ignores, to the binge-drinking uncle who endangers himself by helping Circassian tobacco smugglers. These rebels influence Zabel's personality.

Zabel the writer portrays herself as a headstrong child: garrulous, mischievous, and unruly. A great uncle once said of her, "You have to shut this kid up! Is this how you've raised her? She is going to be a real terror one day! But hey, God knows what he's done. He's stopped a disaster before it happened by making her a girl."[10] Echoing him later, she claims, "Oh, if I had only been a boy [...] I would have fought for justice and gladly died for it."[11]

In these passages, Zabel seems to write with a socialist mindset, representing ideas of equality and class struggle and detailing the corrupt nature of money within her family and community. When she attends a private school for Armenian students, she describes the servants bringing full barbecued picnics to the wealthy students while the poor students eat dry crusts of bread.[12] She also writes scathing critiques of the local parish priests and the harsh means they use to govern the Armenian population, imprisoning people for cooking meat on Sundays.[13] Later, when she attends a church school, she torments a failed priest by adorning him with fake flowers during his daily nap.[14]

One can't help but wonder if parental abandonment exacerbated Zabel's strong will. Her mother suffers a severe depression that commits her to bed for days, beside herself with sadness and unable to speak. Her mother's illness "consumes" the adult members of the household so that there is little attention left for Zabel and her younger sister, who she says are "practically orphans in our own home."[15] In contrast, Zabel portrays her joyful father as living beyond his means, and the family as moving between polarities as their fortunes rise and fall: when debt increases, they scale down to a smaller house, and when times are good, they throw lavish parties. She describes her spirited father as her champion, always listening to her and supporting her. However, even his patience runs out when she turns twelve and attends a new school:

My personality was met with fierce resistance. I was continuously forced to fight both physically and mentally, but I never thought that the fight was beyond my capabilities, and I had no intention of retreating. I was in a constant struggle against my family, my school and my peers. I would sometimes experience a temporary victory, but I would more often experience defeat. These losses would not embitter me or cause me to lose hope. I would absorb the defeat, neutralize it, immediately accept that I had lost and start a new battle. That approach became a necessity in my life; even as an adult, I found myself behaving in much the same way in many other circumstances and situations.[16]

Much has been written about the reasons for Zabel's political sea change, including accusations that she was a flighty opportunist.[17] However, just before the arrest that caused the premature end to her life, she was not writing with allegiances but with fierce self-determination. I can't help but imagine some Soviet flunky reading this passage and thinking, "This one will be trouble."

7.

In her life, Zabel must have learned this lesson of self-determination most painfully as a witness to chaos, hate, death, and destruction. In the spring of 1909, she observed the results of massacres of 30,000 Armenians in the region of Adana.

By this time, she had established herself as a writer. As she documents at the end of *The Gardens of Silihdar,* she started to publish her writing at the age of eighteen in local Armenian newspapers and journals, which brought her attention. She soon took interest in nationalist ideologies and began attending revolutionary salon circles. During the Hamidian massacres, her father sent her to France for her safety, where she studied at the Sorbonne.[18] In Paris, she met her husband, the painter Dikran Yessayan, who she married in 1900 when she was twenty-two years old. She gave birth to her daughter Sophie the following year; her son Hrant would arrive later, in 1910. The roles of both mother and writer were tested in 1909 as she witnessed the plight of Armenian survivors and documented her experiences in *In the Ruins.* What strikes me most while reading the book is the unimaginable violence. I struggle to read such horrific images but feel I owe it to Zabel to endure them, given that she nearly lost her mind bearing witness.

As she travels with a delegation, sent from the Armenian patriarch in Constantinople to aid the orphans, she encounters the various circles of Hell. Unlike Dante in *The Inferno*, Zabel doesn't have a guide; instead, she is her readers' navigator, showing us the horrible scenes she encounters. Then she grapples with her own despair, which is sympathetically produced in the reader. Documenting must have helped her to witness the violence, which is otherworldly and disrupts the norms of family, particularly the institution of motherhood. Throughout the book, mothers repeatedly "tear at their breasts" as they mourn the loss of their children in torturous ways, rendered inhuman by the atrocities inflicted upon them.

At one point, Zabel encounters a woman who has lost her family. Her home is in ruins, and her son is so emaciated that she can no longer care for him:

> *We faced fire and sword together and survived, but misfortune dogged us like a shadow. I have no one to look after me; I sleep on the ground at night, I go hungry all day, and I've been bled white. If only I'd gone blind and been spared the sight of this day. Take him and keep him. I'm at my wit's end.*[19]

Another mother buries her child in a shallow grave, only to be prompted to use the same spot for the corpse of her other child:

> *When the woman reopened the grave, the worms had half-eaten her older daughter's body. She gazed at the unrecognizable black remains for a long time. She heard nothing and was afraid of nothing [...] Every now and then, other women would come tap her on the arm and urge her to leave, "Let's go. What are you staring at? Hurry up, get it over with." The mother, as unfeeling as a statue, didn't answer, but kept staring, just staring [...] Only with the approach of evening did she turn her back on the body and grave and run off, howling like a wolf...*[20]

She encounters a woman who must kill her own infant when the child cries out because the group hiding in a cellar from a violent mob doesn't want to be detected. The mother tries to strangle the baby but can't, so the father tries:

No one heard the baby's cries again. But when they emerged into the light and the sun, the boy had not yet died. He agonized for a long time. Belly swollen, eyes bulging from their sockets as if surprised by the crime, the poor child gave up the ghost only after a protracted struggle. His mother had already lost her mind.[21]

You think you've read the absolute worst case of suffering in your life, and along comes another. Zabel acknowledges this in relation to the above passage: "So those who had buried their children's bodies with their own hands and those who had seen their children driven mad by hunger [...] could still be considered lucky."[22]

Zabel never mentions within the book that she is a mother: her daughter Sophie, eight years old in 1909, is living in Paris with her father. Her role as a mother is suggested, however, when Zabel realizes that the children see her as a maternal figure. She encounters a girl in the orphanage who "had been abducted,"[23] and who—like Sophie—is eight years old:

...something in her mournful soul entered into communion with mine. All at once a veil of quiet sorrow fell over her somber tortured gaze, and her pupils turned the dull blue-gray color of coal that has long since burned out and is covered in ash. She hunched up her bony shoulders and, despite the sweltering midday heat, started shaking from top to toe. Her little jaws, chattering, made a sinister sound. Her gaze followed my troubled thoughts and, beneath the veil of her sadness, a brightness seemed to be sparkling in her eyes, flickering and flaring in phase with the waves of my inner agitation.

Oh that slight, tormented [...] forlorn creature. Where in that tiny body was such redoubtable grief lodged? How her muscles still trembled, fiber by fiber, with indignation over the outrage she had endured!

I felt a maddening fever assailing my brain.

"Mama! Mama!"

Had she uttered that supreme cry, like the other orphans, who often looked for their mothers when they were in pain or longed for affection? Or had I blurted out those words? I do not know. I took her in my arms, sat her on my knee, and rocked her slight body back

and forth, so that she might, if only for a moment, forget her own frenetic
sorrow for my own, so that she forget herself...[24]

The mother has become a child, and the mother is a child. Lines are blurred as she tries to cope with despair.

By the end of her narrative, she simply wants to flee the victims: "Nameless disjointed, sobbing cries echoed loudly in my mind and suddenly came to my lips: 'Let's get out of this country. [...] For the love of God! This country's sun will never shine on us again! Help us, help!'"[25] The survivors had made these same pleading exhortations to the delegation, and Zabel internalized the pain of the survivors so much that she has become one with them. Though she also documents a few cases of individuals, families, and villages fighting and surviving, she is clearly writing at the limits of her abilities as both a writer and a witness. I can't help but ask: if witnessing the aftermath of a massacre during which 30,000 people died was barely possible, what must it have been like for her six years later, to experience the genocide, a tidal wave of hellish human destruction on a scale fifty-times larger?

According to my mother, my great-grandparents arrived in the US around 1895, during the time of the Hamidian massacres that killed roughly 300,000 Armenians. Mari was just ten, and Levon was seventeen. Perhaps their parents sent them away to the US the way that Zabel's father sent her to Paris for her safety. Did they witness some part of this cycling sea of rage? Perhaps experiences like these were what they were unable to express to their granddaughter who played innocently in their garden.

⁓

At the time I am reading *In the Ruins* in 2016, my mother is losing her short-term memory but remembering her childhood. She recalls, for instance, how her family went to the beach one day, and when they returned, all the grapes from their arbor were gone. The boy across the street had eaten them all. Not long afterwards, he contracted appendicitis. My mother tells stories about her family, her neighborhood, and what was going on in the world at the time, all in a way that's similar to Zabel recounting life amid the gardens.

Mom says she is grateful that she was a child during World War II, because if she had really understood the implications of the Nazis winning the war, she wouldn't have been able to tolerate it—she'd have been too scared. She remem-

bers her grandparents sitting on either side of the radio trying to piece together the meaning of the events as reported. Perhaps my mother's realization is
a hint about her grandparents' feelings: did they fear for their lives while war
projected from their radio into their home in Cranston, Rhode Island? What
memories were surfacing for them?

Mom remembers going to see *The Outlaw*, starring Jane Russell, when
she was twelve years old after the indecency ban on it had been removed;
the movie house was so packed that she had to share a chair with her friend.
Movies loomed large in their lives, and her mother liked to visit the cinema
every week. I suspect Vivian was depressed after her separation, as a single
mother struggling to care for her family. Movies might have been her escape.

While reading *In the Ruins*, I become listless and depressed. I wake up one
morning while visiting my parents' home in Massachusetts feeling extremely
tired. It isn't until we set out for the day to the DeCordova Art Museum and
take a walk in the surrounding gardens that my mood shifts. I walk a trail
through the woods and up a hill until I come to a clearing through which I
can see the lake below, glistening. Something breaks in me, and I cry. I am
safe. I am not in the world of Adana, 1909.

As I stroll inside to find my parents in the galleries, immersed in the art,
I recall how my mother often sought refuge in museums when she felt troubled. I remember that Zabel escaped madness through the art of the written
word, documenting mad mothers while she was far from her family. And
yet, they were always with her. In her letters to her husband, included in an
appendix at the back of the book, she often asks about her daughter. "And
why doesn't my Sophie write to me? Is it just because she is lazy, or is there
some other reason?"[26] She clearly loves her very much. "I miss my Sophie
terribly; give her lots of kisses for me."[27]

I wonder if all the images of mothers, distraught and despairing, caused
Zabel to remember her own mother who had abandoned Zabel to her disease.

ᶜᵉ

After I read countless descriptions of mothers tearing at their breasts,
my mother seems to enact a similar role. It is a rainy, foggy Saturday morning in the middle-class suburb where my parents live. I planned to attend a
traditional forty-day memorial for a friend who recently passed away. I let
my parents know that I'm leaving, and I retrieve the keys to the car from my

dad. The church is about a forty-minute drive away.

My mother can't tolerate this. She sees no need for it. Having played a role in this scene with her a few times before, I take a deep breath and try to quell the situation by telling her calmly that it's not a big deal; I'll be home in the afternoon.

"You don't have to go. You don't have to make me upset like this!"

"I'm not making you upset. You're choosing to get upset."

She continues to make claims: my friend who passed away isn't very important; it's not like she's family; if it were my mother's memorial, I wouldn't even go. She's making no sense.

"You need to relax," I tell her.

As I pull open the front door, she is actually screaming. Shrieking. Her uvula trills and tears spring from her eyes. "Why are you doing this to me!?" It's as though she is witnessing the murder of her child.

Shaken, I rush to the car and drive away. The skies are drizzly, and the roads are slick. Perhaps this is what upsets my mother: her own mother's car accident took place in the rain.

Later in the afternoon, after I have celebrated the life of a beloved mentor and friend, I walk through my parents' front door, and my mother does not apologize for her behavior. She doesn't even acknowledge it. This is her typical MO. But it's also possible that she just doesn't remember.

On the last morning of my visit, I sit in the kitchen with my mother, we eat scrambled eggs for breakfast, and she tells me about her grandfather's chicken coops. "He had a little business selling eggs out of his truck. They were organic, you know. I never appreciated those fresh eggs."

I've heard her chicken-coop stories countless times. But now she details the three structures, little shacks bordering a courtyard where the chickens freely ranged. "I used to play with the chickens; their feathers were so soft. You know, when you go near them, they lift up their wings"— in her fuzzy pink bathrobe with metal snaps down the front, she mimes the chickens' wings, raising up her elbows gleefully —"because they liked to be petted underneath!" She says this with childlike awe. Perhaps her coming undone a few days before wasn't caused by an imminent separation from her daughter but by the loss of her mother: a reaction rooted in trauma.

8.

How did trauma affect Zabel? Her book *My Soul in Exile* offers a clue. In a letter, she describes writing this book as a "refuge [where] there is neither massacre, nor deportations, nor Bolsheviks, nor anything else, but only sunshine, roses, and the eternal song of love, beauty, and grace..."[28]

This beauty comes upon the reader gradually. *My Soul in Exile* takes place in Constantinople in April, sometime after the sultan's counterrevolution, which prompted massacres of Armenians in 1909, before the genocide of 1915. In other words, it was a lull of relative peace between two storms of violence. Her protagonist, Emma, a young female painter, returns to the city after time spent away in Europe.

On a trolley ride, Emma runs into an older poet, Mrs. Siranoush Danielian,[29] who expresses a desire to view Emma's paintings. But Emma is somewhat shy and overwhelmed by the prospect. Mrs. Danielian responds, "It's as if we were exiles in a remote foreign country. We're exiles in the land of our birth because we're deprived of the kind of environment that our people's collective existence would create around us. Only fragile, loose threads bind us to our native land."[30]

I'm struck that Armenians felt like exiles in the Ottoman Empire, where they had been living for centuries. It could also be that Mrs. Danielian is expressing a nationalist sentiment: the real struggle wasn't in Constantinople but much further east, in the regions where the majority of Armenians lived as poor, oppressed farmers. In any case, it gives me a sense of the alienating climate that my great-grandparents must have experienced as well.

Emma then speaks about her soul in abstract terms, which doesn't really grab me, but all of a sudden, she describes making rose jam, and I am riveted:

> *[T]he whole house and even the street is full of the pungent, penetrating scent of roses. It is an excess of fragrance; the maid, another woman who has come to help out, and even my aunt, their heads spinning from a mild case of rose-poisoning, have to interrupt operations from time to time and leave the room for a breath of fresh air. But the smell of roses pervades the whole house, the stairs, and the kitchen, where some of the petals are already boiling away in wide-mouthed copper pots.*
>
> *In the spacious room in which I've hung my paintings, the roses'*

unrelenting fragrance pursues me, saturates me. The air I breathe seems to grow thicker and makes me tipsy. Dizziness, a sudden malaise, rubber knees—and the reflection of my face in the mirror is pale, blanched white, even if my eyes are burning with fever.

The whole neighborhood is permeated by that smell. It is rose season and many different houses exhale the gradually diminishing aroma. Slipping out of open windows and doors standing ajar, the fragrant waves spread through the air, while the ladybugs, entranced by their favorite flower, buzz in the sun and fly every which way, instinctively trying to find their way to the roses piled up on the divans, trays and tabletops.

The maid brings rose jam for us to taste in small crystal dishes. It is wonderful. This is not eating, but rather feeling, assimilating what is the most intangible and fleeting for our senses: aroma and color. [31]

Alongside such descriptions of sublime beauty are accounts of the unsavory realities of the Armenian community of Constantinople. In the following passage, Emma explains how the Armenian patriarch of the Apostolic Church in the early-eighteenth century persecuted Armenian Catholics, a small religious minority. Fearing that Armenian Apostolics would convert to Catholicism and thus be lost from his jurisdiction, the patriarch convinced the sultan that Catholics were foreign agents infecting the empire with European influence. Backed by the sultan's authority, he decreed that Armenian Catholics must attend the Apostolic church, and he banned them from performing their own services. Catholics who resisted conversion to the Apostolic church were met with harsh penalties: "There was not an Armenian Catholic family that did not have its exile and its prisoner." [32]

Considering this dynamic alongside Mrs. Danielian's claim that everyone is an exile, I feel the compounding effects of oppression on the Armenian community. But it's also clear that Zabel is delving into the complexity of the Armenians: there were good and bad among them. In the genocide of 1915, Armenians had been crushed. In *My Soul in Exile*, Zabel depicts them enjoying the highest beauty the world has to offer but also reveals them at their most base and brutal, manipulating power to harm their own. In short, writing some years after 1915, Zabel is restoring Armenian existence.

Emma summarizes the history of the Catholic Armenians as a way to introduce her visitor, Diran bey, [33] an Armenian Catholic man whose once-wealthy

grandfather was stripped of his riches and killed during the patriarch's perse-
cution. In the book, when Diran bey walks into the room, the light suddenly
becomes magical, and the two size each other up. "A strange torpor has come
over me and it is as if I were in a dream," Emma recounts, and then her aunt
serves them the rose jam. It seems clear that she's overtaken with love: "I experience an unaccustomed feeling of peace and inner harmony [...] his words,
his voice, his gestures, the smile on his lips, his pensive, dreamy gaze—everything appears to correspond to my inner, secret harmony, which, it seems, has
only just now been revealed..."[34]

Emma proceeds to show Diran bey her paintings. In response to her
self-portrait, he tells her, "There is intelligence and restrained power in
your art."

But then he comes out with this gem: "It doesn't seem as if a woman's
hand had held your brush; your portrait, for example: only a man could
have painted it that way. I find it difficult to formulate my feelings and
thoughts at present, but this much is clear: only a man is capable of painting
a woman affected by her most tumultuous, most electrifying emotions."

Emma replies that she wants to talk to him about her work some other
time, "after [he's] freed [him]self from the influence of [his] first impression."[35] She tells him that she's having trouble expressing herself, too. The
novella ends two pages later, after "months and years have gone by" (which
perhaps is a euphemism for the passage of time after the genocide), with her
report of how the love ended between her and Diran bey that afternoon.
Emma explains how she often revisits her life of joys and sorrows:

> *The people who pause in front of an artist's works cannot imagine
> that we have to relive a past grief a hundred times, that we have to
> make our heart bleed a hundred times, in order to be able to commu-
> nicate to the apathetic, indifferent multitude passing by the impression
> that grief left on us when it was present and real."*[36]

This seems to explain why Emma didn't pursue Diran bey's love: he,
whose people suffered as Catholics, can't apply that experience of oppression to understand the grief she faces as a woman; instead, he questions if it
even exists, claiming that a woman can't possibly create a work of art that
expresses herself as a human being.

The passage also suggests that no one could understand the grief that pre-vented Zabel from writing directly about the genocide—for she would have had to relive it and make her heart bleed for it a hundred times—which would have been impossible. In the end, Emma chooses beauty over pursuing love. The last line reads, "It is better to remain alone and listen to the murmurs of my heart; that I make my way to the remotest recesses of the garden beneath the blossom-ing cherry trees, whose white petals, in moments of such great beauty, came raining down on us."[37]

I'm astonished that Zabel chose to retrieve a time and place of beauty. All the contemporary second- and third-generation Armenian-American writers I know have journeyed to a place of ugliness in imagining genocide, drawn to it over and over and over again, as if we are soldiers endlessly dressing the same wounds. Even in this project of mine to retrieve my mother's memory, I am walking the same outdated warpath back to the theater of battle. In the archiving of our family's stories, many of us would say that it's about mourning the past and recovering from our collective trauma. This is valid; subsequent generations can sometimes perform the emotional work that our predecessors couldn't. Though Zabel was not physically able to imagine in writing the hell and the void that was the genocide, her work is crucial in bringing us to a time before memory. In her portrayal of beauty, she reminds us that it is life, it is a part of us, and we can choose to be healed by it. But she doesn't deny reality. Her description of rose-poisoning—the intense, physical intoxication of the perfume that forces Emma from her home—retrospec-tively points to the violence that was to come, but it also indicates an under-standing that violence can exist within even the most beautiful moment.

9.

As I try to understand what compelled Zabel to seemingly shift political gears, a four-day war erupts in Armenia, and I gain a glimpse of understand-ing the impact of violence.

On the evening of April 1, 2016, Azerbaijan attacks the disputed region of Karabakh and violates a twenty-two-year-old ceasefire. News reports are spotty, and it is upsetting to not know what is happening. I am having trouble getting any work done because all I want to do is search for more information online. Fearing things are going terribly wrong, I helplessly watch videos from European and Armenian news outlets with white, male pundits analyzing the situation, and I can barely understand their lingo. The women and queers have no voices in this chatter. Young and old soldiers are shown marching off to war, but the people most affected—those who live in poverty in the war zone in Karabakh, who are most at risk of losing their lives—are invisible.

Is this the moment when Armenia will no longer exist, after decades of threats? Suddenly, Armenia is very vulnerable. Suddenly, people who are progressive aren't anymore; the Azerbaijanis are bad and the Armenians are good. The president of Armenia, who has been proven to be corrupt countless times, is suddenly trusted. Radical progressives begin to sound like conservative nationalists within a day, in contrast to Zabel changing allegiances over the course of several years. People I know who are analytical, complex thinkers are suddenly blaming Aliyev, never questioning how the great powers in the Organization for Security and Cooperation in Europe have been just as complicit in creating this mess, or how Russia profits directly from the eternal cease-fire, selling arms to both Armenia and Azerbaijan.

It seems that no one cares about Armenia. No one cares. Turkey, France, Europe, the US, and Iran: they all want to fuck up Armenia. My insights have flown out the window, and I feel like a failure: what have I done to create conversations that resist the national borders and binaries that separate and oppress people? How many of my friends are Turkish or Azerbaijani? How stupid have I been this whole time, thinking that Armenia would always exist? If this four-day war unsettles me so deeply, then what must have Zabel felt as she watched violence enacted against her people for decades? Did she feel both helpless and responsible? Perhaps, as a woman living during global changes at the turn of the twentieth century, such feelings were compounded—and damning.

I'm reminded of two male perceptions of Zabel. The first, by writer Gostan Zarian, condemns an overemotional and narcissistic diva. The second, published two decades later by Rouben Zarian, a former student of Zabel's (and no relation to Gostan), praises the thoughtful and caring professor. Gostan Zarian scathingly portrays Zabel in *The National* as a "Turkey Hen" at the same time that he documents her panic upon arrival in Bulgaria immediately after escaping the genocide:

She has arrived. An outlandishly tall hat on her head, a tight-fit-

*ting dress, quaintly large feet, narrow eyes—a plucked, old turkey hen
who, after crossing the flatlands of Thrace and the closed frontiers, had
fallen in the streets of Sofia and is now squawking with a shrill, ardent
voice. She speaks volubly, with the accents of the Scutari dialect, her
tragic voice shaking, her thick fingers folding and unfolding, and the
centuries-old sorrow of the Armenian nation perched on her weakened
shoulders. The lady thinks in all modesty that her sudden arrival in the
Bulgarian capital is an event of national, perhaps even international,
import. She is under the impression that her literary fame will perform
miracles...*[38]

When the local officials ignore her, Zabel turns to the Armenian community. Gostan Zarian describes a visit to her "chamber" in which he finds her beside herself with worry about the intellectuals who have been left behind to perish. She insists that the Armenian community must act, and she hatches unrealistic plans with the French and British to rescue their compatriots.[39] Clearly, Zabel is looking for any help she can get. She is prompted by loss and violence, a destruction she knows all too well as a witness to the aftermath of the Adana massacres.

Rather than seek to understand this impulse, as he might have done for a male survivor, Zarian makes fun of her appearance, pointing out her yellow teeth and the way she shifts her belly when she sits—as if a woman shouldn't even have a belly. He shows little sympathy for the state she is in but mocks her desperate urge to rescue others as outsized self-importance: "...her voice flutters like a victorious banner. 'Me, me, me, me!'"[40]

Zarian was known for his proclivity to satire; he wrote this portrait many years later in 1930, and he, too, was a survivor of trauma, like Zabel—he escaped the Ottoman Empire, but his family did not, and he was mistreated in the Soviet Union in the 1920s—so he likely resented her role as a mouthpiece for Soviet Armenia at the time. Even so, it seems that Zabel is vulnerable not just as an Armenian after the genocide. Zarian's hateful depiction makes it clear that she was doubly so as a woman. Nearly twenty years later, when Zabel relocated to Soviet Armenia in 1933, she taught a literature class at Yerevan State University and made a positive impact on Rouben Zarian, a student from her class who later wrote a tribute to her in his memoir (published in 1978), identifying her sophistication and intelligence as she taught French literature.

The students hear of her reputation before she arrives, and so are already awestruck when she does, even more so by her first pronouncement that if they become bored with her lectures, they just shouldn't come: "I have always believed that one should avoid the use of coercion in these matters, because coercion offends the soul."[41] Here, Zabel is almost blasé as she cautions against the use of force, even as mild as it may be in a college classroom.

Rouben Zarian writes, "She went on to speak and we grew very fond of her. We just loved her." Zabel engages the students personally by advising them on their love lives and encouraging them to think for themselves. He recounts how she offers her analysis on French literature, expertly painting the historical backdrop behind each author: "...she went about it like a craftsman —a watchmaker who took apart the mechanism of the watch and put it together again with knowing hands."[42] She truly loves her students, and that love creates inspiration in them. Rouben explains that the students weren't just enamored with Zabel but also with the French literature she presented.

Rouben also mentions her love of Armenia. When the students ask how she can adjust to a provincial place after living in Paris, she says, "These inconveniences are meaningless in my eyes because I take an active part in the building of our country. Does that answer your question?"[43] Another Zarian might have mocked her as self-important for this stance, but Rouben admires her for it. On the last day of class she gives an informal talk:

> Her cigarettes and matches remain on her desk. "Her words came from the depths of her heart, they were the words of a mother who is about to be separated from her children [...] she spoke of the country and its prospects; she urged us to have faith in the future, to live and work for it, regardless of whether or not we should live to see it."[44]

Rouben's portrayal suggests a woman who has grown into herself over the years and who has found in Armenia a place where she could thrive. In a letter to writer Hagop Oshagan in 1935, she expresses her sense of belonging in Armenia: "I have been here for exactly two years and I am endlessly happy and comfortable. I can say that there has never been a period in my life where I have felt like I was living in accordance with my wishes and feelings as much as since I've come and settled here..."[45]

After considering the global, violent changes we're witnessing now and reading about Zabel finally finding a place of safety, I can't help but ask: how can I, or anyone else, judge what happened to the changing arc of Zabel's politics? When violence erupts, you do what you can to survive. You protect your loved ones, your people, your country, and your culture. Over time, however, this protective instinct can turn into a hard, rigid shell, transforming love into blind defense; perhaps we can only shed it when we are not traumatized. After the four-day war, I wondered if my generational trauma was so multilayered that only violence could unsettle me enough to the point that I could love myself as Armenian. But love for self didn't seem confusing for Zabel; her love for her people, country, and culture grew exponentially over the years, despite the horrors she witnessed and the disappointments she experienced.

10.

In the film *Finding Zabel Yessayan*, scholars interpret Zabel's life and work in vastly different ways, pointing to her shift in politics, her depictions of a woman's life, and her mind's utopia that she found in the reality of the Soviet Union.[46] Such diverse interpretations speak to Zabel's complexity—and how her love of people, country, and culture was reciprocated.

Shortly after she taught her class at Yerevan State University, Zabel attended the First Conference on Soviet Writers in Moscow in 1934, and it was there that Stalin identified her as someone to monitor like he did other Armenian writers, including the renowned poet Yegishe Charents. In 1936, after Charents was censored by the regime, Zabel spoke up on his behalf at a conference, calling him a visionary. "The names of many of us will be lost," she said, "but not that of Charents, not for many generations to come. We may, however, be remembered, but only in reference to Charents, and only to whether we were fair or unfair when talking about his genius."[47]

Here Zabel fights for what's right: she's not deferring to the regime but standing up for her fellow writer. In her claims about memory, she seems to be urging others not to bow to pressure. It was this literary form of activism that brought about her demise. In 1937, when she was arrested by the Soviets as "an enemy of the people" in Yerevan, Zabel told her daughter to keep preparing her grandchildren for their summer plans, at the same time that she told her in French, with an ironic tone in her voice, "I'm in trouble."[48]

In prison, she was harassed and tortured on a daily basis. At one point, she was forced to hang by her legs for two days; she could barely walk afterwards, and it took her three weeks of bed rest to recover. Still, she was tortured. Finally, she relented, signing a statement in 1938 that stated that she was an anti-revolutionary, a former member of the Tashnag party,[49] and a French spy. The form was in Russian, and she didn't know the contents. Zabel later filed a complaint that the statement was extracted from her by illegal means; as a result, her death sentence was commuted to ten years in prison. Still, she went on fighting: the prisoners weren't allowed to read or listen to the radio, so she banded the women together to discuss French literature.

Her last letter to her family was dated March 22, 1942. Her friend Clara Terzyan surmises that Zabel was either beaten to death or became ill on the way from Baku to Siberia, and that her body was dumped at sea. No one will ever know how she died, and her death was never properly mourned. Like other victims of the Stalinists' purges, Zabel's name was cleared by Soviet authorities in the late fifties. But her death was taken from her, struck from the record, erased as a historic moment, and stolen from memory.

At the beginning of *Finding Zabel Yessayan*, a taxi dispatcher in Yerevan says that he has never heard of the street named after her. Once the street is found, a woman who lives there says she doesn't know who Yessayan is, and neither do any of her neighbors. In agitation, she announces: "They should have named it after some great hero or leader." How ironic that Zabel claimed she would only be remembered in relation to what she said about Charents: she seemed to anticipate not only her own death but her life after death. In the years after the genocide, Zabel traveled for her work, but she could never return to Turkey after 1922 because of new laws in the Republic of Turkey that limited access to those who had threatened the Ottoman nation. In a sense, Zabel had already lived and died when she arrived in Yerevan. Perhaps she saw it as a rebirth.

How tragic, then, to die a second and even a third time, as a woman and again as a writer. In the film, Zabel's grandson (Hrant's son), and her great-granddaughter discuss how Zabel was never really mentioned much in their family, that a cloud of fear surrounded her. Her friend Clara explains that during the Stalinist purges, people were targeted by association—being related or married to someone suspected of espionage was enough to get you arrested. So, Zabel wasn't just forgotten by Armenians, but banished by her family, too. In her final letter in 1942, Zabel expressed concern that she hadn't received anything from her family since January, though her fellow prisoners regularly received mail: "I'm fine but concerned about the fact that there is no news from you, especially from Sophie. Please don't hide from me if she is sick. Is she working?"[50]

Here's an echo of her question about Sophie when she wrote to her husband from Adana in 1909: "And why doesn't my Sophie write to me? Is it just because she is lazy, or is there some other reason?" During Sophie's childhood, Zabel was frequently apart from her.[51] In March of 1914, Zabel wrote from Constantinople to her daughter in Paris:

> *You belong to a people who may be small in number but is large in pain, strife and hope. You've been called upon to participate in their struggle, in their work of realizing their aspirations. With the propensities of your people and their heritage, you've been called upon to play a major role in your country, where you must not only work, but also organize life and even create it. Is there a more interesting or even beautiful vocation than that?*[52]

Such a letter to a thirteen-year-old girl must have been both inspiring and intimidating. In 1920, Sophie seemed to take inspiration, moving to Constantinople to teach French in an Armenian school, which was an act of bravery after the genocide. Then, she was a librarian in Yerevan when she moved there with her mother. Sophie married and had a child, but after her mother's disappearance, Sophie lost both her husband and child during World War II. She had a psychological breakdown from experiencing an unimaginable loss of loved ones. How painful must it have been for Sophie not just to lose her mother but also to see her memory struck from all public record in a place that Zabel had considered her home?

⸘

My mother often repeats a line that her grandmother told her when Vivian died. "The greatest pain is losing a child," Mari would say. Did Mari's grief outweigh my mother's and take away my mother's ability to grieve? A young woman losing her mother needn't be quantified in relation to a mother witnessing the death of her adult child, because both losses possess their own unique quality. I think of those wailing, bereaved mothers in *In the Ruins* and helplessly question whether Mari was among them, even though her age, hometown, and immigration history wouldn't place her in Adana in 1909. According to her tombstone, Mari Biberjian, my great-grandmother, was born in 1883, so she would have been twenty-six in 1909. But wasn't she already in the US in 1895? I know her date of arrival through family folklore: a lady at a church picnic once told my mother that when she first came to Providence in 1915, Mari told her she had already been in the US for twenty years.

A need for certainty leads me back to Ancestry.com. According to a passenger list of the La Lorraine from Le Havre, France, a one Marie Papazian (her maiden name) from Constantinople arrived in New York on June 4, 1904, and her age is listed as twenty. Her final destination? Providence, Rhode Island. According to the marriage records of "Marry Papazian and Levon Bibeargian" of Rhode Island, they were married just one month later on July 2, 1904. Vivian was born the following year, in 1905. When I ask my mother if she remembers Vivian's birthday, she can't quite recall but thinks it was April or May, which would have been nine months after Levon and Mari's wedding.

According to his naturalization papers, Levon arrived in Providence in 1891 when he was fourteen years old. So her husband arrived before the Hamidian massacres of 1894–96, but Mari arrived ten years later. Who knows what she saw or witnessed as an eleven- to thirteen-year-old child? Something must have propelled her toward marriage and a family, but was it her own desire, or was her marriage arranged? At a time when Armenians embraced family as a method of survival, why did she and Levon have just one child? As I consider Marry and Marie and Mary Papazian in the files at Ancestry.com, I can't be absolutely certain that this Marie arriving on La Lorraine is my great-grandmother Mari.

"It was so hard for my mother," my own mother says. "Her parents were so old-fashioned, and because she was an only child, they really gave her a hard time when her marriage didn't work out."

Regardless of whether Mari left Constantinople in 1895 or waited until 1904, I won't ever know what contours of oppression and violence passed through my mother's family. I'm back to where I started before I read Zabel's books: all I know is that some kind of pain persisted.

When I visit my mother for Mother's Day, we shop at Marshall's, and I surreptitiously buy some cosmetics for her present. Then I find her strolling around the homewares section, and she asks what she can get for me. In women's clothing, she asks again. I look at her, pushing her cart and wobbling a bit from her arthritic knee. There is a whole lot of love in my mother, which has been emerging more as the pain recedes.

The next day, as she sits on the porch surrounded by her children and opening her Mother's Day presents, another story surfaces. The last night she stayed at her grandparents' home before her wedding, a hummingbird flew by her window. She had never seen a hummingbird before.

"Is this a good sign?" she asks, as if we are back with her in Cranston. The following week, I overhear her tell the story again, but this time, it's a rainbow that she sees. Beautiful images are floating through her mind, motifs that she might be inventing. In any case, the story gives me a glimpse of my mother as a young woman imagining her future married life. She has found strength and self-definition through images of beauty in her shifting memories. This prompts me to ask myself if I need to know the facts of my family history—with all the pain and trauma—in order to know myself. Loss of memory can be a form of love, too.

Perhaps not knowing how Zabel died, as wretched as her death might have been, makes us focus more on the beauty of her life. After all, do we have to know how she died to know that she was betrayed? That she fought her whole life? That she found beauty in a world of violence? Perhaps disappearance is a consolation. The unknown is a gift after all of the trauma.

Even if her death was stolen from her, and even if she was forgotten for many years, Zabel is remembered now. Actually, so much more is known about Zabel Yessayan than about countless other Armenian women. It turns out that she wasn't the only woman on the blacklist of intellectuals in 1915: there was a second named Mari Beylerian about whom little has been researched. As the historian Lerna Ekmekcioglu told me, the more Zabel is found, the more other Armenian feminists from her generation will be recognized as well.

My mother calls me one day to let me know she has been reading a recent *National Geographic* magazine, and that there is a spread on the ancient city of Ani. "Did you know it was a city of 1,001 churches?" she asks. It occurs to me that forgetting can allow opportunities to learn and relearn.

Letting go also allows chance into our lives. Most of my mother's family photos of Vivian have been lost, but as I was completing this essay, one surfaced: she is a young mother holding her firstborn baby on a beach in Rhode Island, smiling into the sun. I have been spiraling through lost memories and Zabel's stories, trying to sort them into numbered sections, when the picture of Vivian comes along to remind me: she was a real person. When I now consider the number of Armenians alive today, I realize our eight million is also the population of New York City. Perhaps we are not just a small race of people but an extraordinarily large, vibrant family, made up of individuals.

During the summer of 2016, violence seems to surge: terrorist attacks; mass shootings; police brutality; the Syrian refugee crisis; the violence of the 45th American president's campaign rallies; the coup in Turkey that prompted another blacklist, this one in the thousands; and attacks by militarized police on civilians and journalists protesting their corrupt government on the streets of Yerevan. Writing about Zabel and my mother helps me to sort through the insanity, and the ability to write reminds me that it is a manageable madness. Though the act of writing springs from me, it doesn't have a time, nor a place, nor a homeland, and it affords me the opportunity to learn and relearn through memory and lost memory.

Like all human beings, I come from deep roots of pain, loss, and love. This is enough certainty and uncertainty for me. And this is my existence. ❧

To Jennifer Manoukian, for her sensitive translation
of Zabel Yessayan's words and spirit.

Trek Across a Trackless Land

By Claudia Smith

O n June 9, 1909, Alice Ramsey begins a 3,800-mile journey from Hell Gate, Manhattan to San Francisco, California. It will take fifty-nine days across fourteen states—a vast trek across a "trackless land," as the Automotive Manufacturers Association put it.[1] Only 152 of the 3,800 miles that will be traversed by Alice and her companions across America are paved.[2] The journey is sponsored by the Maxwell-Briscoe Company, which was absorbed by Chrysler in 1926. She drives a green 1909 Maxwell DA, and to start the car, it must be hand cranked. In a grainy old photograph, she stands in front of the Maxwell-Briscoe Co. glass storefront with the three women who accompanied her.

She is the only one smiling for the camera, giving it a side-glance. She looks like a rascal, like someone who would cheekily say, "Good driving has nothing to do with sex. It's all above the collar."[3] The two older women, her sisters-in-law, are there to protect, to guide, to make it proper. The younger looking woman, a sixteen-year-old friend, is there to bookend the group. Alice is the only one who knows how to drive a car; she had been scouted for this adventure after completing a 200-mile round-trip race to Montauk, NY.

The summer after third grade, my grandparents, aunt, uncle, cousin, and I took a road trip to a family reunion. It was the only family reunion I've ever attended, and the first time I'd ever been to the Northeast. My grandparents were Yankees, and although my mother moved down to Texas with them when she was eleven and she sounded as Texan as anyone I've ever known, she always called herself a Yankee, too. They drove from Waco to New Bloomfield, Pennsylvania. We all fit into my grandfather's new white Crown Victoria. Even then, I thought of it as a boat of a car, with its powerful air conditioning and plush burgundy seats. We all fit, but barely. My cousin and I took turns in the middle seat in the back.

My grandmother had Parkinson's and couldn't drive, so the other three grown-ups took turns. They packed a cooler of sandwiches, but we also stopped at Kip's Big Boy or HOJO's. It's the best long drive I can remember. There is no drama, no sudden decisions, and no long stretches of perfect silence, which my father would have demanded had he been present. My grandparents have a plan and a budget. We stop by botanical gardens, and we stay in motels. My uncle consults AAA TripTiks. When it's my turn to sit in the window seat, I choose to look at the mesmerizing landscape pass for hours rather than play the car games my cousin keeps track of. I don't tell her that. We play *Mad Libs*. Once we get into the Deep South, we roll down the windows with the electric lever—you don't have to roll these windows down manually—and I can smell the Earth changing. The trees are hanging with moss, and everything smells heavy, like syrup. We progress north and get closer to Pennsylvania, the place my mother still calls home, but a place I've never been.

It must have been then that I fell in love with the American road trip. It was the best time I'd ever had on the road, although it was certainly not the first. I can't remember a first road trip. There were many with my parents, but they were usually fraught. I can vaguely remember riding in between my parents in a green pickup truck, traveling the country, going from point to point: the Southwest, the Midwest, the Northeast. I'm not sure you would call it a trip; there was no clear destination on the map. The destination was to find employment and security. Or was it? I'm not sure, exactly, because my mother always recalled our wanderings so fondly, as if those times were magic. But those trips, unlike Alice's adventure, had no clear end in sight.

The trip I took with my Grandma and Grandpa was a family trip, and I recognized it as one. It reminded me of the scrapbook pictures of family trips they'd taken in the 1950s, the Polaroid colors, my mother and my aunt standing in front of road stop signs, dressed for travel in white bobby socks and pleated skirts, squinting into to the sun.

❦

I found Alice online. In 1961, Alice Ramsey wrote and published the story of her journey titled, *Veil, Duster, and Tire Iron* while she was living in West Covina, California. It is out of print now and difficult to purchase, but the biography *Alice's Drive*, carefully researched, annotated, and written in large part by Gregory M. Franzwa, is affordable and easily found on Amazon. Franzwa's book contains Ramsey's account. I bought a used copy and was pleasantly surprised to find an inscription, "To Ron and Lunn, with best wishes, Gregory M. Franzwa, 2006." I wonder how much of history ends up with used booksellers. Franzwa wrote most of the book, and his work provides context, statistics, and historical and contemporary photographs, tracing the route in modern terms.

Alice now has entries on Wikipedia and in *Smithsonian Magazine*. Vassar College Archives and Special Collections library houses a scrapbook and printed materials about her automobile trip along with correspondence and audiotape. Various blogs and articles even show several women reenacting the centennial anniversary, in 2009, of Alice's historic drive across the country in, variously, a 1915 Model T, a 1909 Cadillac, and a 1909 Maxwell DA.

❦

Alice Ramsey was the daughter of a lumber dealer. She was a Vassar girl. She was educated, upper class, and she married well. In short, she was respectable. She was attractive. Her husband, John Rathbone Ramsey, was a congressman. She called him "Bone."

My own grandmother would be well over one hundred now; she was a small girl when Alice took to the road. She did not come from a sturdy middle-class background. Her father was a Methodist minister. She told me about her own vocation as a nurse; about Clara Barton, the founder of the Red Cross; and about service. At twenty-two, she was a nurse and was engaged to a doctor. All of the other nurses who worked in her ward died of tuberculosis. All but she. Her best friend, Sue Armstrong, died when she was the same age

Alice was when she began her journey. My grandmother contracted tuberculosis as well, returned her ring to the doctor, and lived in an asylum for almost ten years, preparing for death. She did not die but lost a lung. She returned to New Bloomfield, Pennsylvania and married my grandfather, a man twelve years her junior. She left for Texas with him after the war, after he'd failed in his business of selling and repairing cars, and they started all over again in Waco.

In their front driveway sat old cars, some without engines. Her husband Billy, my grandfather, still liked to repair cars, although he had given it up as a profession—instead, he taught welding. He had kept a copper-colored, penny-replica key chain in his pocket, inscribed with "A Penny A Day Drives A Henry J," which he got from a different failed business selling cars. When he died, he was fixing up a peach-colored Pacer for me.

With her Eastern sensibilities, my grandmother was what I considered a to be a lady when I was growing up. She never cussed, and she didn't use racial slurs. Once a week, she went to have her hair fixed, and sometimes I would go with her and get my hair washed, too. She smelled like apple-blossom perfume and once told me that a lady never paints the half-moons on her fingernails. She read, and I would later discover that she wrote poetry. After she died, I found some of her poetry in a box in their room. I also found a picture of her standing with all her friends, the nurses who had died. Their hair was cut straight across their cheeks, and they kicked their legs in the air playfully, pretending to be chorus girls. She worked until she was too sick to work anymore.

Only in dire circumstances could I imagine her driving across the country on her own. Despite having her own career, she followed my grandfather down to Texas. Staying in the town where they both grew up or staying for her job—I don't think they even considered it. I don't believe it would have occurred to either of them, not in the 1940s.

I only have one fickle, flickering memory of my grandmother driving. We have just arrived home from the Piggly-Wiggly grocery store. She is wearing driving gloves, and her hair is pulled back in a translucent red scarf. "Home again, home again, jiggidy-jig," she says.

⁓

There is a romance about the American road. It's a genre all its own:

the road trip movie, the road trip novel, the road trip memoir. The first road trip films and books I read and watched were about men. *On The Road, Fear and Loathing in Las Vegas*, and *The Electric Kool-Aid Acid Test* were the books I was drawn to at first. Why didn't I read Simone De Beauvoir's *America Day by Day?* I don't think I ever discovered it, and if I did, I took only a passing interest. I wanted to read about Raoul Duke and Dr. Gonzo going on a surreal journey filled with drug-induced hallucinations, tearing apart hotel rooms, wrecking cars, ruminating about the busted up American dream. It wasn't a pain I knew; I couldn't make a beast of myself, and if I did, it would have to be disguised as something else. If they were brave enough, the world was theirs for the taking. It was a broken world, but they could kick it around some.

&

Alice writes with a certain pride in herself, her achievements, with a kind of wry sense of humor that I recognize; it reminds me of my grandmother's. It is winking at me just a little bit, and it pisses me off at times but also charms me. She takes her journey with her husband's sisters—she calls them "the girls"—in tow. They wear "the daintiest of French heel footgear," and they are conservative. "Could such dressy and fastidious women manage with so little in the way of fancy clothes for so long a period?" she wonders. And yet, that's why the girls go along, right? They keep it looking civilized. And yet, Bone has no qualms about Alice's potentially unseemly adventure:

> *More than twice my age and with many years as a counselor-of-law and county official, Bone was a recognized political figure of considerable stature. Although he was better qualified than I to pass on matters concerning us, nevertheless he kept an open mind, allowed me to hold an independent opinion, and never "fenced me in."*[4]

I like her husband, with his open-minded sweetness. It's Alice I find myself unreasonably annoyed with as I read on. Why does she have to put so many words in quotes? I know she wants to go on that drive more than anything and that to do it, she has to be clever. She has to tuck things in a bit. This is what I'm in the habit of calling "generational," but it is also gendered. She has to be capable and controlled; she can never be a beast like Dr. Gonzo.

I found a picture of John Rathbone Ramsey online. He has a beautifully groomed mustache, kind eyes, and the kind of excellent posture I associate with portraits of well-to-do middle-aged men. It was a forgettable picture, a pleasant picture. Alice is not forgettable. The camera loves her as she leans in to the twentieth century; she is instantly recognizable in all photographs. In one of my favorites, she is changing a flat tire as one of her companions gazes demurely down at her. She manages to look comfortable and capable in spite of her heavy clothing; no wonder the sales manager of the Max-well-Briscoe Company called his idea to send her across the country "the greatest promotional idea of [his] career."[5]

I put the book down. I miss my grandmother. She died when I was twelve, in 1982, a year ahead of Alice. What frustrates me about Alice is also what frustrates me about my grandmother. I wish I could find those poems, but I'm not close to my mother or to any of the family members I grew up with. There are things Alice Ramsey won't tell. She isn't a proper writer like Beryl Markham, the adventurer who became known for her memoir *West with the Night*; instead, she is a storyteller.

It happens on the second page of *Veil, Duster, and Tire Iron*: Alice is proud of the beast in her, but it has to be subdued. It is something to joke about. She is clearly excited about the trip, and not interested in fashion. "The adventure," she writes, "is not going to be a 'style show.' It will be only slightly above the Hottentot version of clothing."[6]

Well, okay, Alice. I can't sanitize you or pretend you away. I wonder if I would have noticed this if I'd read the book when I was a girl. Probably not. It wasn't until I grew up and went away that I noticed Laura Ingalls Wilder's Ma telling her to put on her bonnet so that she won't look like a little pickaninny, or Gatsby's Nick Carraway noticing the "young buck" in the car passing him on the road with his merry, rich friends.

On page 41, Alice and the girls are invited to the Cobe Cup Race at Crown Point. They show up with dusty, sun-goggled faces:

> *Hats, veils and dusters failed to keep us protected or clean, and by the time we arrived, people were calling out to us "Oh, you kid!" and "Why don't you wash your dirty faces?" We were truly sights! Where our goggles fitted around our eyes, exciting the dust, there were circular patches of skin several shades lighter than the rest of the face. We looked as if we belonged to another race! (No pun intended).*[7]

Alice isn't doing anything I haven't seen other writers of her generation do over and over again. She is imagining herself as another race to allow herself some wildness. I could imagine my own grandmother saying this quietly, drolly, as she wraps a rain bonnet over her unruly white hair on the way to the Piggly-Wiggly; she isn't crass. Overtly racist comments are horrifying now, although they were an accepted practice at the time. And now that I'm the mother of a biracial child in 2018, Alice's wry asides, like my grandmother's, which were once upon a time subtle and quirky to me, strike me as arising out of thoughtlessly smug and coy privilege. The words make me cringe. I wish Alice would stay away from Hottentot references, as well.

A few years after I'd been pining over a picture of the beautiful Jack Kerouac in his motorcycle jacket, I noticed a poster of him on the wall in the media arts room of my high school. He looked askance, cigarette in his mouth, sexier than James Dean because he was the man James Dean only played in a film. I never got over crushing on that photograph or on the poster. I wanted to kiss his mussed hair, to be one of the women in the black-and-white photograph. I liked him because he knew things I didn't, because he'd slept with that waitress and eaten all that pie. I couldn't be him. It would wreck me and ruin me to let the beast out.

My freshman year of college, I read Mona Simpson's *Anywhere But Here*. I loved it. It reminded me of my favorite required reading from sophomore year of high school, Fitzgerald's *The Great Gatsby*. It is the story about Ann and her mother Adele driving to California in pursuit of Adele's dream to make her daughter a star. Adele—dreamy, beautiful, and self-absorbed—is the heart and soul of the book for me, but she needs Ann's canny and sobering narration to make her so. They would later turn it into a pretty good film starring Susan Sarandon, but the film would have none of the darkness, depth, and dreaminess of the book.

Ann, like Jay Gatsby's Nick, sees the blows coming when Adele cannot and will not. The sheer force and magic of their dreaming carries them in moments, but also like Gatsby, it can never sustain them. Adele takes (steals?) credit cards, finagles (bilks?) old people out of their Lincoln Continentals, and sleeps with men who never fulfill promises in the way that she imagines they will. Like Gatsby's, her dream isn't really about wealth or power but about the depth it promises. Adele and Ann drive from point to point, always unsettled.

Alice Ramsey is no Adele. She begins her journey with a clear desti-nation and arrives, with much fanfare, fifty-nine days after her departure. She is ensconced into a comfortable life and what appears to be a comfort-able and loving marriage. After her adventure, she settles into upper-class motherhood and fidelity.

The energy of her memoir comes from the sheer joy and pleasure she takes in her work, although it isn't called "work" or a "career"—it is adven-ture. I love that her infant son is barely mentioned, if at all; the book is best when she is immersed in the details of her passion. She devotes a page and a half to describing the 1909 Maxwell "30" touring car. She revels in changing a tire before an audience of men who don't really know what to do other than pump the gas for her. The landscape is her ocean, the Maxwell her ship. She follows a *Blue Book* automotive guide that can't keep up with the changing landscape and effectively ends at the Mississippi River. It instructs her to turn at a yellow barn, but the farmer has only recently painted it another color. When the *Blue Book* fails her, she follows the telephone wires to civilization.

"I was born mechanical, an inheritance from my father. As I grew up I showed great curiosity about the working of any device and by the time I was almost out of grade school I had elected to take manual training in-stead of some feminine art," she writes.[8] Both her father and her husband encourage her; it is Bone who gives Alice her first car and driving lessons. "I didn't even ask for the shining red Maxwell that was delivered to our door,"[4] she writes.

Her delight in mechanical and technical details reminds me of my grandfather: "Where modern automobiles use tires which measure perhaps 15 x 7 or 8 inches, the 1909 autos ran on wheels which utilized casings of 32 x 4 inches. This greater wheel diameter raised the chassis higher above ground and helped the transmission and differential escape possible dam-age from high centers between ruts made by wagon traffic." Command of the road was essential, until roads designed for motoring, she writes, "did away with those ridiculous [corrugated] differentiations."[9]

I was twenty-one the summer Ridley Scott's *Thelma and Louise* was released. I was a sophomore at Bard College, a small liberal arts school that was miles away from where I grew up, but it could have been a different planet, for all my understanding. I was just beginning to see the class differences between myself and many of my friends; even now, as my Chinese husband and I raise our blended family—my son is white, and our daughter came from both of us—I have a hard time understanding those differences. Space, geography, and time are different now. I, the wife of a Chinese immigrant, can log in to Facebook to see my brother's most recent white-nationalist-leaning post, a quote from *InfoWars*, perhaps, or a meme that seems a few clicks away from Holocaust denial. My husband holds a Ph.D. in biochemistry from China and is completing his second fellowship at Baylor College of Medicine. We are what I'd call middle class, and we live in a small, two-bedroom apartment that is well maintained but does have a chronic roach problem. What social class are we? I'm not sure. But I am not and never have been Alice. I've never had her resources. In this respect, I'm more of a Louise, one of the tough, canny, hardscrabble heroines of the film.

I went to see it with my friend Jen; on the way back, I was quiet for a while, thinking, "What the hell did I just see?" It was a man's buddy movie, but it was nothing like a man's buddy movie. Louise, a waitress, and Thelma, a restless housewife, were nothing like women I'd seen in films or television. Louise was no gum-smacking Flo from the sitcom *Alice*, saying, "Kiss my grits!" She was funny, and she was smart, but she wasn't cutesy.

When their story begins, Thelma and Louise are about to leave for a fishing trip together. They are excited and happy. Thelma's marriage is unhappy; her husband Darryl isn't as nice as Alice Ramsey's, and he isn't encouraging. At the start of their journey, both women are looking forward to some drinks in a bar and some time in the mountains. Louise is with a good guy, but she is tired of the crap she has been through and is a little cynical.

They put on their scarves and their lipstick, driving off in Louise's gorgeous car. When I watched the film again recently, I didn't remember the make—my grandfather would have. Had Alice lived to see the film, she would have, too. I looked it up. It's a mint-condition green '66 T Bird.[10]

You can read the screenplay online at IMSDb.[11] Screenwriter Callie Khouri won an Academy Award for best original screenplay in 1992, and in 2018, she is still only one of a few women to win in that category.[12] Watching Susan Sarandon and Geena Davis on screen makes the following scene move differently than it does on the page. There is laughter, and the whole scene has energy and verve. The wording is a little different as well.

> **THELMA**
> I've never had the chance to go out
> of town without Darryl.

> **LOUISE**
> How come he let you go?

> **THELMA**
> 'Cause I didn't ask him.

> **LOUISE**
> Aw, shit, Thelma, he's gonna kill you.

> **THELMA**
> Well, he has never let me go. He
> never lets me do one goddamn thing
> that's any fun. All he wants me to
> do is hang around the house the whole
> time while he's out doing God only
> knows what.

> *They are both silent for a minute.*

> **THELMA**
> [*looking straight ahead*]
> I left him a note. I left him stuff
> to microwave.

In the film, the two laugh when Louise tells Thelma that Darryl is going to kill her. And then, a little ruefully, she says quietly, "Well, I guess you get what you settle for." The whole film is filled with rueful lines and sad, funny moments like this one.

Thelma and Louise's fishing trip becomes a flight from the law when Louise shoots and kills a man they meet in a bar who has assaulted her friend in the parking lot. The film was as fast and charged as any outlaw Western I'd ever seen, but this was different. Thelma and Louise are traveling a charted America that is inhabited and "civilized"—and they are doomed. The now-iconic ending of the film shows the two women flying into the Grand Canyon to their deaths; it's the best kind of ending, one that feels inevitable. The movie was a blockbuster; everyone was talking about it the summer I came of age, the summer I was old enough to go to a club without a fake ID, drink a bit, and weave my way through potential men like Harlan, Thelma's would-be rapist.

After we left the theater, I think I said, "Wow. I've never seen anything like that."

And Jen said something like, "That was no *Terms of Endearment*."

"Yeah."

It was different, Jen said, because whenever Thelma or Louise did something to escalate the violence and their predicament, it was by turns horrifying and thrilling. It wasn't quite like watching Mel Gibson and Danny Glover blowing things up; much of the humor, the pathos, and the thrill came simply from the fact that Thelma and Louise don't respond in the way everyone expects them to respond.

Thelma and Louise's story takes a turn before Louise kills Harlan; the assault of Thelma was realistic, frightening; the camera never eroticizes Thelma's experience. The camera angles, and quick cuts to Thelma's struggle, from body parts to her facial expression, are closer in tone to battle scenes than anything I had seen before then. The moment we argued over and dissected was the moment that Louise shoots Harlan; after she's pointed her gun, and the women have successfully made their escape, Harlan gloats, "I should have fucked her!"

It's this moment that lingers, that makes all that follows resonate with humor and pathos. After this moment, I saw causal links everywhere, in every potential leering asshole, and so do Thelma and Louise. The violence that follows felt transformative; it was a movie, not my real life, but for the first time, I felt myself embracing the violence with gusto. I wanted Louise to shoot that fucker.

The first time I saw the film, I almost couldn't believe what they had done. They couldn't, at one point, either; the camera spends a moment taking their expressions in. "Shoot the radio, Louise!" Thelma shouts before they disarm a policeman and leave him locked in his trunk, careful to leave an air hole for him. Louise shoots the radio.

"I meant the police radio, Louise!"

By the end of the film, we watch them in pensive moments, looking into the eyes of elderly people who seem almost like visions and driving under pitch-black sky in the desert on the way to escape to Mexico. It all begins to feel like a fantastic dream. They blow up a tanker truck simply because the driver is being an asshole—he calls them "beavers." The viewer wants to laugh and to cry as he stands in front of his exploding truck, screaming, "You fucking bitches!"

Near the end of the film, they can both see there is no way out, and Thelma begins to laugh hysterically, recalling the look on the rapist's face right before Louise shot him, which was the action that set the whole film into frenetic motion in the first place.

INT. CAR - DESERT HIGHWAY - DAWN
They are quiet for a moment, then Thelma starts quietly laughing to herself. She is trying to stop but cannot.

THELMA
Boy, he wasn't expectin' that!

LOUISE
[*scolding*]
Thelma!

THELMA
[*impersonating Harlan*]
Suck my dick ... Boom!!

Thelma is laughing wildly.

LOUISE
[*quietly*]
Thelma. It's not funny.

Thelma has just crossed the line from laughing to crying.

THELMA
[*trying to catch her breath*]
I know!

They both get quiet.

Thelma leans back just watching Louise. She studies her as if she's never really seen her before. All of a sudden a look of shocked realization comes over Thelma's face.

She jerks upright and startles Louise.

THELMA
[*carefully*]
It happened to you ... didn't it?

The summer we saw the film together, Jen and I were rooming together on campus, working shifts for the food-services department during the day. That night, Jen drove a gray Jeep down a dark, long country road in the Hudson Valley in upstate New York, and we both laughed as she hit bumps in the road and hydroplaned on our good mood—on the gusto of that film. Until watching Davis and Sarandon on screen, I hadn't imagined that a road-trip movie could be like that one—the characters had gleefully allowed to let loose the beast.

⌇

If we return to Alice, we find a joyful narrative. There is no tragedy lurking around the corner, at least not in her telling, although beneath the surface, I can't help but feel that she's perturbed with the publicity stunt. Maxwell-Briscoe would claim that upon their arrival, Alice and her crew completed their journey without "a particle of trouble." Alice Ramsey's book makes the opposite claim:

> [She] had fixed at least one tire blowout and had called for a mechanic to repair a coil in Syracuse, waiting near their car as someone in the crowd cried "Get a horse!" Or the time the women came upon a sheriff's posse out hunting a killer in Ogallala, Nebraska. Perhaps intimidating at first, these men were only curious about the strangeness of finding women alone in a car at the edge of the road. In Nebraska, the car bottomed out in two separate holes within one mile of each other. They had to be pulled out, she later recalled, "The farmer's son caught one of their horses in pasture and pulled us out—for a fee—then walked on to the next hole, repeated his towing, but doubled his fee!" And in Opal, Wyoming, Alice and crew suffered a serious case of bedbugs from a roadside motel.[13]

Additionally, although most newspaper coverage of her journey was supportive, Alice later said, in response to the naysayers, "...criticism, of course, merely whetted the appetites of those of us who were convinced that we could drive as well as most men [...] It's been done by men and as long as they have been able to accomplish it, why shouldn't I?"

Indeed. Why shouldn't she? And why shouldn't her tale have all the trappings of an adventure story, with all the scrapes, humor, and triumph? Alice prides herself on her resourcefulness, on her crew. Her narrative makes it abundantly clear that this is no publicity stunt, that the challenges she faces are no less than that of any man's. If the road trip is essentially an American story, what is our story? Certainly, women in this country have reached the point in our journeys with some "particle of trouble." Long before Jack Kerouac's *On the Road*, we read and followed adventures because of the quest, not the journey.

Women continue to take to the road, in fiction and nonfiction. There is Mona Simpson's *Anywhere but Here*, Cheryl Strayed's emotional memoir *Wild*, and Mary Miller's coming-of-age road trip novel *The Last Days of California*, to name just a few.

꿏

If *Thelma and Louise* is a ballad, then *Veil, Duster, and Tire Iron* is a fireside story—a bright yarn. And, as with any rich and resonant mythos, we need both, don't we?

My own road trips are both—and neither. I'm a middle-aged, white, twenty-first century woman; I can't call myself a lady, because a word that feels so lovely when applied to my grandmother just does not apply to me. My mother has very different opinions on sexual politics and rape than I do; she was not a *Thelma and Louise* fan. I wonder if my own grandmother would approve of the middle-aged me. I've taken countless road trips on my own, and I like to think that she would approve. I imagine she would rather that I had married as a virgin and had remained married to the same man. I imagine that she would love my daughter, who is not white. I don't want to believe she would say the things my mother said, that my daughter looks nothing like me. My mother said that Chinese was "the ugliest language she had ever heard," which she later qualified by saying, "Well, maybe what I was hearing was Cantonese."

In so many ways, we fail our mothers. And they fail us.

I'd like to think she would be mostly proud of me.

⌒

I drove a yellow Dodge Dart from Virginia to New York to leave a boy-friend who would later take all the money from our joint bank account, trans-ferring it into an account only in his name. He was able to convince the teller that he was my fiancé and therefore did not need my permission. I spent the night in a YMCA, watching movies from my bunk bed and sipping Coke that I bought from a vending machine. I had fifty dollars to my name. I spent several months on friends' couches and a lot of quarters on pay phones.

I drove with a friend from graduate school from Mississippi to North Car-olina in a green Neon to deliver my son to his father for a summer visitation. I was broke and had not received child support for some time, but I was deter-mined to follow the court order and deliver my son on time. There were many privacy controls on his health insurance, including a withholding of informa-tion that meant I couldn't file claims. When he contracted pinkeye, it ended up being a few hundred dollars on my debit card, which only made me sore. After being directed to the parking lot of what appeared to be a nice condominium in an upscale, artsy neighborhood, I said goodbye to my kid, got myself some pie, and then drove all night, fueled by bad gas station coffee and a metallic, hollow taste in my mouth.

I would not cry. I would not cry.

There was a kind of romance, I suppose, in these travels. I listened to music, felt sorry for myself, and did a lot of daydreaming. Once, after leaving my son in Houston, I drove all the way back to Hattiesburg, Mississippi, an eight-hour drive, without stopping to pee. I pulled up to our family-housing apartment and passed out for twelve hours. How strange it was to wake up late, in a heavy daze, without a little boy to cook for.

I remember driving him from Texas to our new beginning in Hattiesburg, Mississippi, where I was going to start graduate school, in that same green Neon. I was scared but certain. I listened to a lot of Cyndi Lauper, and my son slept half the time. In Texas, there were rest stops every few hundred miles, and the sky was as I remembered: vast and blue during the day, full of stars at night. When we crossed over to Louisiana, the landscape changed, and once I made it to Mississippi, the pine trees made the world seem cozier and less intimidating.

We drove over swampland across the Atchafalaya—a very long, un-interrupted bridge. "It almost looks like dinosaurs could be munching on vegetation out there, don't you think?" I asked my son.

He agreed.

↵

In Chicago, Alice Ramsey and the girls were overcome by a drove of pigs. The pigs, she writes, are everywhere, "big pigs, little pigs, all different sizes and all different colors, all over the roads as well as the fields." She hadn't realized there were so many pigs. "They seemed to tickle our risi-bles,"[14] she writes.

This is the serendipity of adventure. This is what Alice revels in. Perhaps this is what I seek—what so many of us seek when we take to the road. Most of us in this country came from somewhere else, or our grandmothers did, or their grandmothers did. We drive into places that are new, or not so new, or changing, always changing.

I Google "women" and "road trip." I cause an avalanche:

> *Women On The Road, Empowering Women Through Travel*
> *The Wild Woman Roadtrip Guide*
> *The Female Survivalist: Surviving the Road Trip*
> *How to Travel As a Woman By Herself*
> *Women on Road Trips Aren't Tragedies Waiting to Happen, We're Free*, a great opinion piece in *The Guardian*.

There is a list of road trip movies, including a Brittany Spears movie from the 1990s. Thelma and Louise tops that one. There is "BlackGirlTravel.com: One-Stop Travel Resources for Black Women." It's great. I think of all the narratives of women on the road, traveling, that have been written and are going to be written.

Yarns, ballads, movies, and blogs.

If I write one, what will my granddaughter think of it? What will she see that I can't see? What do I know that she doesn't, that she won't know? Should I tell her about stopping at a rest stop in Texas, climbing out of an old blue Ford Escape, and trying to read the sweaty printouts of Google

Maps before GPS was common? We still had flip-phones. I felt sorry for myself and worried, thinking that in spite of the fancy schools I'd attended and the scholarships I'd earned, I was still lost and scared. I couldn't even get a secured credit card.

Should I tell her that?

And then it occurs to me that among all these Google hits, there is no Alice Ramsey. You have to know her name to find her. I try other searches, such as "road trip alone female" and "solo road trip female," but I can't find her. Later, I discover an obituary for Alice's daughter, Alice Ramsey Bruns, who died at 105. In 2009, at age ninety-eight, Bruns said about her mother to *The Record*, on the 100th anniversary of her mother's cross-country drive, "Nobody thought too much at the time about what Mother did […] she was not recognized. The car should have gone into the Smithsonian, but instead, Mother said it burned up in a garage in Passaic."[15]

~

I Google her name. I look at her picture and at her face, which is a remarkable face. She is behind the wheel, looking down at the camera. She's not sitting on her perch in the car that had to be tall like a wagon, lest it be torn apart. She's Alice. She follows the telephone wires when the *Blue Books* steer her off course, back to civilization.

For my Grandmother

Reader's
Guide
Questions

Reader's Guide Questions

**Developed by Stephanie Cohen, Heather Klinkhamer,
Tiffany Morris, and Margaret Seiler**

These questions are grouped into shared themes, with questions that are specific
to each individual essay followed by broader questions about the book as a whole.

CONTENTS

WOMEN AS BODIES AND VESSELS

Questions for *Nangeli: Her Defiant Breasts* by Meera Nair

1) Meera Nair discusses "a woman finding joy in the experience of privacy and relishing her autonomy." Today, some places prevent women from wearing concealing garments such as head scarves. Why and how might women who seek privacy and modesty be a threat, particularly in modern times? —*H.K.*

2) Why do you think Nair chose to structure *Nangeli: Her Defiant Breasts* in the form of two linked tales about related situations in the past and the present? How would your understanding of Nangeli's historical tribulations and Nair's present-day societal concerns about women's bodies as "sign and spectacle" (p. 24) change if the essay had been written instead as two separate narratives? —*S.C.*

3) In *Nangeli*, Nair closely examines how class structures objectify the body (particularly those bodies coded as female). She also examines how she has internalized these societal structures and messages. In what ways do we subconsciously absorb these messages? How do we confront them, and what can be done with that confrontation? —*T.M.*

4) Nair writes about disowning the conventions of her caste: "I had discarded it easily, and to my mother, it likely felt like I was disowning not only our traditions but her." If you choose to reject the traditions, religion, or rules that you grew up with, how do you grapple with the cognitive dissonance of your loved ones' differing opinions and the potential interpersonal fallout? Is it possible to educate people who are set in their ways? Is it even desirable to do so? In extreme circumstances, your non-conforming views may expel you from your family or community. Does taking a stance require sacrificing relationships? Does not taking a stance equal cowardice? How do you weigh a rupture with loved ones against doing the right thing? —*K.K.* (*editor*)

5) Discuss the significance of "the body" in the tale of Nangeli—from the ancient Vedic texts describing the caste system in India as moving from the lowest part, the feet, to the highest, the head, to her rebellious act of cutting off her breasts. How does the representation of women's bodies still manifest itself in various cultures? How can we understand the personal motivations of Nangeli's sacrificial act and the resulting social response to it? —*M.S.*

Questions for *Victorine and Laure in Manet's* Olympia: *Seeing and Not Seeing a Famous Painting* by Debra Brehmer

1) Debra Brehmer uses the word "consumed" to describe the state of being naked and on display for another, both in art and in her own personal experience. Much has been written about the "male gaze." How does the "gaze" embody itself—masculine, feminine, bisexual, white, black? How does contemporary identity politics affect our understanding of art history? —*M.S.*

2) Both women in Manet's painting *Olympia* are depicted in the context of work, but the nude figure is shown in a moment of rest whereas the maid is shown to be actively performing labor. How does the portrayal of labor in art reinforce power structures? How can we contextualize the figures of Olympia with Brehmer's statement that "capitalism was and still is a steamroller that does not respect difference or realignments of power"? —*T.M.*

3) We know little about the real Victorine Meurent, but we know even less about "Laure," the black maid figure in Manet's *Olympia*. However, from a design perspective, the maidservant takes up just as much room on the canvas as the supine white prostitute does. What does the typical interpretation of this aspect of the painting reveal about the ideals and stereotypes of Western art? What do you make of Brehmer's hypothesis that there might be a Madonna-and-child situation occurring in the painting? —*S.C.*

4) Brehmer shows that women can be simultaneously recorded and erased. How is this possible? Can presence also be an absence? Brehmer also suggests that women's work can be placed alongside that of

men to illuminate the past. How does adding women's work to the historical context change the conversation? — *H.K.*

IDENTITY

Questions for *Rose-Poisoning: Beauty, Violence, and the Unknown History of Zabel Yessayan* by Nancy Agabian

1) Nancy Agabian returns to Yessayan's ability to see beauty in a world of violence throughout the essay. To what extent do you think both Agabian and Yessayan use beauty to cope with hostility and destruction? Can you think of any other writers who balance the dueling realities of beauty and violence to create their messages? What other messages might be conveyed in addition to hope and resilience? —*T.M.*

2) Two unrelated men with the surname Zarian (Gostan and Rouben) wrote vastly different accounts of Yessayan. Gostan compared her to a "Turkey Hen," unfavorably focusing on her appearance and manner. However, Rouben, her student, wrote a glowing tribute to Yessayan's lovability, intelligence, and sophistication. What are the positive and negative attributes of each kind of impression? If this example shows a microcosm of divergent male attitudes toward women, how can it inform a strategic reaction to addressing broader Feminist issues? —*K.K.* (*editor*)

3) Agabian's essay speaks to intergenerational history and suffering within a single family as well as to how a community as a whole is impacted by prejudice, violence, and genocide. Agabian was drawn to research Yessayan because of their shared identities —"Armenian, woman, writer"— but what other parallels do you spot between Yessayan's story and that of Agabian's grandmother and mother? —*S.C.*

4) Agabian said that her mother "talked herself into existence," but the author endeavors to piece her history together based on snippets of information from her mother. To fill the gaps of her family narrative, she relies on Yessayan's story as a possible

guide. When the facts of a story are unknown, how does placing it within its larger context honor its fuller history? —*H.K.*

Questions for *Origins* by Taté Walker

1) How are feminism and colonialism intertwined? What are the differences between: (1) rights and responsibilities, (2) equality and equity, and (3) autonomy and collectivism? How might these differences—combined with colonial-based feminism—harm, displace, and erase Indigenous womxn? Can feminism be a more inclusive space for Indigenous womxn? If so, in what ways? —*T.W. (author)*

2) Taté Walker explores the intersecting issues of cultural appropriation and Native American representation in pop culture, for instance in children's literature, movies like *Dances with Wolves* and *The Revenant*, and racist sports team mascots. How do these forms of storytelling dominate stories about Native American peoples, especially women's stories? What popular culture generated by Native American peoples have you encountered that refute or complicate white-led narratives about Native Americans? What Native-American-created pop culture would you like to see made more visible? —*T.M.*

3) Lakota oral history relates that a woman's actions are the basis of all Lakota ceremony. How can students of women's history give equal value to oral history and the all-powerful primary document? Also, Walker writes, "feminism was built for white, middle-class women who never experienced gender equity," whereas pre-Columbian Indigenous peoples had a much more gender-fluid culture. How is contemporary, mainstream feminism the outgrowth of a patriarchal worldview? Does it embrace a genderless ideal?—*M.S.*

4) Walker describes being raised in an Indigenous Lakota culture that valued feminine energy and strength. How did this worldview contrast with the misrepresentation, underrepresentation, cultural appropriation, and "casual racism" they experienced as they grew older? What does their research on how children of color perceive the world's impressions of them reveal? —*S.C.*

5) As Walker writes in *Origins*, cultural appropriation and "casual racism" stems from a romanticized and biased view of Native American Culture that ignores the responsibilities that come with it. For example, they may want to experience teepee glamping, but, "few want the Indigenous leadership, historical trauma, and systematic oppression that comes attached." What does this opinion infer about the bond (or lack thereof) between privilege and education about that privilege? —*S.C.*

6) Walker lists the ways of what could be called "white dissembling" on page 58, including "Midwest nice," "Southern hospitality," "not seeing color," and "playing devil's advocate," to name a few. It calls attention to the way racism can subtly and subconsciously—if not deliberately—be rationalized. Women similarly come up against these forms of dissembling about their lived experiences by men, often by way of some "mansplaining." How do you become more mindful and change your own dissembling rationalizations? What is the most effective way to make other dissemblers aware of their bias, whether toward you or others? —*K.K.* (*editor*)

Questions for *Radiant Identity: Chicaba Herstories* by Chicava HoneyChild

1) What does Chicaba's life story elucidate about the manipulation of the spiritual lives of the enslaved? How do we discern the life of her true inner soul from the original proposed narrative of her life? —*C.H.* (*author*)

2) What is the power Chicava claims when she names herself? How does it reflect a larger reclamation of power? —*H.K.*

3) After examining the "path to sainthood" timeline provided on page 185, consider how society classifies both Chicaba, the historical figure, and Chicava, author. The Victorian (and honestly, age-old) figures of the "fallen woman" and the "angel" provide dichotomies that history tries to separate, but HoneyChild notes that they are all intertwined. How do both

Chicaba and Chicava defy those boxes and provide knowledge and healing to other women in the community, despite the bias against them? —*S.C.*

4) How does the devotion to a religious or spiritual life both detract from and add to a woman's power or independence? How did Chicaba's devotion to the Catholic faith and her scholarly ability both change her lot as an enslaved woman and also undermine her cultural heritage as an African? —*M.S.*

5) Chicaba is brought to her spiritual path through a series of mystical experiences and visions. How do we situate the roles of mysticism and piety with Chicava HoneyChild's own intuited interpretation of Chicaba's life? Discuss this in the context of HoneyChild's statement that "true piety is rejoicing in the fantastical orchestration of your very existence." —*T.M.*

Questions for *Reveling and Rebelling: A Look at the Life of Ada "Bricktop" Smith* by Kara Lee Corthron

1) Ada "Bricktop" Smith had a vivid and colorful life that was framed, in large part, by a sense of self-determination. Yet she was still expected to perform emotional labor in many different areas of her life. To what extent do you think this expectation is gendered? Racial? Has society advanced in this expectation of women? How has this expectation impacted black women, specifically? —*T.M.*

2) Kara Lee Corthron writes, "Our cultural lust for drama (and, let's be real: trauma) often neglects the stories of people who lived fascinating lives and who ultimately lived WELL." How are such accounts romanticized, and how is this romanticized view different among genders? —*S.C.*

3) Despite identifying as a member of several marginalized communities in Western Europe during her life, Bricktop conformed to certain "traditions" of her time such as requiring women to be escorted by men in the otherwise freewheeling experience of Parisian nightlife as well as refusing to acknowledge interracial marriages. What are your thoughts on the motivations that might lie behind adhering to

these strict rules, especially for a liberated woman of a minority community who prided herself on her hospitality? —*S.C.*

4) How did traditional societal norms and archetypes for women, and particularly black women, play out in Bricktop's life? What can we make of the good female/bad female dichotomy imposed by society in relation to Bricktop? It is also useful to consider her life in the context of colorism, a form of prejudice based on gradations of skin color. How does that discrimination still play out today? —*M.S.*

5) What do you make of Bricktop's decision to identify as what was most convenient and "safe" at a given moment? What does this speak of the environment she was raised in and the new environment she cultivated in her nightlife hotspots? Though she gained notoriety as a famous black and female hostess, she rarely acknowledged her heritage during her life. —*S.C.*

DEFYING TRADITIONAL ROLES

Questions for *Up From the Rubbish Heap: The Persistence of Julie D'Aubigny* by Caitlin Grace McDonnell

1) Caitlin Grace McDonnell zeroes in on fencing, which was practiced both by her grandmother and Julie D'Aubigny, as a symbol of strength and daring. She writes about sparring, her high school debate club, and her young daughter's ability in public speaking. How does fencing function as a metaphor for the "dance of power" in women's lives? How can voices be used as swords? —*M.S.*

2) In *Up From The Rubbish Heap*, McDonnell expresses her own ambivalence about her participation in "heteronormative coupledom" and uses D'Aubigny and her family as inspiration for operating outside of its confines. Yet, there is a class component to their freedom to subvert heteronormative coupledom as well. In what ways does class uphold or subvert heteronormative coupledom? How does the class of women like D'Aubigny and Eleanor Cass factor into its upholding or subversion? —*T.M.*

3) Through telling the story of D'Aubigny and her own grand-mother, McDonnell mentions that her female predecessors, both blood-related and not, become "both hero and cautionary tale" (see also Berger's quote on page 160). She both committed to her-self and to the patriarchal society she was raised in. What do you make of this internal divide that many women experience? How did D'Aubigny defy these traditions and live life on her own terms: physically, mentally, and emotionally? —*S.C.*

4) D'Aubigny was an outrageous and charismatic personality. Even so, is it shocking to learn that she stashed the corpse of a nun in a bed as a placeholder, all the better to traipse off in the night with her amour?! Is this mischief, or is it criminal behavior? Is it trans-gressively thrilling that she got away with this act without serious consequences? Why or why not? —*K.K.* (*editor*)

Questions for *Baba Yaga Unleashed: The Night Witches* by Betsy Andrews

1) Betsy Andrews references fairy-tale imagery like Baba Yaga and the dark, twisted fantasy world of the Brothers Grimm to sew togeth-er the grim realities that victims of Nazi experimentation and other horrors endured. How else does the fearsome figure of Baba Yaga manifest itself in Soviet Russian culture? How do ideas about this fairy tale creature feed into stereotypes and biases against women's physical, mental, intellectual, and emotional capabilities? —*S.C.*

2) How do you speak about something without giving undue power to it? The rhetorical device of paralipsis gives cursory emphasis to a point—instead of elaborating on it—as a means of elevating the impact of its understatement. Andrews seems to employ it by noting in her essay that her father demanded to know when she was going to write a book about him. Do you think his brief appearance in *Baba Yaga Unleashed* would have satisfied his need to have an entire book written about him? What do you think she was trying to stress by omission of additional details, and how does this link to other aspects of her essay? —*K.K.* (*editor*)

3) Andrews writes that women in the Soviet Union were regarded as both fighters and mothers, and she notes the many ways women suffer during war. They suffer from violence as both civilians and soldiers, and they anguish as mothers, daughters, and wives of those killed, captured, and maimed. Unlike the women sent to the Gulag when the enemy captured their soldier-husbands, the night witches were granted some agency in their wartime fate. Is it better for women to fight in or to resist wars? Why or why not? —*H.K.*

4) In *Baba Yaga Unleashed*, Andrews utilizes the metaphors of birth and motherhood in her examination of war and femininity. In what ways does war undermine the traditional structures and expressions of femininity? Are motherhood and femininity implicitly at odds with violence and war, or are there ways in which these intersect on a social and/or societal level? —*T.M.*

Questions for *Under the Cover of Breeches and Bayonet* by Jessie Serfilippi

1) Gender-bending and cross-dressing, not to mention trans and queer women characters have made quiet but nonetheless impactful appearances in history, both literary (think Shakespeare) and real-life events (Joan of Arc). The discrepancies in Deborah Sampson's story are intriguing, but the questions remain: what was her life really like, and which story is true? Why does society seem intent on spending so much time to "get the facts right" for male historical figures, upholding those facts, but less concerned with getting the story right for women? Feel free to bolster your discussion with other examples of masquerading and androgynous women from films, TV shows, books, and history, and both the power and pain their secret lifestyles afforded them. —*S.C.*

2) In *Under the Cover of Breeches and Bayonet*, Serfilippi establishes her desire to have Sampson's sexual orientation identified, affirmed, and reflected. Serfilippi simultaneously advocates for greater representation in our historical figures, and identifies the deleterious impact of historical erasure in her own life. Do you think that con-

temporary history moved forward in making these identities known? How has this type of erasure impacted your own perceptions of history, and has it extended into your own personal experience? —*T.M.*

3) Sampson impersonated a man to enjoy the freedom of living as a "masterless woman." Although many women today do not need to impersonate men to live freely, they sometimes assume "masculine" behavior or clothing to be taken seriously, especially in the workplace. For example, they may wear suits or speak in a lower register. Is this a form of deliverance? How can modern women enact deliverance in a world still dominated by men? Can deliverance be found when abiding by dominant systems and structures? —*H.K.*

4) The concept of "deliverance," which can be defined as "the action of being rescued or set free," is emphasized by Serfilippi in Sampson's story. Consider this concept in relation to Sampson, other historical figures, and/or yourself. Do you agree that her story, as we know it, is a good example of deliverance or liberation? —*M.S.*

FIGHTING FOR RIGHTS

Questions for *Audacious Warrior: Ernestine Rose* by Edissa Nicolás-Huntsman

1) Independently embarking into the realities of the world at a young age, Ernestine L. Rose defied many barriers placed in front of her based on her identity: race, religion, age, and gender. She spoke of the importance of self-care and the need for "social recreation to restore a healthy equilibrium to the system." What is the significance of female self-care in our society today, and how is it advocated for or suppressed? —*S.C.*

2) In *Audacious Warrior*, The Queen of the Platform says it is easier to "take a fortress" than it is "to storm a citadel of prejudice." Is it easier to win a physical battle than hearts and minds? Why? —*H.K.*

3) Ernestine Rose is quoted as saying, "The world is my country, and to do good my religion." Although she became atheist at a

young age, Ernestine was raised in a Jewish household, and she both identified with Jewish culture and was coded as Jewish socially. Her work in social justice, as noted with the quote above, was performed from a humanist perspective. How does Ernestine's experience of religion and culture inform her embrace of social justice and the belief that "human freedom and true democracy are identical?" —*T.M.*

4) What does The Queen of the Platform mean when she asks us to consider, "What is wrong in one sex, can be right in the other?" William Rose supported Ernestine's social reform efforts. What can we learn from their relationship? How does this pertain to the task of fostering allies today? —*H.K.*

Questions for *Firebrand: The Radical Life and Times of Annie Besant* by Leah Mueller

1) In her exploration of Annie Besant's life, Leah Mueller touches upon the different forms of violence executed by the state, most vividly and concretely shown in the "Bloody Sunday" incident. To what extent do social justice movements anticipate the violence of the state as inevitable? In what ways did Besant's activism attempt to lessen its impact? Discuss contemporary parallels. —*T.M.*

2) Besant was a radical: a women's rights activist, trade unionist, and atheist. She was a vehement defender of the woman's right to control her own body and also spoke out against English colonial rule. Later in life, she threw herself into the religion of theosophy. How do you reconcile these two aspects of Besant's life: political activist and spiritual seeker? —*M.S.*

3) Besant's story, as do many of the women depicted in this anthology, centers around an unhappy marriage (or two, in some cases) and a choice to forgo having biological children, which was often disapproved of (and still is, sometimes). Besant even advocated for women's sexual rights and moral methods of contraception. What kind of emotional impact does this sort of conflicting dichotomy

(loving, doting wife and mother versus lonely, successful spinster) have on women, especially women during Besant's era? As Mueller describes in her anecdote about a man who was repulsed by her because she was not "an unspoiled column of pure light," what types of effects do these unrealistic and often contradictory standards and rules have on women? —*S.C.*

4) In Mueller's essay on Besant, the possibility is explored that the women's rights and family planning advocate knew of her co-president's inappropriate treatment of young men, yet still kept Leadbeater instated in his role. The essay includes the statement, "Besant resided in a paternalistic society and surrounded herself with men." In the face of the time, her position, and these circumstances, how much are women expected to succumb to the traditional opinion and hypocrisy rather than uphold their own personal values? —*S.C.*

TRAILBLAZERS

Questions for *The Blazing Worlds of Margaret Cavendish* by Robyn Kraft

1) In *A True Relation,* Margaret Cavendish assumes a male voice and is uncharitable toward members of her sex. Did she internalize the sexism she endured, or does her attitude reflect ambition and privilege? —*H.K.*

2) Cavendish remarked that "it is within everyone's power to create their own world as they see fit, be it on paper or in reality." This idea can be applied to everything from social justice to utopian fiction like Cavendish's own *The Blazing World*. Notable for its heroine protagonist, it is an early example of the intersection of gender and utopia. What role does gender equality play in the concept of a utopia? How does the concept of gender itself influence or corrupt the idea of a utopian society? —*T.M.*

3) Robyn Kraft discusses the identification of different literary genres as masculine or feminine; comic books, for example, are often seen as masculine. We know that "male-identified" spac-

es have evolved since seventeenth-century writer Cavendish lived. And, yet, they still exist. How do you think those spaces have contracted, expanded, or stayed the same? In particular, what genres, authors or literary works do you think either fit, or explode, societal gender norms? —*M.S.*

4) Cavendish was a trailblazer in several respects, which include penning one of the earliest examples of science fiction. Cavendish even referred to herself as a writer with masculine pronouns, despite publishing proudly under her own name. How does Cavendish's choice of language tie into Kraft's anecdote about being made to feel unintelligent, inexperienced, or unwanted in specific primarily male-dominated, niche-specific communities that are also of interest to women? Do you think some of Cavendish's confidence in the sciences, publishing, and the community can be transferable to women today in spheres they may feel outnumbered or uncomfortable in? —*S.C.*

Questions for *Trek Across a Trackless Land* by Claudia Smith

1) The road trip is a particularly American phenomenon because the country is vast (and some years after Ramsey's journey) was covered by a network of easily accessible "tracks." Claudia Smith comments on the "beasts"—mainly men—who act destructively and dangerously as they road trip across America. Consider Ramsey's journey as a female-centric road trip. How does the road trip express a uniquely American identity? What part does the road trip play in the American dream? How has that dream changed over time and across generations? —*M.S.*

2) Smith brings up several interesting points about being raised in a paternalistic society in her essay. Her own American road-trip idols were initially all male, from the cast of *Fear and Loathing in Las Vegas* to *On the Road* and *The Electric Kool-Aid Acid Test*. She describes simultaneously wanting to *be* and *be with* James Dean at the height of his "cool" phase. What do you make of this par-

adoxical desire of being infatuated with a man while wanting to emulate him? —*S.C.*

3) Throughout *Trek Across a Trackless Land*, Smith expresses both dismay and discomfort at the racism implicit in the social conditioning of the past and connects it to present day issues. How can we best navigate the racism practiced by historical figures, especially female ones? How does this tie into Smith's statement that "in so many ways, we fail our mothers. And they fail us?" —*T.M.*

4) Smith writes, "And then it occurs to me, among all these Google hits: there is no 'Alice Ramsey.' You have to know her name to find her." What do Smith's revelations that the American road trip has become a tale that romanticizes male fictional and real-life protagonists, "beasts" et al., as well as the fact that Ramsey, and the vehicle she accomplished her cross-country feat in, have been mostly forgotten, tell readers of the subversion of *her*story, the female-led, factual series of events? —*S.C.*

5) Ramsey writes that she inherited her mechanical skills from her father, and Smith agrees that mechanical and technical processes remind her of a male role model in her own life, her grandfather. Because male family members can have a positive impact on their daughters, granddaughters, nieces, and sisters, it seems to suggest that the barriers in male-dominated workspaces may be systemic. What do you think Smith and Ramsey's remembrances imply about the opportunity for women to relate to prominent female figures in male-dominated STEM fields? Is it a lack of same-gender mentors and role models, systemic barriers, or both that impede full participation in such positions? —*S.C.*

BROADER QUESTIONS ABOUT ALL ESSAYS

1) All of these essays intertwine personal reflection and historical research. To what extent do we internalize history in our own narratives? How do we center history and historical figures in our daily lives? What does this mean for claiming and reclaiming narratives about female historical figures and the issue of whose stories get told? —*T.M.*

2) How have women and their achievements been suppressed in the arts, culture, and other aspects of our society? Consider the anecdote in *Rose-Poisoning* about Emma and her interest in the handsome gentleman caller, Diran bey, until he flatly notes about her painting:

> *"It doesn't seem as if a woman's hand had held your brush; your portrait, for example: only a man could have painted it that way. I find it difficult to formulate my feelings and thoughts at present, but this much is clear: only a man is capable of painting a woman affected by her most tumultuous, most electrifying emotions."*

And in *Baba Yaga Unleashed,* as Soviet women precision-dropped bombs upon Germans and killed them, a Nazi general remarked, "We simply couldn't grasp that the Soviet airmen that caused us the greatest trouble were, in fact, women." Have you ever been in a situation where your obvious ability to do the work was blatantly disbelieved, minimized or dismissed, even though its impact was undeniable? How could you strategically overturn underestimation of your abilities to your advantage? —*S.C./K.K.*

3) Both Taté Walker, in their essay on Lakota and Indigenous origins, and Robyn Kraft's essay on Margaret Cavendish explore definite usages of preferred pronouns. Other essays in the anthology, such as those on Deborah Sampson and Julie D'Aubigny, explore themes of diverse identification by how a woman chooses to dress or by their romantic/sexual partner preferences. How did these modes of identification create adversity for these historical trailblazers? How do they still do so today? How did these women overcome those biases against them and their choices? —*S.C.*

4) Some of these essays (e.g., Deborah Sampson, Zabel Yessayan) discuss masquerade survival techniques used by women throughout history, whereas others (e.g., Ernestine L. Rose, Chicaba, Annie Besant) promoted their identities freely to achieve their goals. Still others (Bricktop) relied on convenience depending on

situations to flaunt their true selves or stay back in the shadows. What were the pros and cons of taking each of these stances? Were any of these routes more of less effective than others? —*S.C.*

5) In *Firebrand: The Radical Life and Times of Annie Besant*, *Radiant Identity: Chicaba Herstories*, and *Origins*, spirituality is tied inextricably to social justice movements. What role does spirituality have in the feminist movement, both historically and currently? What undercurrents exist in the disparate forms of spirituality that unite these historical figures in their championing of social causes? —*T.M.*

6) Caste, colorism, colonialism, and settler colonialism as discussed in *Reveling and Rebelling*, *Nangeli*, and *Origins* are different systems of dehumanizing. Identify what structural components of each of these oppressive classifications are similar, dissimilar, or related. How can these systems be rejected, dismantled, and made obsolete? —*K.K.* (*editor*)

7) Many of the subjects in *Fierce* were never given proper tribute for their contributions during their lifetimes; some were eventually remembered long after their passing, but many were overlooked or forgotten altogether. Consider how Alice Ramsey's car was burnt in a garage in New Jersey rather than given a place of honor in a museum, or the throwaway comment about how the street named after Zabel Yessayan in Yerevan should have been named after a hero. What does this say about society's current historical priorities? —*S.C.*

8) Reproductive justice and motherhood, whether literal or figurative, are recurring themes in many of these essays. How does reproductive justice inform other forms of social justice, in general and in these essays? What are some contemporary examples of intersection between the two? —*T.M.*

9) Several of these essays traverse the sometimes painful, and even taboo, subjects of mental health, mental illness, and trauma. What kinds of effects do you think that mental well-being, mental illness, and self-care had upon women activists, teachers, and

mothers? See Ernestine L. Rose, Zabel Yessayan, and Bricktop essays for examples. —*S.C.*

10) From fables about unicorns resting their heads in the laps of virgins, to the timeless and tiresome virgin/whore tropes, women throughout history have had the burden of "purity" placed upon them, often twinned with the assumption of performative attractiveness for others. Several essays explore how purity expectations impacted both their subjects and themselves, whether by caste rules, like Nangeli with her "polluting breath," Chicaba the nun and Chicava the stripper, or the "column of unspoiled light" question asked of essayist Leah Mueller. How does purity culture continue to manifest today, and how is it detrimental to women? —*K.K. (editor)*

11) Discuss the role of formal education (or a lack thereof) in motivating these female figureheads to achieve their goals and fight for what they believed was just and fair. See Julie D'Aubigny, Lady Cavendish, Victorine, and Chicaba for examples. —*S.C.*

12) To quote a line from Nancy Agabian's essay on Zabel Yessayan, "The mother has become a child; the mother is a child; lines are blurred as she tries to cope with despair." Discuss the intergenerational contexts of essays like *Up from the Rubbish Heap, Trek Across a Trackless Land*, and *Reveling and Rebelling*, wherein past heroines influence those to come. Some ideas on mothering not only flesh-and-blood children but also brainchildren include child-rearing as a single parent, the idea of "Mammifying women," the epigenetics of trauma endured by past generations, and conversely, being positively influenced by past generations. —*S.C.*

13) Land is at the forefront of Indigenous justice movements, as is seen in Walker's *Origins*. It can also be a source of inspiration, whether it's the beauty of roses in *Rose-Poisoning*, or something to be explored, as in *Trek Across A Trackless Land*. What roles do ecology, land, and nature play in social justice movements, especially feminism? In what areas are they overlooked? How do

the dichotomies of ownership and stewardship of land factor into social justice? —*T.M.*

14) HoneyChild notes that Eurocentric scholars are quick to mistakenly conflate various African and Caribbean traditions (including those of the Ewe, Igbo, and Yoruba) to flesh out their knowledge of Chicaba's spiritual life. A similar issue is also referenced in Taté Walker's essay. How are these assumptions and mass groupings of cultures and beliefs both dangerous to historical records and the true understanding of a figure, a people, or an entire community? —*S.C.*

15) Women often assume male forms or manners to live on their own terms and be taken seriously. D'Aubigny and Sampson dressed as men. Soviet women openly fought in World War II—a male prerogative at the time—and contemporaries of Cavendish published under male pseudonyms. Do the advantages of this approach outweigh the downfalls? What are the drawbacks and advantages? —*H.K.*

16) Several women in *Fierce* were self-created economic powerhouses. Ernestine Rose, Annie Besant, and Bricktop all created their own financially successful businesses. Rose and Besant used the money they made to make an impact for social justice in their worlds, and Bricktop donated to Catholic charities later in her life. Walker also notes in *Origins* that white women try to fit in a system that was not built for them. If you work within conventional economies, systems, and hierarchies but devote your life and economic power to social justice, does it offset being a part of the system? Why or why not? —*K.K.* (*editor*)

FIERCE *Timeline*

Oral History	1600	1650	1700	1750	1800	1850	1900	1950	2000

NANGELI LIVED IN THE EARLY 19TH CENTURY.

THE NIGHT WITCHES WERE ESTABLISHED ON OCTOBER 8, 1941 AND DISBANDED ON OCTOBER 15, 1945

PTESÁŊWIŊ

ADA BRICKTOP SMITH (AUGUST 14, 1894 – FEBRUARY 1, 1984)

ANNIE BESANT (OCTOBER 1, 1847 – SEPTEMBER 20, 1933)

VICTORINE MEURENT (FEBRUARY 18, 1844 – MARCH 17, 1927)

JULIE D'AUBIGNY (C. 1670 – 1707)

ERNESTINE ROSE (JANUARY 13, 1810 – AUGUST 4, 1892)

MARGARET CAVENDISH (C. 1623 – DECEMBER 15, 1673)

CHICABA – TERESA, SISTER JULIANA OF SANTO DOMINGO (C. 1676 – DECEMBER 6, 1748)

DEBORAH SAMPSON GANNETT (DECEMBER 17, 1760 – APRIL 29, 1827)

ZABEL YESSAYAN (FEBRUARY 4, 1878 – C. 1943)

ALICE RAMSEY (NOVEMBER 11, 1886 – SEPTEMBER 10, 1983)

Bibliography and Notes

Foreword

1 A. Padnani and J. Bennett, "Remarkable People We Overlooked in Our Obituaries," *New York Times*, last modified March 8, 2018, http://www.nytimes.com/interactivE/2018/obituaries/overlooked.html.

2 S. Goldberg, "For Decades, Our Coverage Was Racist. To Rise Above Our Past, We Must Acknowledge It," *National Geographic*, March 12, 2018, http://www.nationalgeographic.com/magazine/2018/04/from-the-editor-race-racism-history/.

3 Adrian Piper, "Ideology, Confrontation and Political Self-Awareness," *High Performance*, 1981.

4 Mary Beard, *Women & Power: A Manifesto* (New York: Liveright, 2017).

5 Ernestine Rose, "Speech at the Second National Woman's Rights Convention in Worcester, Massachusetts: 'Unsurpassed'" (October 15, 1851), quoted in Paula Doress–Worters, *Mistress of Herself: Speeches and Letters of Ernestine Rose, Early Women's Rights* (New York: The Feminist Press at CUNY), 91–103.

6 K. Reilly, "'Nevertheless, She Persisted': Women's History Month Theme," *Time*, March 1, 2018, http://time.com/5175901/elizabeth-warren-nevertheless-she-persisted-meaning.

7 Ibid.

8 James Earl Carter, Jr., "Liberty University Commencement Address," in *Liberty University Commencement* (Lynchburg, VA: Liberty University, 2018).

9 K. Todd, *Chrysalis: Maria Sibylla Merian and the Secrets of Metamorphosis* (Orlando: Harcourt, 2007).

10 C. C. Miller, K. Quealy, K., & M. Sanger–Katz, "The Top Jobs Where Women Are Outnumbered by Men Named John," *New York Times*, April 24, 2018, https://www.nytimes.com/interactive/2018/04/24/upshot/women-and-men-named-john.html.

11 A. Garcia, "Trump Gets Caught Saying 'Grab Her by the Pussy'" YouTube video, 01:12, October 7, 2016, https://www.youtube.com/watch?v=o21fXqguD7U.

12 M. Yglesias, "Trump's Enduring Political Strength with White Women, Explained," *Vox*, July 25, 2018. https://www.vox.com/2018/7/25/17607232/trump-white-women.

13 H. Cixous, "The Laugh of the Medusa," *Signs* 1, no. 4 (1976): 875–893, doi:10.1007/978-1-349-22098-4_19.

14 Ursula K. Le Guin, "Bryn Mawr Commencement Address," in *Bryn Mawr Commencement* (Bryn Mawr, PA: Bryn Mawr College, 1986).

15 C. Wingfield, "Witches' Ladder: The Hidden History," England: The Other Within, accessed April 13, 2018, http://england.prm.ox.ac.uk/englishness-witchs-ladder.html.

Nangeli: Her Defiant Breasts

1 "The Agenda with Steve Pitkin: Anupama Rao: The Caste Question" YouTube video, 16:21, January 23, 2011, https://www.youtube.com/watch?v=OH_u0uCr59E.

2 Robin Jeffrey, *The Decline of Nayar Dominance: Society and Politics in Travancore 1847–1908* (London: Sussex University Press 1976), 9–10.

3 Patrick Orville (trans.), The Law Code of Manu (New York: Oxford University Press, 2004), 19.

4 Ambedkar Rao Babasaheb, *Who Were the Shudras?: How They Came to Be the Fourth Varna in the Indo-Aryan Society* . (Calcutta: Thackers Press, 1972), 4, archive.org https://archive.org/stream/in.ernet.dli.2015.527572/2015.527572.Who-Were_djvu.txt

5 Ambedkar Rao Babasaheb, *Who Were the Shudras?*, 5.

6 Orville, *Law Code of Manu*, 19.

7 Babasaheb, *Who Were the Shudras?*, 4.

8 Sasha Riser–Kositsky, "The Political Intensification of Caste: India Under the

Raj," *Penn History Review* 17, no. 1 (2009): 32.

9   Riser–Kositsky, "The Political Intensification of Caste," 32.

10   Udaya Kumar, "Self, Body and Inner Sense: Some Reflections on Sree Narayana Guru and Kumaran Asan ," *Studies in History* 13, no. 2 (1997): 249.

11   CNN Staff, "Sexually abused and seen as the lowest of the low: life as an 'untouchable' Dalit woman," CNN, last modified July 25, 2016, http://www.cnn.com/2016/07/25/asia/india-dalit-caste-women.

12   John Berger, *Ways of Seeing* (London: British Broadcasting Corporation and Penguin Books, 1972), 54.

13   Vivek Deshpande, "Khairlanji Massacre: From Khairlanji to Kopardi, Full Circle in 10 Years," *The Indian Express*, last modified September 20, 2016, https://indianexpress.com/article/india/india-news-india/khairlanji-kopardi-rape-case-maratha-protests-3053443/.

Baba Yaga Unleashed: The Night Witches

1   Anne Noggle, *A Dance with Death: Soviet Airwomen in World War II* (College Station, TX: Texas A&M University Press, 1994), 86; Reina Pennington, *Women, Wings, and War: Soviet Airwomen in World War II Combat* (Lawrence, KS: University Press of Kansas, 2002), 82; Samantha Vajskop, *Elena's War: Russian Women in Combat* (Ashland, OH: Ashland University), 18.

2   Noggle, "Interview with Major Mariya Smirnova," in *A Dance with Death*, 31.

3   Pennington, *Women, Wings, and War*, 72.

4   Pennington, 72.

5   Thomas Robisheaux, "The German Witch Trials," in *The Oxford Handbook of Witchcraft in Early Modern Europe and Colonial America*, ed. Brian P. Levack (Oxford, UK: Oxford University Press, 2013), 179.

6   David Frankfurter, *Evil Incarnate: Rumors of Demonic Conspiracy and*

Satanic Abuse in History (Princeton, NJ: Princeton University Press, 2008), 87.

7   Noggle, "Interview with Captain Larisa Litvinova–Rozanova," in *A Dance with Death*, 68.

8   Noggle, "Smirnova," 31.

9   Noggle, "Litvinova–Rozanova," 64.

10   Noggle, "Litvinova–Rozanova," 69.

11   Noggle, "Interview with Senior Lieutenant Yevgeniya Zhigulenko," in *A Dance with Death*, 55.

12   Noggle, "Interview with Polina Gelman," 38.

13   Vajskop, *Elena's War*, 18.

14   Vajskop, 17.

15   Henry Sakaida, *Heroines of the Soviet Union 1941–45* (Oxford, UK: Osprey Publishing, 2003), 18.

16   Noggle, "Interview with Lieutenant Serafima Amosova–Taranenko," in *A Dance with Death*, 46.

17   Joanna Hubbs, *Mother Russia: The Feminine Myth in Russian Culture* (Bloomington, IN: Indiana University Press, 1993); Andreas Johns, *Baba Yaga: The Ambiguous Mother and Witch of the Russian Folktale* (New York: Peter Lang, 2004).

18   Douglas Martin, "Nadezdha Popova, WWII 'Night Witch,' Dies at 91," *New York Times*, July 14, 2013.

19   Vajskop, *Elena's War*, 28.

20   Pennington, *Women, Wings, and War*, Appendix A; Pennington, 87.

21   Vajskop, *Elena's War*, 9.

22   Vajskop, 27.

23   Noggle, *A Dance with Death*, 97.

24   Noggle, 47–48.

25   Orlando Figes, *The Whisperers: Private Life in Stalin's Russia* (New York, NY: Picador, 2008), 111.

26   David Hosford, Pamela Kachurin, and Thomas Lamont, *Gulag: Soviet Prison Camps and Their Legacy* (Cambridge, MA: National Park Service and the National Resource Center for Russian, East European and Central Asian Studies, Harvard University) 2, http://gulaghistory.

org/nps/downloads/gulag-curriculum.pdf.

27 Amy Goodpastor Strebe, *Flying for Her Country: The American and Soviet Women Military Pilots of World War II* (Lincoln, NE: Potomac Books, 2009), 17.

28 Marianna Yarovskaya, director, "Interview with Yelena Glinka [in Women of the Gulag (film in progress)]," YouTube video, [14:24], [October 10, 2015], https://www.youtube.com/watch?v=z9Y2EvrM4R0

29 Pennington, *Women, Wings, and War*, 77–78.

30 Noggle, "Interview with Senior Lieutenant Nadezhda Popova," in *A Dance with Death*, 81.

31 Bryce Myles, *Night Witches: The Amazing Story of Russia's Women Pilots in World War II* (Chicago, IL: Chicago Review Press, 1997), 62.

32 Anna Akhmatova, "Requiem," in *The Complete Poems of Anna Akhmatova*, ed. Roberta Reeder, trans. Judith Hemschemeyer (Brookline, MA: Zephyr Press, 1994), 384. Akhmatova was a great Russian poet born in Odessa in 1889. She has been lauded ever since the publication of her first book, Evening, in 1912. She was a star of St. Petersburg's literary scene. Following the Russian Revolution, her work was banned, first unofficially by the Bolsheviks and after World War II by official decree under Joseph Stalin, when she was expelled from the Writers' Union. Her son, Lev Gumliyov, was arrested, and she spent 17 months waiting in prison lines—an experience she describes in her long poem, "Requiem," written in secret throughout the 1930s and dictated in fragments to friends for safekeeping. "Requiem," which was not published until 1987, is dedicated to Stalin's victims and is a witness document by a poet beloved by the Russian people. Following Stalin's death, state repression against Akhmatova was lifted. In 1964, two years before her death at the age of 76, she was named president of the Writers' Union.

33 Nadezhda Mandelstam, *Hope Against Hope: A Memoir* (New York: Atheneum, 1970), 4. Mandelstam was the wife of acclaimed Russian poet Osip Mandelstam, who died in 1938 in a transit camp en route to the gulag.

She authored two astonishing memoirs of her life in Soviet Russia: Hope Against Hope, which documents her husband's final years, and Hope Abandoned (1974), which is about their early years together and her own existence after her husband's death. Both are essential reading for insight into life under the Stalin regime.

34 Noggle, "Smirnova," 37.

35 Noggle, "Interview with Senior Lieutenant Nina Raspopova," in *A Dance with Death*, 21–26.

36 Associated Press, "Russian Guards Order Stalin's Police-Style Coats," *San Diego Union–Tribune*, June 19, 2011.

37 Neil MacFarquhar, "A New Vladimir Overlooking Moscow," *New York Times*, November 4, 2016.

38 Ibid.

39 Rosemary Sullivan, *Stalin's Daughter: The Extraordinary and Tumultuous Life of Svetlana Alliluyeva* (New York: Harper Perennial, 2015), 92.

40 Sullivan, *Stalin's Daughter*, 85.

41 Sullivan, 66.

42 Sullivan, 78.

43 Scott Neuman, "Trump Lashes Out at McCain: 'I Like People Who Weren't Captured,'" *The Two-Way: Breaking News from NPR*, July 18, 2015.

44 "Interview with Nenila Platonovna Bazeleva," in *Life Stories of Russian Women: From 1917 to the Second World War*, eds. Sheila Fitzpatrick and Yuri Slezkine (Princeton, NJ: Princeton University Press, 2000), 241.

45 Anna Krylova, *Soviet Women in Combat* (Cambridge, UK: Cambridge University Press, 2010), 15.

46 Catriona Kelly, "Riding the Magic Carpet: Children and the Leader Cult in the Stalin Era," *Slavic and East European Journal* 49(2) (July 2005): 206–07.

47 Krylova, Soviet Women, 41.

48 Krylova, 27.

49 Krylova, 12.

50 Krylova, 43.

51 Noggle, 47.

52 Noggle, 39.

53 Noggle, "Interview with Senior Lieutenant Alexandra Akimova," in *A Dance with Death*, 92.

54 Sullivan, p. 85.

55 Noggle, "Amosova–Taranenko," 45.

56 Noggle, "Interview with Major Irina Rakobolskaya," in *A Dance with Death*, 26.

57 Noggle, "Interview with Captain Klavdiya Ilushina," in *A Dance with Death*, 51.

58 Noggle, "Interview with Lieutenant Olga Yerokhina–Averjanova," in *A Dance with Death*, 58.

59 Noggle, "Raspopova," 26.

60 Noggle, "Zhigulenko," 57.

61 Noggle, "Interview with Senior Lieutenant Irina Sebrova," in *A Dance with Death*, 77.

62 Noggle, "Interview with Senior Lieutenant Zoya Parfyonova," in *A Dance with Death*, 70.

63 Noggle, "Interview with Major Mariya Smirnova," in *A Dance with Death*, 32.

64 Noggle, *A Dance with Death*, 94.

65 Kevin Maurer, "She Kills from 7,850 Miles Away," *Daily Beast*, October 18, 2015, http://www.thedailybeast.com/articles/2015/10/18/she-kills-people-from-7-850-miles-away.html.

66 Noggle, *A Dance with Death*, p. 56.

Origins

1   John G. Neihardt, *Black Elk Speaks: Being the Life Story of a Holy Man of the Oglala Sioux*, (New York: William Morrow & Company, 1932), 294.

2   A note on racial terms: I use the word "Indian" sparingly and only in a direct quote or when referring to the legal and historical name thrust upon Indigenous people of the United States by the federal government. "American Indian" is the legal term used most often today, though "Native American" is also accepted as a legal term as of 2016. Whenever possible, I use "Native," "Indigenous," or specific tribal names.

3   Neihardt, *Black Elk Speaks*, 295.

4   "Sioux" was adapted by French fur traders from "Nadouessioux" (a pejorative meaning "enemies"), a name originally applied to them by the Ojibwe, who competed with the Dakota for resources. *Encyclopædia Britannica*, "Sioux," accessed December 13, 2016, https://www.britannica.com/topic/Sioux.

5   Anh-Thu Cunnion, Lakota Winter Count: *The Teachers' Guide* (Washington, DC: National Anthropological Archives, Smithsonian Institution, 2005), 4.

6   Shannon Smith, "Once upon Their Time," in *Native Daughters* (Lincoln, NE: University of Nebraska–Lincoln, 2010), 68.

7   Lydia Whirlwind Soldier, Stephanie Charging Eagle, Dorothy LeBeau, Earl Bullhead, Dan Snyder, and Corrie Ann Campbell, *Oceti Sakowin Essential Understandings and Standards* (Pierre, SD: South Dakota Department of Education, Office of Indian Education, 2012), 24.

8   Vine Deloria, Jr., *God Is Red* (New York, NY: Dell Publishing, 1973), 114.

9   Smith, *Native Daughters*, 69.

10 Deloria, *God Is Red*, 111.

11 D.M. Dooling (ed.), *The Sons of the Wind: The Sacred Stories of the Lakota* (New York: Parabola Books, 1984), 139.

12 Dooling, *Sons of the Wind*, 3.

13 Dooling, 3–5.

14 Whirlwind Soldier et al., *Oceti Sakowin*, 15.

15 Neihardt, *Black Elk Speaks*, 295.

16 Border towns are majority-white communities situated near Indian reservations. In border towns, systemic oppression and racially based violence committed by non-Natives against Natives is disproportionately higher than in other communities. "In constant and close proximity to the perceived 'threat' posed by...[a large Indigenous] presence to the supremacy of U.S. common sense, border town residents uphold, reinforce, and inhabit practices of colonization in their assumptions and everyday dealings with Indigenous Peoples (sic)." Melanie K. Yazzie, "Brutal Violence in Border Towns

Linked to Colonization," *Indian Country Media Network*, August 22, 2014, https://indiancountrymedianetwork.com/news/politics/brutal-violence-in-border-towns-linked-to-colonization.

17 Mike Anderson, Samuel Blackstone, and Jennifer Naylor Gesick, "Safety Concerns Arise About Downtown Rapid City," *Rapid City Journal*, January 22, 2017, http://rapidcityjournal.com/news/local/safety-concerns-arise-about-downtown-rapid-city/article_eb679ec0-8333-536b-b223-2af0a79d24fc.html.

18 Deloria, *God Is Red*, 210.

19 Susan Hazen–Hammond, *Spider Woman's Web: Traditional Native American Tales About Women's Power* (New York, NY: The Berkley Publishing Group, 1999), 2.

20 Virginia Driving Hawk Sneve, *Sioux Women: Traditionally Sacred* (Pierre, SD: South Dakota Historical Society Press, 2016), 21, 23.

21 Roxanne Dunbar–Ortiz, *An Indigenous Peoples' History of the United States* (Boston, MA: Beacon Press, 2014), 110.

22 Dunbar–Ortiz, *An Indigenous Peoples' History*, 142.

23 Dunbar–Ortiz, 158.

24 Dunbar–Ortiz, 211, 212.

25 Neihardt, Black Elk Speaks, 295.

26 Wikipedia, "Ralph Englestad," accessed January 28, 2016, https://en.wikipedia.org/wiki/Ralph_Engelstad#cite_note-18.

27 I've written extensively about Indian mascots, so I am intimately familiar with the responses generated by this statement. I address most of those here http://everydayfeminism.com/2015/01/argue-against-racist-mascots/.

28 Audre Lorde, *Sister Outsider: Essays and Speeches* (Berkeley, CA: Crossing Press, 2007), 138.

29 This is an inclusive way of spelling "woman" or "women" that embraces queer women, transwomen, and women of color, while also rejecting the biblical notion that womxn are separate entities from "man." See Asia Key, "Woman, Womyn, Womxn: Students Learn About Intersectionality in Womanhood," Standard, March 27, 2017, http://www.the-standard.org/news/woman-womyn-womxn-students-learn-about-intersectionality-in-womanhood/article_c6644a10-1351-11e7-914d-3f1208464c1e.html.

30 David Huyck, Sarah Park Dahlen, and Molly Beth Griffin, "Diversity in Children's Books 2015 Infographic," sarahpark.com, September 14, 2016, https://readingspark.wordpress.com/2016/09/14/picture-this-reflecting-diversity-in-childrens-book-publishing.

31 Maile Arvin, Eve Tuck, and Angie Morrill, "Decolonizing Feminism: Challenging Connections Between Settler Colonialism and Heteropatriarchy," Feminist Formations 25, no. 1 (2013): 26.

32 "Ending Violence Against Native Women," Indian Law Resource Center, accessed February 21, 2017, http://indianlaw.org/issue/ending-violence-against-native-women.

33 Andre B. Rosay, "Violence Against American Indian and Alaska Native Women and Men: 2010 Findings from the National Intimate Partner and Sexual Violence Survey," National Institute of Justice Research Report, May 2016, https://nij.gov/publications/pages/publication-detail.aspx?ncjnumber=249736.

34 "Ending Violence Against Native Women."

35 Sarah Deer, *The Beginning and End of Rape: Confronting Sexual Violence in Native America* (Minneapolis, MN: University of Minnesota Press, 2015), x.

36 Peter A. Leavitt, Rebecca Covarrubias, Yvonne A. Perez, and Stephanie A. Fryberg, "'Frozen in Time': The Impact of Native American Media Representations on Identity and Self-Understanding," *Journal of Social Issues* 71 , no. 1 (2015): 39.

37 Andrea Carmen and Vi Waghiyi, *Indigenous Women and Environmental Violence: A Rights-Based Approach Addressing Impacts and Environmental Contamination on Indigenous Women, Girls and Future Generations* (New York, NY: United Nations Permanent Forum on Indigenous Issues Expert Group Meeting, United Nations Headquarters, 2012), 16.

38 Winona LaDuke, *The Winona LaDuke*

Reader: A Collection of Essential Writings (Stillwater, MN: Voyageur Press, Inc., 2002), 218.

39 Neihardt, *Black Elk Speaks*, 296.

IMAGES

p. 53, map: Wikipedia, "Great Sioux Reservation, 1888; established by Treaty of Fort Laramie (1868)," accessed October 4, 2016, https://en.wikipedia.org/wiki/Sioux#/media/File:Great_Sioux_reservation_in_1888.png. The text under the provided image on Wikipedia reads, "Great Sioux Reservation. 1888 Map showing the location of the Indian reservations within the limits of the United States and territories, compiled from official and other authentic sources, under the direction of the Hon. Jno. H. Oberly, Commissioner of Indian Affairs; Wm. H. Rowe, draughtsman." Ibid.

p. 57, photograph: Provided by the author.

p. 63, illustration: 2015 Diversity in Children's Books. Huyck created this with a Creative Commons BY-NC-SA 4.0 license (Huyck, Dahlen, & Griffin, 2016). Used with permission. https://readingspark.wordpress.com/2016/09/14/picture-this-reflecting-diversity-in-childrens-book-publishing/

p. 67, photograph: Sarah Sunshine Manning, © 2016. Used with permission.

Reveling and Rebelling: A Look at the Life of Ada "Bricktop" Smith

1 "TOBA" stands for "Theatre Owners Booking Association."

2 James Haskins and Ada Smith, *Bricktop* (New York, NY: Atheneum Press, 1983), 26.

3 Haskins and Smith, *Bricktop*, 134–35.

4 Haskins and Smith, 135.

5 Nadra Kareem Nittle, "What Is Colorism—Skin Tone Discrimination in America," ThoughtCo., last modified July 22, 2018, https://www.thoughtco.com/what-is-colorism-2834952.

6 The Brown Paper Bag Test was used to determine whether an individual could have certain privileges. Only individuals whose skin was the same color as a brown paper bag or lighter were given these privileges. The test was used in many African American and multiracial settings such as fraternities, sororities, churches, and professional organizations. "Brown Paper Bag Test," *Wikipedia*, accessed January 21, 2018, https//en.m.wikipedia.org/wiki/Brown_Paper_Bag_Test.

7 Haskins and Smith, Bricktop, 96.

8 Haskins and Smith, 225–26.

9 Haskins and Smith, 126.

10 Haskins and Smith, 190–91.

11 Haskins and Smith, 144.

12 Haskins and Smith, 106.

13 Jean–Claude Baker, Josephine: *The Hungry Heart* (New York, NY: Cooper Square Press, 1993), 120.

14 Haskins and Smith, Bricktop, 108.

15 Haskins and Smith, 109.

16 Haskins and Smith, 109–10.

17 Haskins and Smith, 180.

18 Haskins and Smith, vi.

19 Haskins and Smith, 158.

20 Haskins and Smith, 289.

21 There is a musical called *Bricktop*, but from the little information I could find, it seems that it's more of a jazz revue than a traditional musical with a story.

Firebrand: The Radical Life and Times of Annie Besant

1 Archana Singh, "Annie Besant," The Varanasi Society, accessed February 20, 2017, http://www.varanasi.org.in/annie-besant.

2 Andrzej Diniejko, "Annie Besant's Multifaceted Personality. A Biographical Sketch," The Victorian Web, last modified November 20, 2014, http://www.victorianweb.org/authors/besant/diniejko.html.

3 Diniejko, "Annie Besant's Multifaceted Personality."

4 "Annie Besant," in *Encyclopedia of Occultism and Parapsychology* (Farmington Hills, MI: Gale, 2001), accessed February 16, 2017, link.galegroup.com/apps/doc/K1656000167/

BIC1?u=tacomapl&xid=dab40ac0.

5   "Bradlaugh–Besant Trial (Birth Control),"
    What-When-How, accessed February
    20, 2017, http://what-when-how.com/
    birth-control/bradlaugh-besant-trial-birth-
    control.

6   *Wikipedia,* "Margaret Sanger," accessed
    January 23, 2018, https://en.wikipedia.org/
    wiki/Margaret_Sanger.

7   "Bradlaugh-Besant Trial (Birth Control)."

8   John Simpkin, "Annie Besant," Spartacus
    Educational, last modified April 2017, http://
    spartacus-educational.com/Wbesant.htm.

9   "Bradlaugh-Besant Trial (Birth Control)."

10 Simkin, "Annie Besant."

11 Ibid.

12 Ibid.

13 *Who Decides? The Status of Women's
    Reproductive Rights in the United States*
    (Washington, DC: NARAL Pro-Choice
    America Foundation, 2017).

14 Ibid.

15 Diniejko,"Annie Besant's Multifaceted
    Personality."

16 John Simkin, "The Matchgirl's Strike,"
    Spartacus Educational, last modified April
    2017, http://spartacus-educational.com/
    TUmatchgirls.htm.

17 Greg Guma, "19th Century Protest and the
    Matchgirl[']s Strike (1888): Annie Besant,
    London's First Wonder Woman," Counter
    Information, last modified February 11,
    2017, https://counterinformation.wordpress.
    com/2017/02/11/19th-century-protest-and-
    the-matchgirls-strike-1888-annie-besant-
    londons-first-wonder-woman.

18 Simkin, "The Matchgirl's Strike."

19 "What is Democratic Socialism? Q & A,"
    Democratic Socialists of America, accessed
    February 21, 2017, http://www.dsausa.org/
    what_is_democratic_socialism.

20 "London, 13 November 1887," *Socialist
    Review,* November 1998, http://pubs.
    socialistreviewindex.org.uk/sr224/charlton.
    htm.

21 Guma, "19th Century Protest and the
    Matchgirl[']s Strike (1888)."

22 Ibid.

23 *Wikipedia,* "Theosophy," accessed February
    21, 2017, https://en.wikipedia.org/wiki/
    Theosophy.

24 "Annie Besant," The British Empire,
    accessed February 21, 2017, http://www.
    britishempire.co.uk/biography/anniebesant.
    htm.

25 "Annie Besant."

26 "Charles W. Leadbeater," The Open
    University, accessed February 22, 2017,
    http://www. open.ac.uk/researchprojects/
    makingbritain/content/charles-w-leadbeater.

27 J. Michael McBride, "Serious Scientific
    Lessons from Direct Observation of Atoms
    through Clairvoyance," Yale University,
    December 6, 1999, https://webspace.yale.
    edu/chem125/125/history99/8Occult/
    OccultAtoms.html.

28 Philip Ball, "Clairvoyant Chemistry," The
    Royal Society of Chemistry, March 15,
    2013, https://www.chemistryworld.com/
    opinion/clairvoyant-chemistry/5984.article.

29 Ibid.

30 "J. Krishnamurti (1895–1986)," TS Adyar
    Organization, accessed February 22,
    2017, http://www.ts-adyar.org/content/j-
    krishnamurti-1895-1986.

31 "An Overview of Krishnamurti's Life
    and Work," J Krishnamurti Online,
    accessed February 22, 2017, http://www.
    jkrishnamurti.org/about-krishnamurti/
    biography.php.

32 "Annie Besant," The British Empire.

33 "Annie Besant (1847–1933)," TS Adyar
    Organization, accessed February 22, 2017,
    http://www.ts-adyar.org/content/annie-
    besant-1847-1933.

34 "Remembering the Life and Times of
    Annie Besant," *Business Standard,*
    October 1, 2015, http://www.business-
    standard.com/article/current-affairs/
    remembering-the-life-and-times-of-annie-
    besant-115100100808_1.html.

35 David Jones, "C.W. Leadbeater: Saint or
    Sinner?," *New Dawn,* March 16, 2013, http://
    www.newdawnmagazine.com/articles/c-w-
    leadbeater-saint-or-sinner.

36 "Jiddu Krishnamurti," Freepaperz,
    accessed February 23, 2017, http://www.
    freepaperz.com/biographies/Jiddu-

Krishnamurti-30781.html.

37   "Maitreya in the Light of Real
     Theosophy," Blavatsky Theosophy
     Group UK, June 2015, https://
     blavatskytheosophy.com/maitreya-in-the-
     light-of-real-theosophy.

38   Michel Snoeck, "Jiddu Krishamurti,"
     Wise Old Goat, last modified August
     18, 2015, http://www.wiseoldgoat.com/
     papers/krishnamurti.html.

39   Snoeck, "Jiddu Krishamurti."

40   "J. Krishnamurti (1895–1986)," TS Adyar
     Organization.

41   "Jiddu Krishnamurti," Freepaperz.

42   *Annie Besant, The Changing World
     and Lectures to Theosophical Students*
     (London, UK: The Theosophical
     Publishing Society, 1910), 332

43   "Annie Besant's Funeral," CW
     Leadbeater, June 4, 2016, https://
     cwleadbeater.wordpress.com/2016/06/03/
     annie-besants-funeral.

44   "Funeral of Dr. Annie Besant, Madras,
     India, 1933," Science and Society Picture
     Library Prints, accessed February
     24, 2017, http://www.ssplprints.com/
     image/124974/funeral-of-dr-annie-besant-
     madras-india-1933.

45   "Annie Besant (1847–1933)," TS Adyar
     Organization.

Victorine and Laure in Manet's *Olympia*: Seeing and Not Seeing a Famous Painting

1   Eunice Lipton, *Alias Olympia: A Woman's
    Search for Manet's Notorious Model and
    Her Own Desire* (Cornell Univ. Press,
    1999).

2   For analysis regarding the role of the
    prostitute in 19th-century France and
    the historical context of *Olympia*, see
    Timothy J. Clark, *The Painting of Modern
    Life: Paris in the Art of Manet and His
    Followers* (Princeton Univ. Press, 2008).

3   For a discussion of the painting and its
    potential cultural context/interpretation,
    see Charles Bernheimer, "Manet's
    Olympia: The Figuration of Scandal,"
    Poetics Today 10, no. 2, Art and
    Literature II (Summer 1989): 255–277,

    http://www.jstor.org/stable/1773024.

4   See Beth Gersh–Nesic, "Spotlight on
    Laure, Manet's Other Model in *Olympia*
    in the Musée d'Orsay," Bonjour Paris,
    Feb. 21, 2017.

5   See Darcy Grimaldo Grigsby, "Still
    Thinking About *Olympia's* Maid," *Art
    Bulletin* 97, no. 4 (Dec 2015): 430; Emma
    Jacobs, "What's to be said' for Laure:
    Reconceptualizing the Maidservant in
    Manet's *Olympia*," (Senior Capstone
    Projects Paper 519, Vasser College, 2015).

6   cited in Grigsby, "Still Thinking About
    Olympia's Maid."

IMAGES

p. 118, photograph: Provided by the author.

Audacious Warrior: Ernestine L. Rose

1   Paula Doress–Worters, *Mistress of
    Herself: Speeches and Letters of
    Ernestine Rose, Early Women's Rights*
    (New York: The Feminist Press at CUNY,
    2008), 360. Doress–Worters also says
    that "it's nearly certain that a Jewish
    rabbi didn't name his daughter Ernestine.
    Ernestine's Louise Susmond Potowski
    Rose, mysterious origins, her true name,
    her genealogy, her ancestral lineage and
    much of her civic history—most of this
    information is lost forever to aggressive
    European anti-Semitism, as well as the
    slow erasure of her legacy by intentional
    omissions and revisions. Born in 1810 in
    feudal Russian-Polish Galicia, Ernestine's
    first 26 years of her life comes from
    an account by her Parisian friend and
    confidant, Jenny d'Héricourt, to whom
    Ernestine recounted the details of her
    youth during her 1856 visit to Paris. Her
    story, while almost entirely unverifiable,
    is completely credible and remarkable,
    since during some four decades as a
    public figure, Ernestine seldom discussed
    her private life." Ibid., [360].

2   Yuri Suhl, *Ernestine Rose: And the Battle
    for Human Rights* (New York: Reynal &
    Co., 1959), 113.

3   Ernestine Rose, "Speech at the Fifth
    National Woman's Rights Convention: 'A
    Great and Immutable Truth'" (October 18,

1854), quoted in Doress–Worters, *Mistress of Herself*, 179.

4   Quoted in Paula Doress–Worters, *Mistress of Herself: Speeches and Letters of Ernestine Rose, Early Women's Rights* (New York: The Feminist Press at CUNY, 2008), 300.

5   Carol A. Kolmerten, *The American Life of Ernestine L. Rose* (Syracuse, NY: Syracuse UP, 1999), 24.

6   Kolmerten, *The American Life*, xix

7   Quoted in Doress–Worters, *Mistress of Herself*, "Letter to the Editor: 'Mrs. Rose and the Bangor Mercury,'" (December 1855), 198.

8   Owing to multiple Jewish pogroms and the Holocaust in Europe, many records have been lost to us. It is clear that Ernestine's father was a rabbi, but exact details are unavailable.

9   Joseph Roth, *The Wandering Jews: The Classic Portrait of a Vanished People* (New York, NY: W.W. Norton & Company, 1976), 28. The worse life became for Polish citizens, the more the Jews—who experienced "the countryside only as beggars or vagrants" (Joseph Roth, *The Wandering Jews: The Classic Portrait of a Vanished People* (New York, NY: W.W. Norton & Company, 1976, p.28)—stood out, becoming the recipients of the peasants' anger and malcontent. In this world of brutality, which was a bleak existence for most, the Jews were free. No one owned them. Though Ernestine's parents most likely remembered the Russian Polish pogroms of the late 1700s, by the early 1800s, it was a golden age for Jews in Polish shtetls— a time of relative prosperity for the surviving Jew. Times were changing, and a newly emergent Jewish Fundamentalism such as Hassidism with its "wonder-rabbis" (Joseph Roth, *The Wandering Jews: The Classic Portrait of a Vanished People* (New York, NY: W.W. Norton & Company, 1976, p.35) had spread.

10 James P. Duffy and Vincent L. Ricci, *Czars: Russia's Rulers for Over One Thousand Years* (New York, NY: Barnes and Noble, 1995), 266. Ernestine's ancestral homeland is perhaps forever unknowable after numerous wars before and after her birth.

Among the Russians, Poles, Prussians, and Vikings, there was hardly room for the Turkish, Cossack, or Mongol warriors to fight. It would be easy to think of these times on a large scale of the migrating humans looking for opportunity and building a society on the steppes of the Orient for posterity, but look past the classifications of nations and the warring factions, and you find the people of the land—the peasants, the ones with no title, no name, no land, no power, no sway, and no say in their own lives.
The winters were bitter and rulers were cruel. Russian peasants were a commodity, used as a form of trade and a measure of wealth during several centuries of Czarist rule. By the 1790s, half of Russia's peasant population was in bondage under serfdom. The peasants and their progeny had absolutely no rights thanks to Czar Alexis, who bound them to their ancestral lands and went as far as providing for runaways to be returned to their landholders. Life was cheap: a person could be slaughtered by invading forces or be beaten to death by a detestable master. The egregious acts of violence against peasants were so notorious during that time when the famous writer Nikolai Gogol wrote the famous mocking satire, Dead Souls, in which dead peasants' souls are owned, bought and sold in perpetuity, even after their death. Peasants were traded like coins from noble's hand to aristocrat's pocket, and could never gain their freedom as they were bonded to the land. The peasants endured a cruel form of Eastern European slavery akin to what Black Americans suffered under Jim Crow laws. Like African Americans on a distant continent, the abused peasants led hopeless lives, totally uneducated and without means for betterment.

11 Duffy and Ricci, *Czars*, 238. Czar Alexander reigned from 1801 to 1825; Jewish people joined Napoleon to fight against the aristocrats for money, land rights and the international allegiances they thought would gain them citizenship.

12 Suzan F. Wynne, *The Galitizianers: The Jews of Galici*a, 1772–1918 (New York: Wheatmark, 2006), 43.

13 Suhl, *Ernestine Rose*, 20.

14 Roth, *The Wandering Jews*, 32; Wynne, *The Galitzianers*, 50.

15 Doress–Worters, *Mistress of Herself*, 2; Wynne, *The Galitzianers*, 40.

16 Roth, *The Wandering Jews*, 50.

17 Suhl, *Ernestine Rose*, 9.

18 Roth, *The Wandering Jews*, 35. Roth explains the egalitarian nature of rabbis: "Some wonder-rabbis really do hold court." Roth, *The Wandering Jews*, 28; Wynne, *The Galitzianers*, 26. Wynne explains that official rabbis were regionally appointed.

19 Roth, *The Wandering Jews*, 35.

20 Herman Kantor I. *The Bear and the Baby: Still More Tales My Great-Great-Grandfather Might Tell About Life in a Ghetto of Russia in the Time of the Czars* (New York: Fithian P, 1995), 183–91.

21 Based on Wynne, Suzan F. The Galitizianers: The Jews of Galicia, 1772-1918, regional maps, Doress-Worters, Paula. *Mistress of Herself: Speeches and Letters of Ernestine Rose, Early Women's Rights* and Suhl, Yuri. *Ernestine Rose: And the Battle for Human Rights* I believe and speculate that Ernestine lived in Piotrkow, a village in Poland.

22 Suhl, *Ernestine Rose*, 14.Yuri Suhl believes she was stopped for some six hours or so.

23 This is one of the oldest towns in Galicia with a municipal court building.

24 Wynne, *The Galitzianers*, 26. Each district had an official rabbi.

25 Wynne, 34. Before WWII, most Jews in Galicia—after 300 years in residence—were unrecognized by the government, lacked surnames, and refused to register births or marriages because they would have incurred a heavy tax.

26 Wynne, 3. Ernestine was never able to return to Poland, though she tried two times. See also Doress–Worters, *Mistress of Herself*, 3; Suhl, *Ernestine Rose*, 13–15.

27 Suhl, *Ernestine Rose*, 21.

28 Roth, *The Wandering Jews*, 6. Describing the harsh conditions of the Jewish enclaves a century after Rose left the region, Roth writes, "He is not allowed to live in villages or in big cities. Here Jews live in dirty streets and collapsing houses. Their Christian neighbor threatens them. The local squire beats them. The official has them locked up. The army officer fires his gun at them with impunity," (Roth, *The Wandering Jews*, 6).

29 Suhl, *Ernestine Rose*, 21–22.

30 The Eastern Jewish struggle against intolerance lasted until WWII.

31 Ernestine Rose, "'Freedom or Slavery' Speech at the Thomas Paine Celebration," (January 29, 1861), 291–94, quoted in Doress–Worters, *Mistress of Herself*, 292.

32 In the 18th- and 19th-century shtetls, giving was organized in a way that ensured the equal distribution of resources to all Jews, especially those too meek to beg for alms; in the Polish Ghettos, Jews organized the charitable sharing of food, clothing, and other resources. *A Yiddish World Remembered*, directed by Andrew Goldberg (2002), [New York]: Two Cats Production, LTD, (2002), DVD; also Wynne, *The Galizianers*, 47–49. Under the harsh taxation and privations imposed by the monarchs on all Jews, cruel policies such as taxing Sabbath candles and kosher meat were in effect. See also Wynne, 28–29. They were also prevented from employment in most sectors and from agricultural production of any kind, which posed numerous difficulties in the feudal–agrarian society.They struggled to provide each other with the food and money they needed to survive. There was an understanding that a Jewish person should not become a burden to society if preventable. See also Tracey Rich, Judaism 101, accessed [Dec. 15, 2016], http://www.jewfaq.org/index.shtml.

33 Roth, *The Wandering Jews*, 64: Roth takes great pains to describe the living conditions in the Jewish ghettos of Vienna and Berlin. He illustrates the pungent orders of one street; his apartment consists of one room and a kitchen.

34 Alberta Eiseman, *Rebels and Reformers: The Lives of Four Jewish Americans: Uriah P. Levy, Ernestine L. Rose, Louis D. Brandeis, Lillian Wald* (New York, NY: Doubleday & Company, 1976), 43.

35 Doress–Worters, *Mistress of Herself,* 5. This
is based on her account to D'Héricourt in
1856.

36 Suhl, *Ernestine Rose,* 24–25.

37 In this passage, Ernestine Rose quotes
Thomas Paine: quoted in Doress–Worters,
Mistress of Herself, 199.

38 Suhl, *Ernestine Rose,* 25

39 Suhl, 26.

40 Eiseman, *Rebels and Reformers,* 42. "In
the 1830s England was the cradle of social
reform. The industrial revolution had
its beginnings in Great Britain, creating
fortunes for a few manufacturers and at the
same time giving rise to an entirely new
class of overworked, exploited laborers.
Even as a newcomer, just starting to become
familiar with the language, Ernestine gladly
mingled with the workers who would come
to hear speakers demanding higher wages,
shorter hours, and the right to vote for
the working man," Eiseman, *Rebels and
Reformers,* 42.

41 Eiseman, 43.

42 Eiseman, 43; Suhl, *Ernestine Rose,* 27;
Ernestine Rose, "Speech at Robert Owen's
Birthday Celebration" (May 13, 1853),
quoted in Doress–Worters, *Mistress of
Herself,* 131–134.

43 Suhl, *Ernestine Rose,* 28.

44 Eiseman, *Rebels and Reformers,* 44.

45 Ernestine Rose, "Speeches at the National
Convention of the Loyal Women of the
Republic" (May 14, 1863), 303–10, quoted
in Doress–Worters, *Mistress of Herself,* 308.

46 Ernestine Rose, "Letter to Robert Owen"
(1844), quoted in Doress–Worters, 66.

47 Suhl, *Ernestine Rose,* 102–03.

48 Ernestine Rose toasts at the 1840 Thomas
Paine Celebration; quoted in Doress–
Worters, *Mistress of Herself,* 59.

49 Rose toasts at the Thomas Paine
Celebration; quoted in Doress–Worters,
59–61.

50 Ernestine Rose, "Speech at the Thomas
Paine Celebration: Women in International
Freedom Fights" (1850), quoted in Doress–
Worters, 75–79.

51 Suhl, *Ernestine Rose,* 281; Rose, "Speech at

the Thomas Paine Celebration," quoted in
Doress–Worters, 75–79.

52 Suhl, 73–74.

53 All passages in this section are taken from
transcriptions of Ernestine's speeches and
written responses between Ernestine Rose
and several men who were public figures
at the time. The citations are, in order of
appearance: Ernestine Rose, "Attack in the
Albany Register," (March 6 and 7, 1854)
165–68, quoted in Doress–Worters, *Mistress
of Herself,* 167; Ernestine Rose, "Speech at
the 1856 Thomas Paine Celebration," 203–
06, quoted in Doress–Worters, 206; Rose,
"Attack in the Albany Register," (March
6 and 7, 1854) quoted in Doress–Worters,
166; Rose, "Unsurpassed," (October 15
and 16, 1851) quoted in Doress–Worters,
91–103; Rose, "Attack in the Albany
Register," (March 6 and 7, 1854)quoted
in Doress–Worters, 167; Kolmerten, *The
American Life,* (1860) 215; Ernestine Rose,
"Speech at the Thomas Paine Celebration:
'The Rights of Woman'" (January 29, 1855),
181–83, quoted in Doress–Worters, 182;
Otto Weininger, "Emancipated Woman,"
in Sex and Character, 75; Ernestine Rose,
"Letter to the National Woman Suffrage
Convention" (January 14, 1869), 343–44,
quoted in Doress–Worters, 344; Ernestine
Rose, "Speech at the First Anniversary of
the American Equal Rights Association:
'Voices for Votes'" (May 10, 1867) 334–39,
quoted in Doress–Worters, 336; Weininger,
74; Weininger, 71; Rose, "Unsurpassed,"
(October 15 and 16, 1851) quoted in Doress–
Worters, 91–103; Weininger, 71; Susan
B. Anthony, "Diary of Lecture Tour to
the Border South with Ernestine L. Rose,
(1848)" 169–75, quoted in Doress–Worters,
173; Anthony, "Diary of Lecture Tour,"
(March 24 – April 14, 1854) quoted in
Doress–Worters, 173; Anthony, (March 24
– April 14, 1854) quoted in Doress–Worters,
173; Weininger, 71; Ernestine Rose, "A
Defence of Atheism" (1861), quoted in
Doress–Worters, 298; Kolmerten, xcii;
Ernestine Rose, "Speech at the Fourth
Woman's Rights Convention: 'The Double
Standard of Sexual Morality'" (October 7,
1853), 157–62, quoted in Doress–Worters,
159; Ernestine Rose, "Speech at the 7th
Woman's Rights Convention" (November
26, 1856), 222–37, quoted in Doress–

Worters, 234; Suhl, Ernestine Rose, 218; (1862) Doress–Worters, 300; Ernestine Rose, "Speech at the Hartford Bible Convention: 'Trample the Bible, the Church, and the Priests'" (June 4, 1853), 135–44, quoted in Doress–Worters, 144; Suhl, 90–93; Ernestine Rose, "Speech at the Thomas Paine Celebration, 'The 1848 Revolutions in Europe'" (1848), 72–74, quoted in Doress–Worters, 73; Ernestine Rose, "Speech at the 1853 Anniversary of West Indian Emancipation" (1853), quoted in Doress–Worters, 152; Ernestine Rose, "All Free or All Slave," Boston, (May 30, 1855), 187–93, quoted in Doress–Worters, 188, 190; Ernestine Rose, "Debate on the Jews in the Boston Investigator," (1855) quoted in Doress–Worters, 311–33.

54 Suhl, *Ernestine Rose*, 204–07.

55 Rose quoted in Speech at "The Divorce Debate" (May 11, 1860), Doress–Worters, *Mistress of Herself,* 280.

56 Rose quoted in "The Divorce Debate," (May 11, 1860), Doress–Worters, 283.

57 Suhl, *Ernestine Rose*, 212.

58 Suhl, 204–07.

59 Kolmerten, *The American Life*, 202, 219.

60 Rose, "The Double Standard of Sexual Morality," quoted in Doress–Worters, *Mistress of Herself,* 159.

61 Brown Blackwell was the first ordained woman minister in the United States; the two women often shared the same platform.

62 Rose, "Speech at the 1853 Anniversary of West Indian Emancipation," quoted in Doress–Worters, *Mistress of Herself,* 149.

63 Rose, "Freedom or Slavery," quoted in Doress–Worters, 291–94.

64 Rose, "All Free or All Slave," quoted in Doress–Worters, 192.

65 Rose, "Speeches at the National Convention of the Loyal Women of the Republic," quoted in Doress–Worters, 303–10.

66 The Boston Investigator was a free-thought newspaper.

67 Suhl, *Ernestine Rose*, 220–21.

68 Doress–Worters, *Mistress of Herself,* 41; The Jewish Americans, directed by David Grubin (2008); [Washington, D.C.]: Greater Washington Educational Telecommunications Association, Inc. & JTN Productions, 2009, DVD. In South Carolina, German Jews settled and became slaveholders—an irony that must of have caused deep, schizophrenic schisms in their consciousness each Sabbath, when enslaved black men and women served the sacred meal as they gave thanks for their liberty.

69 Ernestine Rose, "Heated Exchange with Horace Seaver," 311–33, quoted in Doress–Worters, 318.

70 Suhl, *Ernestine Rose*, 90–93.

71 Doress-Worters, 41.

72 Rose, "Speech at the 1853 Anniversary of West Indian Emancipation," quoted in Doress–Worters, 152.

73 Rose, "Speeches at the National Convention of the Loyal Women of the Republic," quoted in Doress–Worters, 304.

74 Rose, "Freedom or Slavery," quoted in Doress–Worters, 293–94.

75 Rose,: "The Rights of Woman," quoted in Doress–Worters, 182–83.

76 Quoted in Doress-Worters, Paula. *Mistress of Herself: Speeches and Letters of Ernestine Rose, Early Women's Rights Leader,* the words of Ernestine Rose in "Speech: "A Defense of Atheism": p.300.

77 Suhl, *Ernestine Rose*, 56.

78 Rose, "Speech at the 7th Woman's Rights Convention," quoted in Doress–Worters, *Mistress of Herself,* 232.

79 Kolmerten, *The American Life*, 243.

80 Suhl, *Ernestine Rose*, 200.

81 Suhl, 200.

82 Suhl, 217.

83 Suhl, 228.

84 Rose, "Voices for Votes," quoted in Doress–Worters, *Mistress of Herself,* 336.

85 Suhl, *Ernestine Rose*, 200.

86 Eiseman, *Rebels and Reformers*, 62.

87 Kolmerten, *The American Life*, 250. Stanton is recorded saying, "Think of Patrick and Sambo and Hans and Yung

Tung, who do know the difference between a monarchy and a republic, who can not read the Declaration of Independence or Webster's spelling-book, making laws for Lucretia Mott and Ernestine L. Rose," Kolmerten, *The American Life*, 250. Using Rose's name may have even tipped the scales.

88 Kolmerten, 252. Anthony argued that suffrage be given to "the most intelligent first," (Kolmerten, 252) meaning white women, of course.

89 Kolmerten, 252. Davis went as far as to say black women were more intelligent than black men were because they had learned from white mistresses.

90 Rose is quoted in "The Rights of Woman," Doress–Worters, *Mistress of Herself*, 182.

91 Rose quoted in "Letter to Robert Owen," (1844) Doress–Worters, 66.

92 Ernestine Rose quoted in "Letter to Robert Owen" (1845), Doress–Worters, 66.

93 Doress–Worters, p. 21.

94 This intimate moment was captured by Sallie Holley in her diary when she and Ernestine shared personal details about their lives with each other.

95 Rose suffered from chronic pneumonia, bronchitis, and malaria.

96 Suhl, *Ernestine Rose*, 134–35.

97 Suhl, 136.

98 Suhl, 136.

99 Ernestine Rose, "Farewell Letter of Mrs. Rose" (1856), 207–210, quoted in Doress–Worters, *Mistress of Herself*, 208.

100 Eiseman, *Rebels and Reformers*, 63.

101 Tracey R. Rich, "The Meaning of the Word 'Tzedakah,'" Judaism 101, http://www.jewfaq.org/tzedakah.htm Dec. 15, 2016.

102 Ernestine Rose, "Letter to the National Woman Suffrage Association Convention" (July 19, 1878), quoted in Doress–Worters, *Mistress of Herself*, 350.

103 Ernestine Rose, "Letter to the Editor of the *Boston Investigator*" (September 4, 1851), New York State, quoted in Doress–Worters, 85–86.

104 Rose, "Women in International Freedom Fights," quoted in Doress–Worters, 75–79.

105 Suhl, *Ernestine Rose*, 178.

106 Rose, "Women in International Freedom Fights," quoted in Doress–Worters, *Mistress of Herself*, 75–79.

107 Wynne, *The Galitzianers*, 41. Franz Joseph, who tried to integrate Jews into Polish society, gave Ernestine hope of returning to her fatherland. See also Eiseman, *Rebels and Reformers*, 56.

108 Suhl, *Ernestine Rose*, 266.

109 The Hebrew Leader quoted in Yuri Suhl, *Ernestine Rose: And the Battle for Human Rights*, p.244.

110 "Letter to Susan B. Anthony," Jan. 9, 1877, quoted in Doress–Worters, *Mistress of Herself*, 347–349.

111 "Shirley Chisholm Biography," Biography, last modified February 27, 2018, http://www.biography.com/people/shirley-chisholm-9247015#synopsis.

112 Kolmerten, *The American Life*, 255.

113 Suhl, *Ernestine Rose*, 273–74.

114 Suhl, 49; Doress–Worters, *Mistress of Herself*, xvii.

115 Suhl, 205; Doress–Worters, 19–21.

116 Suhl, 205–06

117 Ernestine Rose, "Letter to Elizabeth Cady Stanton for the National Woman Suffrage Association Convention of 1880" (May 15, 1880, quoted in Doress–Worters, *Mistress of Herself*, 351.

Up from the Rubbish Heap: The Persistence of Julie D'Aubigny

1 Kelly Gardiner, "The Real Life of Julie D'Aubigny," accessed June 15 2017, https://kellygardiner.com/fiction/books/goddess/the-real-life-of-julie-daubigny.

2 J R. Milne, "Why Grow Old? Try Backyard Flip-Flops with the Children," *Boston Sun*, March 20, 1921, newspapers.com.

3 John Berger, *Ways of Seeing* (Banbury, UK: Art & Language, 1978), 55.

4 Eleanor Baldwin Cass, *The Book of Fencing* (Boston, MA: Lothrop, Lee, & Shepard, 1930), 2.

5 Berger, *Ways of Seeing*, 46

6   Jim Burrows, "The Adventures of La Maupin," accessed June 15, 2017, https://www.eldacur.com/~brons/Maupin/LaMaupin.html.

7   Sarah Shulman, *Conflict Is Not Abuse: Overstating Harm, Community Responsibility, and the Duty of Repair* (Vancouver, Canada: Arsenal Pulp, 2016).

8   Cass, *The Book of Fencing*, 83

9   Cass, 51

10 Cass, 15–16

11 Burrows, "The Adventures of La Maupin."

12 Cass, *The Book of Fencing*, 7

13 Burrows, "The Adventures of La Maupin."

14 Victoria Cass, *Dangerous Women: Warriors, Grannies and Geishas of the Ming* (Lanham, MD: Rowman & Littlefield, 1999).

15 "Fencing Is in Favor in Society Again," *Honolulu Star-Advertiser*, June 22, 1924, newspapers.com.

16 Gardiner, "The Real Life of Julie D'Aubigny."

17 Milne, "Why Grow Old?"

18 Gardiner, "The Real Life of Julie D'Aubigny."

19 Gardiner.

20 Theophile Gautier, *Mademoiselle de Maupin* (London, UK: Penguin Classics, 2006).

21 Gardiner, "The Real Life of Julie D'Aubigny."

22 Julie, Chevalier de Maupin. French TV (2004).

23 "LA MAUPIN to Premiere at 2017 Fresh Fruit Festival," Broadway World, July 5, 2017, https://www.broadwayworld.com/article/LA-MAUPIN-to-Premiere-at-2017-Fresh-Fruit-Festival-20170705.

IMAGES

p. 158 scan: Cass, *The Book of Fencing*, cover.

p. 159 scan: Cass, 189.

The Blazing Worlds of Margaret Cavendish

1   Charlotte Ahlin, "10 Struggles All Female Comic Book Fans Understand," *Bustle*, January 22, 2016.

2   Sandra E. Garcia, "The Woman Who Created #MeToo Long Before Hashtags," *New York Times*, October 20, 2017.

3   Margaret Cavendish. *Poems, and Fancies Written by the Right Honourable, the Lady Margaret Newcastle* (1653).

4   Margaret Cavendish, ed. Kate Lilley, *The Blazing World and Other Writings* (New York, NY: Penguin Books, 1994), ix.

5   Cavendish, *The Blazing World and Other Writings*, x

6   Cavendish, *The Blazing World and Other Writings*, xi–xii.

7   Samuel Pepys, *The Diary of Samuel Pepys*, Entry dated April 11, 1667.

8   Cavendish, *The Blazing World and Other Writings*, x.

9   Cavendish, *The Blazing World and Other Writings*, 124.

10 Margaret Cavendish, *A True Relation of My Birth, Breeding, and Life*.

11 Cavendish, *A True Relation*.

12 Cavendish, *A True Relation*.

13 Alexander Kahn, "The Chick Lit of Heian Japan," *Gallatin Research Journal* 2 (2012).

14 Katy Waldman, "How Sci-Fi's Hugo Awards Got Their Own Full-Blown Gamergate," *Slate*, April 8, 2015.

15 Amy Wallace, "Who Won Science Fiction's Hugo Awards and Why It Matters," *Wired*, August 23, 2015.

16 Cavendish, *The Blazing World and Other Writings*, xxv.

17 Kameron Hurley, *The Geek Feminist Revolution* (New York, NY: Tor Books, 2016), 139.

18 Cavendish, *The Blazing World and Other Writings*, 124.

19 Joanna Russ, *How to Suppress Women's Writing* (Austin, TX: University of Texas Press, 1983), 11.

Radiant Identity: Chicaba Herstories

1   *Juan Carlos Miguel Pan y Agua, Oracion Funebre en las Exequias de la Madree Sor Teresa Juliana de Santo Domingo, de Feliz Memoria, Celebradas el Dia Nueve de Enero, en el Convento de Religiosas Dominicas, Vulgo de la Penitrencia, de Esta Ciudad de Salamanca* (Salamanca, Spain: Garcia de Honorato y S. Miguel, 1749), cited in *Voyages and Travel*, Catalogue 1475 (London, UK: Maggs Bros., 2014), 3, https://www.maggs.com/media/139519/ travel and voyages _ maggs 1475 _ dps _ 21 aug 14.pdf. The catalog described the book as an "Extremely Rare Account of a Female Slave." Ibid.

2   A hagiography is a biography and/or legend of a saint, providing a record of his or her life and faith.

3   Supreme Master Television, "The Story of the Ancient Ewe Language," YouTube video, 21:50 , July 2007, http://www. youtube.com/watch?v=dUDrLCB0wQk.

4   Supreme Master Television, "The Story of the Ancient Ewe Language," 14:00.

5   Coleen Wright, "Art and Symbolism in Ewe Religion: Ritual Objects of the Yewe and Tro Mami Worship in Klikor, Ghana," *African Diaspora ISPs* 13 (1999), http:// digitalcollections.sit.edu/african_diaspora_ isp/13.

6   *Wikipedia*, "Canonization Medieval Procedure," accessed January 23, 2018, https://en.wikipedia.org/wiki/ Canonization#Medieval_procedure.

7   Heck Yeah Order of Preachers, Tumblr, "Venerable Teresa Chikaba," December 2013, http://heckyeahorderofpreachers. tumblr.com/post/71228834207/venerable- teresa-chikaba-sor-teresa-juliana-de.

8   *Wikipedia*, "Canonization Medieval Procedure."

9   Lyssa Royal, "Spiritual Sovereignty," February 21, 1992, http://www.galactic- server.com/Planet/spiritual_sovereignty. html. The group consciousness of Germane is channeled through Lyssa Royal. I found their definitions of "Sovereignty" to bring to life what is coming forth in me.

10 Sue Houchins and Baltasar Fra-Molinero, "Afro-Latino Voices Narratives from the Early Modern Ibero-Atlantic World,

1550–1812," in *The Saint's Life of Sister Chikaba, c. 1676–1748: An As-Told-To Slave Narrative* (Indianapolis, IN: Hackett, 2009), 223.

11 Houchins and Fra-Molinero, "Afro-Latino Voices," in *The Saint's Life*, 227–29.

12 Please note the choice of "light" being over a white man in this instance.

13 Daniel P. Manix, *Historia de la Trata de Negros* (Madrid, Spain: Alianza Editorial, 1968).

14 Elivra Melian, "Chikaba, the First Black Nun in the Spanish System," Hispania Sacra LXIV (2012): 565–81, http://hispaniasacra. revistas.csic.es/index.php/hispaniasacra/ article/viewFile/321/322.

15 Houchins and Fra-Molinero, "Afro-Latino Voices," in *The Saint's Life*, 215.

16 The ranking of Marquis and Marchioness is above Duke and Duchess and below Count and Countess, for those who like to keep up with these things.

17 *Wikipedia*, "Juana Inés de la Cruz," accessed January 23, 2018, https:// en.wikipedia.org/wiki/Juana_Inés_de_ la_Cruz. Juana Inés de la Cruz was a self-educated savant. By the time she was 17, she was a lady in waiting in the Marquis's household. The Marquis had her intelligence tested by various scholars, theologians, and intellects.

18 Melian, "Chikaba, the First Black Nun."

19 *Duboisopedia*, "Double Consciousness," December 2013, http://scua.library. umass.edu/duboisopedia/doku. php?id=about:double_consciousness.

20 *Wikipedia*, "Teresa Chikaba," accessed January 23, 2018.

21 Melian, "Chikaba, the First Black Nun."

22 Baltasar Fra-Molinero, "The First Afro-Hispanic Writer: Chicaba," 1999, https://translate.google.com/ translate?hl=en&sl=es&u=http://abacus. bates.edu/~bframoli/pagina/chicaba.html.

23 Melian, "Chikaba, the First Black Nun."

24 Houchins and Fra-Molinero, "Afro-Latino Voices," in *The Saint's Life*, 233.

25 *Wikipedia*, "Third Order," October 2017, https://en.wikipedia.org/wiki/Third_order.

26 Melian, "Chikaba, First Black Nun." "[N]o stranger to the initiative of bringing Chikaba to it. A border shared many convents category "of Penitence", created to redeem marginal groups of women in the street and then converted as needed. To this must be added that during the seventeenth century the number of vocations had been declining exponentially." Ibid.

27 Melian.

28 Pan y Agua, *Oracion Funebre*, 59.

29 Houchins and Fra-Molinero, "Afro-Latino Voices," in *The Saint's Life*, 233.

30 María Eugenia Maeso, *Sister Teresa Chikaba: Princess, Slave and Nun* (Salamanca, Spain: San Esteban Editorial, 2004), 130.

31 Pan y Agua, *Oracion Funebre*, 59.

32 Pan y Agua, *Oracion Funebre*, cited in *Travels and Voyages*, 3.

33 Ibid.

IMAGES

p. 183, map: Nauset Press, source: "World. Gall Projection with Geography Lines," accessed June 13, 2018, www.your-vector-maps.com/world/-144-free-vector-world-maps/?imagelist=wrld-bas.

Under the Cover of Breeches and Bayonet

1 Alfred F. Young, Masquerade: *The Life and Times of Deborah Sampson*, Continental Soldier (New York: Vintage Books, 2004), 190.

2 Young, *Masquerade*, 190.

3 Deborah's last name is sometimes spelled "Samson" instead of "Sampson."

4 Young, *Masquerade*, 24.

5 Young, 29.

6 Young, 29.

7 Young, 30.

8 Young, 30

9 Herman Mann, *The Female Review: Life of Deborah Sampson, the Female Soldier in the War of Revolution* (Boston: J.K. Wiggin & Wm. Parsons Lunt 1866), 59.

10 Young, *Masquerade*, 37.

11 Young, 35.

12 Young, 35.

13 Young, 36.

14 Young, 41.

15 Young, 41.

16 Young, 40.

17 Young, 42.

18 Young, 86.

19 Young, 90.

20 Young, 79.

21 Young, 86.

22 Young, 128–30.

23 Young, 129.

24 Young, 131.

25 Young, 132.

26 Jane Keiter, "Deborah Sampson, Continental Soldier: The Westchester Connection," *The Westchester Historian* 76, no. 1 (Winter 2000): 1.

27 Keiter, *Deborah Sampson*, 1.

28 Mann, *The Female Review*, 173.

29 Keiter, *Deborah Sampson*, 1.

30 Keiter, 1.

31 Mann, *The Female Review*, 173.

32 Mann, 173.

33 Keiter, *Deborah Sampson*, 1.

34 Keiter, 1.

35 Keiter, 1.

36 Young, *Masquerade*, 303.

37 Keiter, Deborah Sampson, 1.

38 Keiter, 1.

39 Young, *Masquerade*, 149.

40 Young, 146.

41 Young, 149–52.

42 Young, 146.

43 Young, 146.

44 Young, 155.

45 Young, 169.

46 Young, 169.

47 Mann, *The Female Review*, 225.

48 Young, *Masquerade*, 171.

49 Young, 171.

50 Young, 174.

51 Young, 171.

52 Young, 171–73.

53 Young, 265.

54 Young, 267.

55 Young, 265.

56 Young, 184.

57 Young, 185.

58 Young, 191.

59 Young, 191.

60 Young, 192.

61 Young, 197.

62 Young, 207–8.

63 Deborah Sampson, *Diary of Deborah Sampson Gannett in 1802.* (Boston, MA: Boston Public Library, 1802), 13.

64 Sampson, *Diary,* 26

65 Stefan Bielinski, "City Streets," People of Colonial Albany Live Here, last modified July 28, 2018, http://exhibitions.nysm.nysed.gov//albany/streets.html

66 Young, *Masquerade,* 228.

67 Young, 234.

68 Young, 229.

69 Young, 229.

70 Young, 236.

71 Young, 265.

72 Young, 265.

IMAGES

p. 223, Photograph: Heidi Hewey Lane, © 2011. Used with permission.

Rose-Poisoning: Beauty, Violence, and the Unknown History of Zabel Yessayan

1 Zabel Yessayan, *The Gardens of Silihdar,* trans. Jennifer Manoukian, eds. Joy Renjilian–Burgy and Judith Saryan (Watertown, MA: AIWA Press, 2014), 17–18.

2 This history was documented by the press at the time. The events have been researched and confirmed as genocide by countless international historians and scholars. It is still denied by the Turkish government.

3 Directed by Lara Aharonian and Talin Suciyan, *Finding Zabel Yesayan,* (2009), film.

4 Aharonian and Suciyan, *Finding Zabel Yesayan.*

5 For more on the racial identity of Armenians in the United States, read my personal essay "Meeting the Man on the Street" in Kweli Journal, December 2015, online.

6 Examples include anthologies edited by poets Diana Der Hovanessian and David Kherdian and the Armenian Poetry Project website, curated by Lola Koundakjian.

7 The result of this search was the memoir *me as her again: True Stories of an Armenian Daughter* (San Francisco, CA: Aunt Lute Books, 2008).

8 Yessayan, *The Gardens of Silihdar,* 37.

9 Yessayan, *The Gardens of Silihdar,* 37.

10 Yessayan, *The Gardens of Silihdar,* 51.

11 Yessayan, *The Gardens of Silihdar,* 58.

12 Yessayan, *The Gardens of Silihdar,* 108–09.

13 Yessayan, *The Gardens of Silihdar,* 7–8.

14 Yessayan, *The Gardens of Silihdar,* 94–95.

15 Yessayan, *The Gardens of Silihdar,* 80–81.

16 Yessayan, *The Gardens of Silihdar,* 101–02.

17 See, e.g., Marc Nichanian, *Writers of Disaster: Armenian Literature in the Twentieth Century,* vol. 1 (Princeton, NJ and London, UK: Gomidas Institute, 2002), 193–94; Krikor Beledian, "My Soul in Exile or Art in Bondage," in *My Soul in Exile and Other Writings* (Watertown, MA: AIWA Press, 2014), 47–48.

18 Jennifer Manoukian, "Zabel Yessayan: Portrait of the Writer as a Young Woman," *Armenite: Culture,* April 14, 2014, http://thearmenite.com/2014/04/zabel-yessayan-portrait-of-the-writer-as-a-young-woman/

19 Zabel Yessayan, *In the Ruins,* trans. G.M. Goshgarian, eds. Judith Saryan, Danila Jebejian Terpanjian, and Joy Renjilian–Burgy (Watertown, MA: AIWA Press, 2016), 32.

20 Yessayan, *In the Ruins,* 51–52. The ellipses are Zabel's, not mine. She used them frequently in *In the Ruins.* Henceforth, three periods indicate Zabel's use of ellipses, and

four periods indicate a quote or text that continues.

21 Yessayan, *In the Ruins*, 54.

22 Yessayan, *In the Ruins*, 55.

23 I assume "abducted" is a euphemism for rape.

24 Yessayan, *In the Ruins*, 30.

25 Yessayan, *In the Ruins*, 183.

26 Yessayan, *In the Ruins*, 227.

27 Yessayan, *In the Ruins*, 230.

28 Zabel Yessayan, *My Soul in Exile and Other Writings*, 44.

29 I assume this character is modeled after Sourpouhi Dussap, a novelist who is a generation older than Zabel and with whom Zabel recounts turning to for advice as a young writer in *The Gardens of Silihdar*.

30 Yessayan, *My Soul in Exile*, 17–18.

31 Yessayan, *My Soul in Exile*, 30–32.

32 Yessayan, *My Soul in Exile*, p. 33.

33 "Bey" is a Turkish social title for men, like "mister."

34 Yessayan, *My Soul in Exile*, 34–36.

35 Yessayan, *My Soul in Exile*, 39.

36 Yessayan, *My Soul in Exile*, 41.

37 Yessayan, *My Soul in Exile*, 41–42.

38 Gostan Zarian, "The National Turkey Hen," in *The Gardens of Silihdar* and Other Writings, ed. and trans. Ara Baliozian (New York, NY: Ashod Press, 1982), 9.

39 Zarian, "Turkey Hen," in *Gardens of Silihdar*, 11–13.

40 Zarian, "Turkey Hen," in *Gardens of Silihdar*, 13.

41 Rouben Zarian, "Reminiscences of Zabel Yessayan," in *The Gardens of Silihdar* and Other Writings, ed. and trans. Ara Baliozian (New York, NY: Ashod Press, 1982), 17.

42 Zarian, "Reminiscences," in *Gardens of Silihdar*, 19.

43 Zarian, "Reminiscences," *Gardens of Silihdar*, 20.

44 Zarian, "Reminiscences," *Gardens of Silihdar*, 22.

45 Lara Aharonian and Talin Suciyan, *Finding Zabel Yesayan*.

46 Lara Aharonian and Talin Suciyan, *Finding Zabel Yesayan*.

47 Lara Aharonian and Talin Suciyan, *Finding Zabel Yesayan*.

48 Lara Aharonian and Talin Suciyan, *Finding Zabel Yesayan*.

49 She was a member of Tashnagtsutioun, or the Armenian Revolutionary Federation, until 1923–24. Tashnagtsutioun founded an independent Armenian Republic from 1918–1920, until the Soviets took over and exiled the ARF members who then established themselves in diaspora.

50 Lara Aharonian and Talin Suciyan, *Finding Zabel Yesayan*.

51 Zabel and her husband, Dikran, were often separated as well but always considered themselves married. He died in 1921.

52 Jennifer Manoukian, "Resisting Armenian Identity: Zabel Yessayan, Innovate Armenia Conference, Los Angeles: USC Institute of Armenian Studies," YouTube video, 11:12 April 2, 2016, https://www.youtube.com/watch?v=Szgyi1OiSFQ.

IMAGES

p. 243, Photograph: Provided by author.

Trek Across a Trackless Land

1 Marina Koestler Ruben, "Alice Ramsey's Historic Cross-Country Drive," *Smithsonian Magazine*, June 4, 2009, www.smithsonianmag.com/history/alice-ramseys-historic-cross-country-drive-29114570/.

2 Jim Kavanagh, "Celebrating an American Trailblazer," CNN, December 11, 2009, www.cnn.com/2009/TRAVEL/12/11/woman.crosscountry.driver/index.html. I found this estimation of paved roads in several articles about Alice's trip, including sources such as *Smithsonian Magazine*, The Automotive Hall of Fame, and Vassar College's website.

3 Deborah Clarke, *Driving Women: Fiction and Automobile Culture in Twentieth-Century America* (Baltimore, MD: Johns

Hopkins University Press, 2007), 28.

4   Alice Ramsey and Gregory M. Franzwa.
     *Alice's Drive: Republishing Veil, Duster,
     and Tire Iron.* (Tuscon: Patrice Press, 2005),
     13.

5   Ramsey and Franzwa. 10.

6   Ramsey and Franzwa, 2.

7   C. E. Dando, *Women and Cartography
     in the Progressive Era* Abingdon, (Oxon:
     Routledge, 2018).

8   Ramsey and Franzwa, *Alice's Drive*, 15.

9   Ibid.

10   "1964–1966 Ford Thunderbird Review @
     Top Speed," Top Speed, March 30, 2016,
     www.topspeed.com/cars/ford/1964-1966-
     ford-thunderbird-ar30575.html. Several car
     aficionado websites have profiled the iconic
     Thunderbird, and the car sold at auction for
     $71,500 in 2008, according to the Barrett–
     Jackson car collector auctions.

11   Callie Khouri, *Thelma & Louise*, June 5,
     1990, www.imsdb.com/scripts/Thelma-&-
     Louise.html.

12   "The Academy Awards Database,"
     Academy Awards, awardsdatabase.oscars.
     org.

13   Ramsey and Franzwa. *Alice's Driv*e, 49.

14   Ramsey and Franzwa, 52.

15   "Alice (Ramsey) BRUNS," *Record/Herald
     News*, November 15, 2015,
     www.legacy.com/obituaries/northjersey/
     obituary.aspx?n=alice-bruns-
     ramsey&pid=176513353.

Contributors

Nancy Agabian (*Rose-Poisoning: Beauty, Violence, and the Uncertain History of Zabel Yessayan*) is a writer, teacher, and literary organizer working in the spaces between race, ethnicity, cultural identity, feminism, and queer identity. She is the author of a poetry and performance collection, *Princess Freak*, and a memoir, *Me as Her Again: True Stories of an Armenian Daughter*. Her novel *The Fear of Large and Small Nations* was a finalist for the PEN/Bellwether Prize for Socially-Engaged Fiction. Her essays have been published in *Poets & Writers*, *The Margins*, *Kweli*, *The Brooklyn Rail*, and elsewhere. Nancy teaches creative writing at the Gallatin School of Individualized Study at NYU, The Leslie-Lohman Museum of Gay and Lesbian Art, and through her own community writing workshops, Heightening Stories. With writers Amy Paul and Meera Nair, she coordinates Queens Writers Resist, a bimonthly reading series and space for creative resistance in Jackson Heights, Queens, where she lives. Online at www.nancyagabian.com.

Betsy Andrews (*Unleashing Baba Yaga: The Night Witches*) is the author of two books of poetry: *New Jersey*, winner of the Brittingham Prize in Poetry; and *The Bottom*, recipient of the 42 Miles Press Prize in Poetry. Her poems and essays have been published widely in publications ranging from the Academy of American Poets' *Poem-a-Day* to the Yemeni newspaper *Culture*. She makes her living as a journalist. Betsy's writing can be found at www.betsyandrews.contently.com.

Debra Brehmer (*Victorine and Laure in Manet's* Olympia: *Seeing and Not Seeing a Famous Painting*) is a writer and art historian who owns and directs a progressive contemporary art gallery called Portrait Society (www.portraitsocietygallery.com) in Milwaukee, WI. She writes about art for *Hyperallergic*: hyperallergic.com/author/debra-brehmer and other publications.

Kara Lee Corthron's (*Reveling and Rebelling*) plays, including *Welcome to Fear City*, *Listen for the Light*, and *Holly Down in Heaven*, have been performed around the US. She's the author of the young adult novel, *The Truth of Right Now*, which won the Parents' Choice Gold Award in 2017. Other honors include the Princess Grace and Helen Merrill Awards. Currently under commission for La Jolla Playhouse. For more: www.karaleecorthron.com.

Chicava HoneyChild (*Radiant Identity: Chicaba Herstories*) is an actor, burlesque danseur, historian, teacher, and producer. She is the proprietress of Sacred Burlesque and New York City's Brown Girls Burlesque. A scholar of performance art, women of color in burlesque heritage, and sacred sexuality and spirituality, she received her MFA from Goddard College. She is currently working on *Sister Shake*, a documentary and companion book on the legacy of *Women of Color* in burlesque.

Robyn Kraft (*The Blazing Worlds of Margaret Cavendish*) is a published poet and periodic academic with a focus on literature. They rescue cats and dogs and pay for their kibble with full time work as a legal editor. When not discussing issues of intersection and privilege, Robyn is usually found in various bars in downtown Cincinnati.

Caitlin Grace McDonnell (*Up from the Rubbish Heap: The Persistence of Julie D'Aubigny*) is a poet, essayist, and fiction writer. She published a chapbook, *Dreaming the Tree* (belladonna), and book, *Looking for Small Animals* (Nauset Press). She lives in Brooklyn with her daughter.

Leah Mueller (*Firebrand: The Radical Life and Times of Annie Besant*) is an indie writer from Tacoma, Washington. She is the author of two chapbooks, *Queen of Dorksville* (Crisis Chronicles Press) and *Political Apnea* (Locofo Chaps); and three books, *Allergic to Everything* (Writing Knights Press), *Beach Dweller Manifesto* (Writing Knights), and *The Underside of the Snake* (Red Ferret Press). Her work appears in *Blunderbuss, Summerset Review, Outlook Springs, Crack the Spine, Atticus Review, Your Impossible Voice*, and other publications. She was a featured poet at the 2015 New York Poetry Festival and a runner-up in the 2012 Wergle Flomp humor poetry contest.

Meera Nair (*Nangeli: Her Defiant Breasts*) is the author of *Video* (NY: Pantheon) and two middle-grade children's books published in India with Duckbill Publishing. *Video* won the sixth annual Asian-American Literary Award and was a Washington Post Best Book of the Year. Her essays and stories have appeared most recently in *Guernica, The New York Times, The Guardian*, and *NPR's Selected Shorts*. Her work has been in several anthologies in the US and abroad, including *Charlie Chan is Dead 2* (Penguin Random House) and *Delhi Noir* (Akashic Books). Meera has won residency fellowships from the MacDowell Colony and writing fellowships from the New York Foundation for the Arts, *The New York Times*, and the Queens Council for the Arts. She teaches writing at NYU, the New School, and Brooklyn College, and she is a co-founder of the reading series, #Queens Writers Resist in Queens, NYC. www.Meeranair.net

Edissa Nicolás-Huntsman (*Audacious Warrior: Ernestine Rose*) holds a BA from Brown University, an MFA from Mills College, and manages www.KarmaCompass.me, a lifestyle blog about wellness and culture. Edissa is a Reiki III Master and founder of Living Artist Project, a non-competitive international artists' collaboration. She identifies with Healing Mountain of the Heart as her dharma name in the Order of Interbeing, Thich Nhat Hahn's community.

Jessie Serfilippi (*Under the Cover of Breeches and Bayonet*) is a writer and historian who lives outside of Albany, New York. She works as an interpreter at an eighteenth-century historic site in Albany. She will receive her MFA in creative writing from the College of Saint Rose in December of 2018. You can follow her on Twitter @Utterly_Jessie.

Claudia Smith's (*Trek Across a Trackless Land*) essays have appeared online in *LitHub*, *The Rumpus*, *The Manifest-Station*, *Prime Number*, and *The Toast/The Butter*. Her stories and flash fiction have appeared in numerous journals and anthologies, including *Norton's The New Sudden Fiction: Short Short Stories From America and Beyond*, the forthcoming *The New Microfictions*, and *Akashic/Cinco Puntos' Lone Star Noir*. She has two flash fiction collections, *The Sky Is A Well and Other Shorts* (Rose Metal Press) and *Put Your Head In My Lap* (Future Tense Books), as well as a short story collection, *Quarry Light* (Magic Helicopter Press). She lives in Houston, Texas where she works as a lecturer at The University of Houston, Downtown.

Anna Torbina (*Illustrator*) was born in the East of Ukraine and lived there until moving to Moscow in 2006. She holds a degree in fine arts from a Ukrainian college, and her current occupation is an art director with a PA agency. See her illustration portfolio at www.behance.net/anntoorama.

Taté Walker (*Origins*) is a Lakota citizen of the Cheyenne River Sioux Tribe of South Dakota. They are a banner-waving Two Spirit feminist, Indigenous rights activist, and a published and award-winning multimedia storyteller. Taté uses their over-fifteen years of experience working for daily newspapers, social justice organizations, and tribal education systems to organize students and professionals around issues of critical cultural competency, anti-racism, anti-bias, and inclusive community building. For more information, visit www.jtatewalker.com.

Appreciation

First, I must express gratitude to each writer who contributed to *Fierce*. Thank you for your trust and patience. You have each brought something complex, meaningful, and essential to this book, and I hope that *Fierce* will further provide a platform to amplify your voices and opportunities.

Many people provided crucial support for the development of *Fierce*, especially Linda Ganjian, who provided thoughtful critical feedback over the course of several years; Kate Novotny, my cousin, who provided worthy and challenging approaches that improved ideas that I was wrestling with; and Leila Merl, whose careful assessments improved the foreword immensely. Heather Klinkhamer provided expanded analysis on thoughts I was holding in my head about the book, and her *Book Broads* group also provided inspiration.

Anna Torbina made exquisite drawings for each frontispiece, and as befits *Fierce*, balanced the line between modern and historic. Kristen Thornton Navas and Joe Navas of Organic Photography photographed the cover with pristine perfection and made the cover shoot more like a party than a work event. Beta readers and question developers Stephanie Cohen, Heather Klinkhamer, Tiffany Morris, and Margaret Seiler did justice to all the essays by devising thoughtful questions, suggestions, and conversation prompts to advocate the ideas within. Stephanie wrote a stellar back cover blurb, and assisted with additional research.

Additional gratitude to Kate Birdsall, Phoebe Brown, Jessica Blake, Samantha Chanse, Heather Dubnick, Meadow Hilley, David Huyck, Melissa Kinski, Heidi Hewey Lane, Violetta Leigh, Eva Mantell, Lynn McNamee, Derek Nguyen, Erika and Gene Montesano, Kayann Short, Christine Stoddard, and Chris Wells for contributing in diverse ways that made the book stronger by initial participation, work, or connections that manifested in contributions.

Immense thanks and much love to my family for their ongoing support. Lucas Cain Cushanick is the silent partner of Nauset Press. His financial backing enabled this project to happen far more quickly than it would have otherwise. Thank you, CLC, for helping me make this idea a reality. Passion, connection, and creative effort became this book that you hold in your hands.

—K.K.

Index

Heroine Mother 39

Hero of the Soviet Union 40

heteronormativity 164, 230

heteropatriarchy 72, 230

higher-caste body 24

Hinduism , 19, 21

Hindu societ 22

Hitler, Adolf 38, 46

Hobbes, Thomas 171

Holocaust 46

homeland, elusive 127

homosexuality 86, 211–213. *See also* LGBTQ people

HoneyChild, Chicava 182–199, 14. *See also* Chicava

Hudson River Valley 206, 207

Hugo Awards 174

human freedom 136

humanism 127, 152

humanist egalitarianism 152

humanitarian issues 137

humanity 33, 8

human rights 126, 127, 145, 10

  human rights movement 145

  international 128

humiliation 32

Hurley, Kameron 177, 178

Hyderabad, India 29, 32

hypersexualization

  of Indigenous women 64–66

  of white women 65, 66

I

identity 230

  racial 197–198

idiot* (Trump, Donald) 42, 43, 44, 58, 11

  campaign rallies of 255

  compared to Stalin 44

  protests against 101

Igbo traditions 184

immigrants 127, 266

immigration 132–134, 136

impurity 24–23, 24, 26

indentured servitude 205

independence 71, 164, 170

India 18–33

  Besant in 103, 103–104

  British colonialism and 103, 106

  British colonialism in 21

  caste system in 12

  progressive movements in 32

Indiana

  abortion laws in 98

Indian Constitution 21

Indian Law Resource Center 65

Indian mascot issue 60–61

Indian National Congress 106

Indian Removal Act of 1830 60

Indigenous activism 60, 62–64, 62–72, 69

  women and 62–72

Indigenous and

  genocide against 58

Indigenous feminism 56–60

  current understandings 60–72

  future of 72–73

Indigenous food sources 72

Indigenous journalists 68

Indigenous languages

Z